Accession no.

D1391258

Conceptualizing Terrorism

Conceptualizing Terrorism

Anthony Richards

LIS - LIBRARY

Date	Fund
30/5/17	h-Cue

Order No.
2814006

University of Chester

OXFORD
UNIVERSITY PRESS

OXFORD
UNIVERSITY PRESS

Great Clarendon Street, Oxford, OX2 6DP,
United Kingdom

Oxford University Press is a department of the University of Oxford.
It furthers the University's objective of excellence in research, scholarship,
and education by publishing worldwide. Oxford is a registered trade mark of
Oxford University Press in the UK and in certain other countries

© Anthony Richards 2015

The moral rights of the author have been asserted

First Edition published in 2015
Impression: 2

All rights reserved. No part of this publication may be reproduced, stored in
a retrieval system, or transmitted, in any form or by any means, without the
prior permission in writing of Oxford University Press, or as expressly permitted
by law, by licence or under terms agreed with the appropriate reprographics
rights organization. Enquiries concerning reproduction outside the scope of the
above should be sent to the Rights Department, Oxford University Press, at the
address above

You must not circulate this work in any other form
and you must impose this same condition on any acquirer

Published in the United States of America by Oxford University Press
198 Madison Avenue, New York, NY 10016, United States of America

British Library Cataloguing in Publication Data
Data available

Library of Congress Control Number: 2015934708

ISBN 978–0–19–874696–6

Printed and bound by
CPI Group (UK) Ltd, Croydon, CR0 4YY

Links to third party websites are provided by Oxford in good faith and
for information only. Oxford disclaims any responsibility for the materials
contained in any third party website referenced in this work.

Preface

In many quarters the death of Osama bin Laden in May 2011 was met with relief, celebration, and proclamations of victory. Once the excitement and clamour dissipated, however, it also provided an opportune moment to reflect on the counter-terrorism responses of the previous ten years from the United States and the rest of the international community. While one can argue that they were flawed in many respects this book focuses on one particular aspect—that is the inability to agree a definition of terrorism. Notwithstanding the formidable obstacles that confront such an endeavour, there are many reasons for persisting with it—not least that, without an agreed definition, states are left to define terrorism as they see fit and remits of counter-terrorism are often (and sometimes dangerously) determined accordingly. 'Terrorism' has been used as a subjective label that is often applied (or not applied) according to where one's interests lie, and has been manipulated to justify all manner of responses.

'Terrorism Studies' has also been found wanting in the development of a theoretical framework as to *what terrorism is* which in turn has limited its usefulness in informing policymakers' own endeavours in defining the term. Such utility, the author hastens to add, would not be in 'service of power' but, as much as anything else, is to prevent the abuse of power. One might have thought, in the context of the voluminous literature on terrorism that has been published since 9/11, that greater attention would be paid to the theoretical development of Terrorism Studies and, in particular, to the definitional issue, for, after all, all other terrorism related theories depend on what we mean by terrorism in the first place. It is as if the increased exposure of terrorism since 9/11 has simply magnified its manipulation as a subjective label rather than prompting a serious refocus or attempt at conceptual scrutiny of the term. While there has been little interest in understanding what we mean by it, however, there has nevertheless been plenty of interest in using it.

This book approaches the definition of terrorism from an academic perspective and is written in the hope that it can make some contribution towards addressing the problem of terrorism studies as something in its 'pre-theory stage' or, to put it more candidly, as something that 'is widely recognized as theoretically impoverished' (see Chapter 1). Far from being irrelevant or of little use to the practitioner or policymaking community, it is argued that more detached academic perspectives can best inform a more objective approach as to what constitutes terrorism in the 'real world'. If there *is* something analytically distinctive about terrorism compared with other forms of political violence then how can this be captured in a general definition of the concept that all can agree upon? Or how can we at least begin to enhance the analytical quality and utility of the concept of terrorism? This book does not, nor cannot, claim to 'speak truth' on defining what is after all a social construction but it does hope to provoke engagement and discussion in this hitherto neglected area within the study of terrorism (although there are some notable exceptions). Above all else, then, this book aims to explore the prospects for instilling some *analytical quality* into the concept of terrorism— something that has proven to be a rare commodity within the burgeoning public, political and academic discourses of this controversial phenomenon.

Acknowledgements

In the course of writing this book I have received generous advice from a number of colleagues, family, and friends. I would firstly like to thank the University of East London for providing me with a sabbatical in order to progress this work. I would also like to thank the following for their helpful and friendly advice: Maureen Azubike, Joel Busher, Jill Harries, Marisa Linton, Torsten Michel, John Morrison, Win Pang, Jill Payne, Andrew Silke, Chandra Sriram, and James Windle. In particular, I would like to express thanks and pay tribute to the late Paul Wilkinson, who was a great source of inspiration in my formative years in studying the phenomenon of terrorism. I also appreciate the constructive comments from three anonymous reviewers of this work which have been very helpful. Of course, all arguments made in the following are my own and none of the above should be held culpable for them! I would also like to extend my warm thanks and appreciation to Dominic Byatt and Oxford University Press for taking on this project. Finally, I would like to express my gratitude and thanks to my family for their continuing support and, in particular, to my wife, Su, and my young son, Connor, for their forbearance and patience during the writing of this book.

Contents

1

Introduction

Shortly after midnight on 2 May 2011 a US Navy Seal team launched an assault on a fortified compound near Abbottabad in north-west Pakistan. The raid, which was personally authorized by the President of the United States, resulted in the deaths of five people. It was an event that was to reverberate across the globe because this was no ordinary 'kill', nor was the target merely another middle-ranking Al Qaeda operative. Remarkably, it appeared that it was Osama bin Laden himself—the symbolic and charismatic figurehead of the Al Qaeda network that had perpetrated the most devastating terrorist attacks in history on 11 September 2001 (9/11) and who had defied the United States ever since.

With the death of bin Laden, theories abounded as to what lay ahead for Al Qaeda and what the contemporary international terrorist threat might look like in the future. Was the leader's demise the beginning of the end for Al Qaeda or would the decentralized movement be galvanized and sustained in memory and honour of their lost 'martyr'? In death would bin Laden continue to be the source of inspiration for current and future followers? By 6 May, four days after the Abbottabad assault, statements in Arabic appeared on 'jihadist forums' acknowledging the death of bin Laden but also defiantly emphasizing that their struggle would continue: 'Are the Americans able to kill what Sheikh Osama lived and fought for, even with all their soldiers, intelligence, and agencies? Never! Never! Sheikh Osama did not build an organisation that would die with him, nor would end with him.'[1]

Whatever the future might hold for Al Qaeda, or any incarnation of it, there is no doubt that the death of bin Laden was an enormous symbolic blow for its followers and adversaries alike. While there was rejoicing in many quarters in

---

[1] S. Maher and A. Soliman, ICSR Insight: 'Al Qaeda confirms death of bin Laden', International Centre for the Study of Radicalisation and Political Violence, May 2011, available at: <http://icsr.info/2011/05/icsr-insight-al-qaeda-confirms-death-of-bin-laden/> (last accessed 27 November 2014).

the West, however, it also seemed to be an opportune time for reflection on some of the counter-terrorism responses of the previous decade since September 2001. While one can argue that the approach to terrorism has been flawed in many respects the focus of this book is on one particular failure that has helped to underpin ill-conceived counter-terrorism policies—that is the inability to agree a definition of terrorism on the part of policymakers and academics, and it is this failure that has undermined endeavours to respond to terrorism in an effective way.[2]

Even before 9/11 the '[t]he term terrorism [was] so widely used in many contexts as to become almost meaningless'.[3] Yet, since the events of September 2001 it has been employed ever more broadly and carelessly in public and political discourse to the extent that there appears to be a wholesale disregard for any serious endeavour to treat terrorism as an analytical concept. It has been shaped to serve the interests of the definers to the point that any common political will or purpose to address the problem of achieving a universally agreed definition has been overridden in favour of perspectives that seek to preserve and enhance those interests. In short, terrorism is defined as one sees fit. Some years before 9/11 Conor Gearty remarked that '[t]he word resonates with moral opprobrium and as such is, as far as the authorities and others are concerned, far too useful an insult to be pinned down and controlled',[4] while Richard English, in his incisive work on how to respond to terrorism, argued that the subjective use of the term has meant that 'one can end up merely with antiphonally chanted, mutually echoing abuse, and as a result with little clarity or analytical illumination'.[5]

'Terrorism' has been coined to refer to protesters in Thailand, Tunisia, and Libya,[6] to the Israeli attack on a flotilla of ships attempting to break the Israeli blockade of Gaza, to the US invasion of Iraq and the Israeli invasion of Lebanon,[7] to US drone attacks in Pakistan, to Western and NATO airstrikes against Libya, to Syrian rebels attempting to overthrow the Assad regime, to the 'Islamic State in Iraq and the Levant' (ISIS) and to Wikileaks founder Julian

---

[2] Much of pages 2–11 of this chapter have been reprinted with the permission of Taylor and Francis LLC from A. Richards, 'Conceptualizing Terrorism', *Studies in Conflict and Terrorism*, Vol. 37, No. 3, March 2014.

[3] L. Richardson, 'Terrorists as Transnational Actors', in M. Taylor and J. Horgan (eds.), *The Future of Terrorism* (Abingdon: Routledge, 2000), p. 209.

[4] C. Gearty, *Terror* (London: Faber and Faber, 1991), p. 6.

[5] R. English, *Terrorism: How to Respond* (Oxford: Oxford University Press, 2009), p. 19.

[6] A Libyan government statement in February 2011 reportedly described protesters as 'terrorist gangs made up mostly of misguided youths', who had been exploited and fed 'hallucinogenic pills' by people following foreign agendas. See 'Libyan leader Muammar Gaddafi appears on state TV', BBC News, 11 February 2011, available at: <http://www.bbc.co.uk/news/world-africa-12533069> (last accessed 27 November 2014).

[7] A. Schmid, 'The Definition of Terrorism', in A. Schmid (ed.), *The Routledge Handbook of Terrorism Research* (Abingdon: Routledge, 2011), p. 88.

Assange who was described by US Senator Mitch McConnell as a 'high-tech terrorist'.[8] Whether or not any or all of these should be classified as terrorism (or terrorists) the point is that the label is all too often used without any real rigour as to what terrorism is and what its parameters are. Martha Crenshaw, a respected scholar in the field, has argued that 'the term is often used in a careless or pejorative way for rhetorical reasons',[9] while a UN High Level Panel in 2004 lamented that 'a lack of agreement on a clear and well known definition undermines the moral and normative stance against terrorism and has stained the United Nations image'.[10]

There are serious consequences of this. The definitional failure, particularly in a post 9/11 context in which public and policy discourse on the phenomenon has expanded beyond measure, has meant that the term has more than ever before been subject to manipulation. If it was difficult to define terrorism before September 2001, then it has become even more so since. Prospects for capturing any qualitative distinctiveness in 'terrorism' therefore seem more remote than ever, the term having been stretched this way and that in the service of strategic interests and rhetorical stances. It is as if the greater exposure of terrorism since 9/11 has simply magnified its manipulation as a subjective label rather than prompting a serious re-focus or attempt at conceptual scrutiny of the term. While there has been little interest in understanding it, however, there has nevertheless been plenty of interest in using it.

Gearty raised the concern in 1996 that 'terrorism' is used so widely by government and the public to describe 'all forms of conduct' that they find morally repugnant that it raises 'the uncomfortable question of the extent to which the academic search for a coherent definition of terrorism is removed from political reality'.[11] Yet, surely this 'academic search' should be integral to *informing* policymaking rather than being shaped by it.

The failure to craft an agreed definition of terrorism has left a vacuum for actors, whether they be state or non-state, to define terrorism in ways that serve their own perceived political and strategic interests, and, in the case of state responses, remits of 'counter-terrorism' are often determined accordingly. Saul has remarked that:

---

[8] See, for example, N. Chittal, 'Sen. Mitch McConnell: Julian Assange is a "High Tech Terrorist"', Mediaite website, 5 December 2010, available at: <http://www.mediaite.com/tv/mitch-mcconnell-julian-assange-is-a-high-tech-terrorist/> (last accessed 27 November 2014).

[9] M. Crenshaw, *Explaining Terrorism: Causes, Processes and Consequences* (Abingdon: Routledge, 2011), p. 206.

[10] Report of the Secretary-General's High-Level Panel on Threats, Challenges and Change, 'A More Secure World: Our Shared Responsibility', 2 December 2004, p. 51, available at: <http://www.un.org/en/peacebuilding/pdf/historical/hlp_more_secure_world.pdf> (last accessed 27 November 2014).

[11] C. Gearty (ed.), *Terrorism* (Aldershot: Dartmouth Publishing, 1996), p. xiv.

Some States have deployed the international legitimacy conferred by [the UN Security] Council authorization to define terrorism to repress or de-legitimize political opponents, and to conflate them with al-Qaeda...Thus China bluntly characterizes Uighur separatists in Xingjiang as terrorists;...and India seldom distinguishes militants from terrorists in Kashmir. In Indonesia, insurgencies in Aceh and West Papua have been described and combated as terrorism, as have a Maoist insurgency in Nepal and an Islamist movement in Morocco. Israel has compared Palestinians with al-Qaeda, with Ariel Sharon calling Arafat 'our Bin Laden'...In the Maldives, an opposition politician was convicted of terrorism offences and sentenced to ten years imprisonment for peacefully protesting against rights violations by the government....Similarly, in Uzbekistan 15 men were convicted of vague terrorism offences for organizing public demonstrations, at which the government indiscriminately fired upon the crowd.[12]

Saul has thus argued that 'the more confused a concept, the more it lends itself to opportunistic appropriation'.[13] This undermines attempts to generate international cooperation against terrorism and can lead to unilateral and (even if unwittingly) counter-productive strategies. Indeed, some have suggested that the failure to define the concept is itself a cause of terrorism. Schmid, for example, has argued that 'a lack of definition is perceived widely as one of the factors likely to encourage future terrorism', and cites a study that places the absence of such a definition at the top of a list of ten factors and conditions 'likely to encourage future terrorism'.[14]

From a legal perspective, Golder and Williams argued for the need to 'describe the concept with as much precision as possible. One danger is that if terrorism is not so defined, the powers of the State may extend very far indeed',[15] while it has also been suggested that 'the absence of an internationally accepted definition of terrorism has led to international lawlessness and unilateral vigilantism'.[16] At the very least, then, the failure to define terrorism has made its own contribution to dubious counter-terrorism responses.

Yet, defining terrorism is no easy task. Indeed, for some academics, it is an endeavour that is hardly worthy of serious contemplation as any attempt to secure agreement on a definition has thus far proved to be a fruitless exercise. The view is that any such aspiration will continue to disappoint and is therefore not worth the effort. Walter Laqueur wrote that although 'terrorism is an

---

[12] B. Saul, 'Defining Terrorism to Protect Human Rights', in D. Staines (ed.), *Interrogating the War on Terror: Interdisciplinary Perspectives* (Newcastle, UK: Cambridge Scholars Publishing, 2007), pp. 201–2.

[13] B. Saul, *Defining Terrorism in International Law* (Oxford: Oxford University Press, 2006), p. 3.

[14] A. Schmid, 'Terrorism: The Definitional Problem', *Case Western Reserve Journal of International Law*, Vol. 36, Nos. 2 and 3, 2004, p. 378.

[15] B. Golder and G. Williams, 'What is Terrorism? Problems of Legal Definition', *University of New South Wales Law Journal*, Vol. 27, No. 2, 2004, p. 272.

[16] U. Acharya, 'War on Terror or Terror Wars: The Problem in Defining Terrorism', *Denver Journal of International Law and Policy*, Vol. 37, No. 4, 2008–2009, p. 678.

unmistakable phenomenon...the search for a scientific, all-comprehensive definition is a futile enterprise',[17] while Edward Said remarked:

> The use of the word terrorism is usually unfocused, it usually has all kinds of implicit validations of one's own brand of violence, it's highly selective. If you accept this norm, then it becomes so universally applicable that it loses any force whatsoever. I think it is best to drop it.[18]

Another remarked that 'a definition of terrorism is hopeless...terrorism is just violence that you don't like',[19] while Andrew Silke argued that the field is 'bogged down in conceptual mire' and that answers to what appear to be fairly basic questions (such as what *is* terrorism and what makes an act a *terrorist* act?) continue to be elusive.[20] He summed up the general fatigue over the issue:

> For some, the definition debate is a hugely wasteful quagmire, undeserving of the energy it has swallowed over the years. Many experienced commentators hold such opinions. Weary of the heated and largely fruitless debates of the 1970s and 1980s, they view the necessity of a shared definition with a jaundiced eye, and consider the research effort expended on such efforts would be better applied to other more amenable issues.[21]

From a policymaking perspective, senior figures have also found the challenge of defining terrorism daunting. Lord Lloyd of Berwick, in his review of terrorism legislation in the United Kingdom in 1996, conceded that 'there are great difficulties in finding a satisfactory definition. Indeed, I was unable to do so and I suspect that none of us will succeed.'[22] Lord Carlile, reviewer of counter-terrorism legislation in the UK from September 2001 to February 2011, conceded that '[h]ard as I have striven, and as many definitions as I have read, I have failed to conclude that there is one that I could regard as the paradigm. Unsurprisingly, I have been unable to achieve what was not achieved by Lord Lloyd—perhaps because it is not possible to do so.'[23] Yet, as Golder and Williams noted above, and as a European Commission Sixth Framework Programme Project on

---

[17] W. Laqueur, *No End to War: Terrorism in the Twenty-First Century* (New York: Continuum, 2004), p. 238.

[18] E. Said, cited in S. O'Lear, 'Environmental Terrorism: A Critique', in S. Brunn (ed.), *11 September and its Aftermath* (London: Frank Cass, 2004), p. 132.

[19] R. E. Rubenstein, cited in Schmid, 'Terrorism: The Definitional Problem', p. 397.

[20] A. Silke, 'The Devil You Know: Continuing Problems with Research on Terrorism', *Terrorism and Political Violence*, Vol. 13, No. 4, 2001, p. 2.

[21] A. Silke, 'An Introduction to Terrorism Research', in A. Silke (ed.), *Research on Terrorism: Trends, Achievements and Failures* (London: Frank Cass, 2004), p. 3.

[22] Lord Lloyd of Berwick, cited in A. Carlile, 'The Definition of Terrorism', 15 March 2007, p. 4, available at: <http://www.official-documents.gov.uk/document/cm70/7052/7052.pdf> (last accessed 27 November 2014).

[23] Carlile, 'The Definition of Terrorism', p. 4.

defining terrorism also remarked, there is from a legal perspective a need for precision and certainty.[24]

Laqueur, however, cautions those engaged in such a conceptual pursuit arguing that 'terrorism is dangerous ground for simplificateurs and general-isateurs',[25] while others have proclaimed that 'it is unlikely that *any definition* will ever be generally agreed upon' (original italics),[26] and another has written of the 'The Indefinable Concept of Terrorism'.[27] In 1986, Levitt summed up the challenge from a legal perspective for those who set out to achieve the seemingly impossible:

> The search for a legal definition of terrorism in some ways resembles the quest for the Holy Grail: periodically, eager souls set out, full of purpose, energy and self-confidence, to succeed where so many others before have tried and failed. Some, daunted by the difficulties and dangers along the way, give up, often declaring the quest meaningless. Others return claiming victory, proudly bearing an object they insist is the real thing but which to everyone else looks more like the same old used cup, perhaps re-decorated in a slightly original way. Still others, soberly assessing the risks, costs and benefits attendant upon the attempt, never set out at all, preferring to devote their energies to humbler but possibly more practical tasks. But the long record of frustrations and failures often seems to spur further efforts; the 99th [United Nations] Congress, for example, saw a dozen bills containing various attempts at legislative definitions of terrorism.[28]

Defining terrorism has thus been a controversial endeavour that has perplexed both academics and policymakers. The political, subjective, and pejorative use of the term has rendered any prospect of achieving a universally agreed definition as remote indeed, and, as such, continuing deliberation over the meaning of terrorism is often seen as a stale and redundant exercise.

In such a context, it may seem strange that anyone should want to write a book on the subject. There are, however, in this author's view, some fundamental reasons for doing so. *Firstly*, as I have argued above, the term has more than ever before been subject to manipulation. Indeed, as English has remarked, 'the post-9/11 response to terrorism has been both analytically and practically flawed in a very dangerous manner' and this analytical failure has 'significantly

---

[24] European Commission Sixth Framework Programme Project, 'Defining Terrorism' (WP3 Deliverable 4), 1 October 2008, p. 121, available at: <http://www.transnationalterrorism.eu/tekst/publications/WP3%20Del%204.pdf> (last accessed 27 November 2014).

[25] W. Laqueur, quoted in Schmid, 'Terrorism: The Definitional Problem', p. 378.

[26] Shafritz et al., cited in A. Silke, 'Terrorism and the Blind Men's Elephant', *Terrorism and Political Violence*, Vol. 8, No. 3, 1996, p. 13.

[27] See G. Fletcher, 'The Indefinable Concept of Terrorism', *Journal of International Criminal Justice*, Vol. 4, No. 5, 2006.

[28] G. Levitt, 'Is Terrorism Worth Defining?', *Ohio Northern University Law Review*, Vol. 13, No. 1, 1986, p. 97.

exacerbated' the failures in the practical realm.[29] While legal practitioners call for a precise definition in order to prosecute terrorist crimes it is the political abuse of the term that has taken on profound and ominous proportions since 9/11, and the nature of some legislative responses is but one symptom of this. In 2004 Sami Zeidan cautioned that 'the political value of the term currently prevails over its legal one... leaving the [then] war against terrorism selective, incomplete and ineffective.'[30] Charles Townshend argued that 'the indefinite reach of President Bush's "war against terror" underlined more sharply than ever the need for some definition—or compartmentalization—of this manipulable term.'[31] For the concept has indeed been available as a 'free for all' label for any actor who wishes to denounce the activities of their political adversaries for as long as there is no general conviction as to what terrorism really means or what its parameters are.

While one can argue that governments and policymakers are culpable in this regard it is also behoven upon academics to address this theoretical vacuum. Yet academic research has also been found wanting in the development of a theoretical framework as to *what terrorism is*. Wight, citing research that suggested 'that there have been roughly three new books on terrorism published every week' since 9/11 ('not to mention new journals, seminars, workshops, conference panels and a whole swathe of public comment in newspapers') lamented that this 'sheer volume of research and comment on the subject has not been translated into a sophisticated understanding of the phenomenon. Why?'[32] This vastly increased coverage of terrorism[33] has not, it seems, advanced theoretical understanding of the concept.

Secondly, therefore, this book is written in the hope that it can make some contribution towards addressing the problem of terrorism as something in its 'pre-theory stage' or, to put it more candidly, as something that 'is widely recognized as theoretically impoverished',[34] or to at least provoke engagement and discussion in this hitherto neglected area of what is otherwise a burgeoning post 9/11 literature on terrorism.[35] The lack of theoretical endeavour as to

[29] English, *Terrorism: How to Respond*, pp. ix–x.

[30] S. Zeidan, 'Desperately Seeking Definition: The International Community's Quest for Identifying the Specter of Terrorism', *Cornell International Law Journal*, Vol. 36, No. 3, 2003–2004, pp. 491–2.

[31] C. Townshend, *Terrorism: A Very Short Introduction* (Oxford: Oxford University Press, 2002), p. 2.

[32] C. Wight, 'Theorising Terrorism: The State, Structure and History', *International Relations*, Vol. 23, No. 1, 2009, p. 99.

[33] See A. Silke, 'Contemporary Terrorism Studies: Issues in Research', in R. Jackson, M. Breen Smyth, and J. Gunning (eds.), *Critical Terrorism Studies: A New Research Agenda* (Abingdon: Routledge, 2009), pp. 34–5.

[34] M. Crenshaw, 'Current Research on Terrorism: The Academic Perspective', *Studies in Conflict and Terrorism*, Vol. 15, No. 1, 1992, p. 1.

[35] This is not to suggest that the definitional issue has been abandoned entirely. Schmid, in particular, has been responsible for the most impressive data collection exercises on the subject.

'what terrorism is' has rendered much of terrorism research in general as foundationally weak.

Yet, one also has to acknowledge that terrorism, like any social science concept, is ultimately a *social construction* and so there is, one has to concede, something of a paradox in trying to be *definitive* about it. As an 'ontologically unstable' term terrorism, therefore, hardly represents a 'brute fact'.[36] Its social construction means that in theory terrorism can indeed be whatever one says it is and that it therefore comes down to who has the power to define or who 'is heard the loudest'. It is also therefore the case that those who claim that the term has been abused are by definition themselves culpable of making some sort of knowledge claim as to what terrorism is and what it is not. In this context it might, therefore, be reasonable to suggest that one should be no bolder than to offer one's own conception of terrorism, that one should pursue this less lofty goal rather than trying to be *definitive* about it or 'to speak truth' on the matter.

Such is the dilemma with all social science concepts—all of which have been socially constructed and whose meanings and applications have changed over time. But does this mean that, because we cannot speak 'truth' in defining these concepts, that we should abandon attempts to capture their meaning in historical and contemporary contexts? The answer is surely a resounding 'no' because not only do the meanings attributed to such concepts, like terrorism, often have major 'real-life' consequences but every academic discipline requires a degree of conceptual clarity to guide research. Otherwise, Wight has cautioned, terrorism research 'will always tend to drift into a form of journalistic speculation'.[37] Moreover, as English has noted, 'the fact is that this word is simply not going to disappear from the political vocabulary (it is far too useful to too many people for this to occur), and so we should probably retain our commitment to establishing precise, coherent definitions of the word, rather than merely jettisoning it.'[38] Besides, as Schmid argues, 'giving up on the scholarly debate would leave the field to those who

---

See, for example, Schmid (ed.), *The Routledge Handbook of Terrorism Research*. Other notable (post 9/11) exceptions include A. Schmid and A. Jongman, *Political Terrorism*, 3rd edn. (New Brunswick, NJ: Transaction Books, 2008); R. Goodin, *What's Wrong With Terrorism?* (Cambridge: Polity Press, 2006); Saul, *Defining Terrorism in International Law*; Schmid, 'Terrorism: The Definitional Problem'; S. Tiefenbrun, 'A Semiotic Approach to a Legal Definition of Terrorism', *ILSA Journal of International and Comparative Law*, Vol. 9, No. 2, 2003; L. Weinberg, A. Pedahzur, and S. Hirsch-Hoefler, 'The Challenges of Conceptualising Terrorism', *Terrorism and Political Violence*, Vol. 16, No. 4, Winter 2004; R. Monaghan, D. Antonius, and S. J. Sinclair, 'Defining "Terrorism": Moving towards a More Integrated and Interdisciplinary Understanding of Political Violence', *Behavioral Sciences of Terrorism and Political Aggression*, Vol. 3, No. 2, 2011.

[36] R. Jackson, L. Jarvis, J. Gunning, J., and M. Breen Smyth, *Terrorism: A Critical Introduction* (Basingstoke: Palgrave Macmillan, 2011), p. 119.

[37] Wight, 'Theorising Terrorism: The State, Structure and History', p. 105.

[38] English, *Terrorism: How to Respond*, p. 21.

simply hold that "terrorism is what the bad guys do" (B. M. Jenkins), or "one man's terrorist is the other man's freedom fighter".[39]

Moreover, while 'terrorism' may be socially constructed, this does not mean that there cannot be a universally agreed definition of the concept, even if we acknowledge that such a definition would not be the 'truth' but the culmination of an agreed understanding at a given time in a contemporary context. Hence 'the acceptance of terrorism as a social construction does not necessarily preclude defining it.'[40] In the academic literature of the past four decades a general consensus *does* appear to have developed as to what the *core essence* of terrorism is (and it is one that this author concurs with)—*that terrorism entails the intent to generate a wider psychological impact beyond the immediate victims.* While such a consensus may not amount to being the 'truth', the endeavour here is to generate an understanding and conceptualization of terrorism around this indispensable psychological dimension.

Simply abandoning the concept of terrorism as incapable of having any meaningful analytical value is therefore not tenable, and indeed would be an abdication of academic responsibility, not just because it would leave terrorism studies without a sufficient conceptual and theoretical foundation but because it would leave policymakers bereft of academic input to inform their own endeavours in defining the term. This is not, the author hastens to add, to be in 'service to power' but, as much as anything else, is to prevent the abuse of power.

A *third* reason for writing this book (which is linked to the notion of the use of 'terrorism' as a delegitimizing tool used by those in power) is that, through the emergence of critical perspectives within terrorism studies (often referred to as Critical Terrorism Studies or CTS), questions have been posed as to how terrorism has 'traditionally' been studied and also, by implication, how it has been defined. There are, of course, many interpretations as to what it means to be 'critical',[41] though in general this author prefers to understand 'being critical' as a *practice* rather than signifying membership of one or other particular genre or school of thought. It is presumably a practice that all serious terrorism scholars engage in. In this sense one should caution against the exclusive (mis)appropriation of the word 'critical' to a particular body of scholars.

That said, some important perspectives have emerged from CTS that need to be seriously considered in any discussion on the definition of terrorism. One of the core arguments is that so-called 'orthodox' or 'traditional' terrorism

---

[39] Schmid, 'The Definition of Terrorism', p. 42.

[40] R. Jackson, 'In Defence of "Terrorism": Finding a Way through a Forest of Misconceptions', *Behavioral Sciences of Terrorism and Political Aggression*, Vol. 3, No. 2, 2011, p. 118.

[41] See, for example, J. Gunning, 'Babies and Bathwaters: Reflecting on the Pitfalls of Critical Terrorism Studies', *European Political Science*, Vol. 6, No. 3, September 2007, p. 238.

studies has tended to exclude the state (including democratic states) as a culpable actor in definitions of terrorism. Furthermore, some CTS scholars have broadened what they mean by terrorism to include 'structural violence', where the political and commercial interests of states are said to have serious negative impacts on local communities, while there is also some question as to the merits of using 'terrorism' as a concept at all, with little distinction drawn between terrorism and 'state violence'. While the acknowledgement that states have been by far the worst perpetrators of 'terror' is certainly not new, and nor is the particular focus within CTS on democratic states as culpable, some of the approaches of CTS scholars merit consideration for their impact on the conceptual debate. Most notably, many such perspectives question the utility of definitions that present Western governments as victims of terrorism, rather than as potential perpetrators.

A *fourth* important reason for focusing on the definitional debate (and one that is not always acknowledged) is that any serious undertaking to theorize 'what terrorism is' is also inherently an endeavour to *understand* the phenomenon. As English has again argued, any explanation and understanding of terrorism 'can be developed only if we clearly, credibly, plausibly, and honestly define the phenomenon that we actually face',[42] and how one conceives of terrorism will inevitably shape how one understands the phenomenon. For example, the following will hope to generate an understanding of terrorism as a particular *method* of violence rather than something that is only peculiar or inherent to particular types of perpetrator, ideology, or cause. There are a wide range of actors that have used the method of terrorism, whether they be terrorist groups or networks, states, guerrilla groups, extreme fringes of social movements, and so on. In other words, if one scrutinizes the activities of just terrorist organizations we are only considering part of the terrorism picture. Similarly, acts of terrorism have been carried out in the name of a variety of different causes or ideologies, many of which are not in and of themselves inherently violent (or, more specifically, not terrorist).

A *fifth* related reason for the book is that a thorough exploration as to 'what terrorism is' has significant implications for the direction of terrorism related research. Imprecise notions of the concept, or what its parameters are, can lead to a waste of research resources. If, for example, terrorism is understood as simply another form of warfare (such as guerrilla warfare[43]), or indeed if it is viewed as a calculated and rational recourse to warfare as 'a weapon of the weak' (and certainly most terrorist organizations see themselves as 'at war') then why should there have been a focus on trying to identify the psychological profile

---

[42] English, *Terrorism: How to Respond*, p. ix.
[43] See, for example, Silke, 'The Devil You Know: Continuing Problems with Research on Terrorism'.

of the terrorist, or the terrorist 'personality type' with certain 'traits', any more than a focus on the profile of those engaged in other forms of political violence? Indeed, state perspectives on characterizing or *defining* terrorism inevitably inform policy responses, directions for research, and resource allocation. As Cooper stated in 1978, 'definition is a prelude to action'[44] and defining terrorism is key to outlining the parameters for terrorism research.

A *sixth* related reason for writing this book is that it has been argued by the author elsewhere that 'radicalization', it turns out, has not been a particularly useful concept upon which to base a counter-terrorist strategy.[45] It has not been clear as to *who the radicalized are* and responses in the UK in recent years have at times confusingly oscillated between tackling 'violent extremism' in particular and broader societal goals such as promoting 'shared values'. Indeed, the contention here is that the concept of 'radicalization' should be dropped and that the focus should return to what people *do* rather than the way they think—in other words there needs to be a refocus on (the *method* of) *terrorism* and not on more opaque notions of radicalization or on *non-violent* (but 'extremist') ideologies.[46]

Indeed, if terrorism is seen as ineluctably about violence or the threat of violence, and certainly conventional academic wisdom views the phenomenon in this way, then it seems rather paradoxical to speak of a non-violent ideology that is 'conducive' to terrorism.[47] Such a concern with non-violent doctrine as part of counter-terrorism provides a good example of how conceptions of the terrorist threat can have an impact not just on the remit and directions of counter-terrorism policymaking but also on the scope of terrorism and counter-terrorism related research. Having been critical of the fact that there has been little consensus as to what is meant by radicalization, it seems therefore natural that calls for a refocus on terrorism should also come with a commitment to revisiting the definition of the term and to reassessing its own conceptual dilemmas, for, like radicalization, it is very difficult (from a policymaking perspective) to respond to something if one cannot agree on what that something is.

---

[44] H. Cooper, 'Terrorism: The Problem of the Problem of Definition', *Chitty's Law Journal*, Vol. 26, No. 3, 1978, p. 106.

[45] A. Richards, 'The Problem with "Radicalization": The Remit of "Prevent", and the Need to Refocus on *Terrorism* in the UK', *International Affairs*, Vol. 87, No. 1, January 2011.

[46] See 'Contest: The United Kingdom's Strategy for Countering Terrorism', July 2011, available at: <http://www.homeoffice.gov.uk/publications/counter-terrorism/counter-terrorism-strategy/strategy-contest?view=Binary> (last accessed 27 November 2014); 'Prevent Strategy', June 2011, available at: <http://www.homeoffice.gov.uk/publications/counter-terrorism/prevent/prevent-strategy/prevent-strategy-review?view=Binary> (last accessed 27 November 2014).

[47] 'Prevent Strategy', June 2011, p. 12.

Theorizing What Terrorism Is

Perhaps the most important of all the above reasons is to make some contribution to the general need of advancing our theoretical and analytical understanding as to what terrorism is. There will inevitably be disagreement with many of the propositions ahead, and along the way there may be many more questions and dilemmas than adequate answers, but the aim is to provoke thought and discussion. In this way it is hoped that the book will make its own contribution to invigorating the often forlorn hope of bringing greater analytical clarity to what terrorism means—for 'research cannot ignore the definition question indefinitely'.[48]

Perhaps one of the first issues to consider, then, is who should have the power to define? Do some have more of a right than others? Schmid identified in 1992 what he called four arenas of discourse on terrorism: the academic discourse, the official state discourse, the public debate and the discourse of those 'who oppose many of our societies' values and support or perform acts of violence against what they consider repressive states'.[49] In 1988 Schmid and Jongman suggested that the 'functionality of a typology is mostly defined by the purpose of the user: different objectives make for different typologies',[50] while in a later piece of work Schmid argued that '[d]efinitions generally tend to reflect the interests of those who do the defining... In many conflicts, the government is the principal "defining agency".'[51] He footnoted a useful quote from Peter Sederberg who argued that:

> The definition of terms, like other human actions, reflects the interests of those doing the defining. Those who successfully define the terms of a political debate set the agenda for the community... Definition therefore involves the exercise of power.[52]

This book is written from an academic viewpoint and this has certain advantages, not least that it provides distance that allows academics 'more perspective'.[53] An important challenge for any academic attempting to investigate the definition of terrorism is to guard against any 'transaction between discursive

---

[48] Silke, 'An Introduction to Terrorism Research', p. 3.

[49] A. Schmid, 'The Response Problem as a Definition Problem', *Terrorism and Political Violence*, Vol. 4, No. 4, 1992, pp. 7–8.

[50] A. Schmid and A. Jongman, *Political Terrorism: A New Guide to Actors, Authors, Concepts, Databases, Theories and Literature* (Amsterdam: North Holland Publishing Company, 1988), p. 39, cited in European Commission Sixth Framework Programme Project, 'Defining Terrorism' (WP3 Deliverable 4), p. 60.

[51] Schmid, 'Terrorism: The Definitional Problem', p. 385.

[52] P. Sederberg, *Terrorist Myths: Illusion, Rhetoric, and Reality*, 1989, p. 3, cited in Schmid, 'Terrorism: The Definitional Problem', p. 385.

[53] Schmid, 'The Response Problem as a Definition Problem', p. 8.

and political mastery'.[54] Such an endeavour must take place independent of the interests of states or the status quo. As Georges Sorel once remarked '[i]t is necessary to be on the outside in order to see the inside.'[55] The challenge is to elevate terrorism as an analytical term rather than to cement its use as a pejorative label used to delegitimize.[56] As Crenshaw neatly puts it: '[t]he dilemma is to arrive at a "neutral" definition of a method rather than a moral characterization of the enemy.'[57]

Related to this challenge is a further impediment that has compromised attempts to achieve a more neutral definition of terrorism. Approaches to the definitional issue are invariably made with a view of the phenomenon as a 'problem' and with a desire to combat it. This is not to suggest that terrorism is not a problem nor that it shouldn't be combated, but that the academic should be a dispassionate observer, and that a more neutral and non-prescriptive stance is likely to enhance the prospects of a more value-free definition. Far from being of little use to policymakers, it is argued paradoxically that, through this detachment, it is strategically beneficial to have a value-free definition that informs state responses, rather than a definition that is distorted by the (often short-term tactical) needs of states to respond to terrorism.

One symptom of the inclination to be prescriptive is that '[t]he study of terrorism has suffered from a focus on remedies to the exclusion of understanding the phenomenon.'[58] It is understandable from a policymaking perspective that 'one of the functions of defining terrorism, to be sure, is to target the crime that we think should be regarded as taboo and subject to punishment'[59] and that often 'the underlying perception of the wrongfulness of terrorism is echoed throughout the definitional elements'.[60] It follows, then, that the 'normative point' of definition is to underpin and facilitate the eradication of, or at least the reduction of, terrorism.[61] Crenshaw, in drawing a distinction between normative and analytical definitions, argued, however, that:

> The danger inherent in the normative definition is that it verges on the polemical. If 'terrorist' is what one calls one's opponent . . . then the word is more of an epithet

---

[54] L. Jarvis, 'The Spaces and Faces of Critical Terrorism Studies', *Security Dialogue*, Vol. 40, No. 1, 2009, p. 8.

[55] G. Sorel, quoted in M. Anderson, 'Georges Sorel: Reflections on Violence', *Terrorism and Political Violence*, Vol. 1, No. 1, 1989, p. 72.

[56] R. Jackson, 'The Core Commitments of Critical Terrorism Studies', *European Political Science*, Vol. 6, No. 3, September 2007, p. 247.

[57] Crenshaw, *Explaining Terrorism: Causes, Processes and Consequences*, p. 2.

[58] Crenshaw, 'Current Research on Terrorism: The Academic Perspective', p. 3.

[59] Fletcher, 'The Indefinable Concept of Terrorism', p. 895.

[60] European Commission Sixth Framework Programme Project, 'Defining Terrorism' (WP3 Deliverable 4), p. 97.

[61] For a discussion on the normative impact on concept formation see W. Connolly, *The Terms of Political Discourse*, 2nd edn. (Oxford: Martin Robertson, 1983), pp. 26–34.

or a debating stratagem than a label that enables all who read it, whatever their ideological affiliation, to know what terrorism is and what it is not.[62]

Hence, although 'the subject matter is not one which invites dispassion, the challenge is therefore to be dispassionate and non-emotive'.[63] There is, for example, something of a paradox in arguing that '[a]n objective definition of terrorism is…indispensable to any serious attempt to combat terrorism.'[64] For one cannot claim to be pursuing an 'objective' definition that is slanted by the desire to combat and eradicate it, just as much as impartiality would be compromised by an underpinning desire to promote and elevate terrorism as a method.

This book will not, therefore, approach the conceptualization of terrorism with any ulterior prescriptive motive, nor with any preconceived notion as to the 'inherent wrongfulness' of the phenomenon. To some extent at least, then, this addresses the following concern that some 'critical' scholars have hitherto had with so-called 'orthodox' or 'traditional' terrorism studies: 'it is this concern [with producing policy-relevant research] that ensures terrorism studies remains constituted around a restrictively narrow conception of academic responsibility: a conception tied not to critical enquiry but to problem-solving analysis.'[65]

The notion of approaching the definition of terrorism without a prescriptive agenda as to how to respond to it, counter it, or indeed resolve it, suggests then that this work is not concerned with 'problem solving'. Although, by suggesting above that ultimately state responses might be better informed by more dispassionate approaches to the definitional issue, this book is not typical of what 'critical' theorists have argued are 'state-centric, problem-solving perspectives that have thus far dominated terrorism research',[66] and is not written with the aim of sustaining the status quo.[67] Of course, use of the concept of terrorism itself (with its pejorative connotation) might to some already suggest a problem-solving approach, but that would assume that one is employing it as a derogatory term rather than as an analytical one. The endeavour to be more analytical and neutral in defining terrorism also entails

---

[62] M. Crenshaw, 'Introduction: Reflections on the Effects of Terrorism', in *Terrorism, Legitimacy and Power: The Consequences of Political Violence* (Middletown, CT: Wesleyan University Press, 1983), p. 2. Also quoted in L. Stampnitsky, *Disciplining Terror* (Cambridge: Cambridge University Press, 2013), p. 134.

[63] Schmid and Jongman, *Political Terrorism*, p. 177.

[64] B. Ganor, cited in Schmid, 'The Definition of Terrorism', p. 39.

[65] Jarvis, 'The Spaces and Faces of Critical Terrorism Studies', p. 12.

[66] R. Jackson, M. Breen Smyth, and J. Gunning, 'Critical Terrorism Studies: Framing a New Research Agenda', in Jackson et al. (eds.), *Critical Terrorism Studies: A New Research Agenda*, p. 233.

[67] Toros and Gunning have argued that 'traditional terrorism studies has essentially served to sustain the status quo' (see H. Toros and J. Gunning, 'Exploring a Critical Theory Approach to Terrorism Studies', in Jackson et al. (eds.), *Critical Terrorism Studies: A New Research Agenda*, p. 91).

separating the cause from the means. One shouldn't, for example, suggest that violent acts cannot be classified as terrorism if they are carried out for a democratic cause in opposition to dictatorship regimes that one might find objectionable.

Having argued above for the need to enhance the analytical utility of the term 'terrorism', one may, however, have to concede the possibility that, in the course of our scrutiny, there might in fact be nothing qualitatively distinctive about it, that from time immemorial it has been nothing more than a superficial and derogatory label—a delegitimizing rhetorical device for violence that is in fact no different in essence to other forms of political violence. Some have suggested that the label 'terrorism' emerged (along with democratic systems of government) as a delegitimizing tool to describe the violence of those who threatened the status quo.[68] In this context, it might therefore be reasonable to suggest that the word 'terrorism' has never had any analytical quality to redeem in the first place, that terrorism really is the violence of those one 'does not like' and that it would be misleading to pretend otherwise. This perspective (and the view of terrorism as merely violence perpetrated by one's adversaries) might help to explain the frustrating endurance of the old (but still potent) mantra that 'one person's freedom fighter is another's terrorist' that has been so prevalent in the Middle East and other theatres of conflict, or the 'national liberation versus terrorism' debate that has plagued United Nations attempts to generate a universally agreed definition.

Wight reminds us that '[t]he history of the development of the modern state can be understood as a long process of appropriation and accumulation (of territory, peoples and resources) achieved through the use of violence, a process that had winners and losers.'[69] He therefore sees the phenomenon of terrorism as inextricably bound up with the development of the state. It would indeed be strange if both 'winners and losers' endorsed the status quo (and its contemporary territorial and political configurations) at any given time. Naturally enough those winning the game, precisely because they are winning, have decided that the game has ended and have sought to consolidate the status quo. In this sense terrorism (at least of the 'powerless' or 'power seekers') can be viewed as a natural part of the 'system' as one of a number of opposing political activities, and not qualitatively different to other forms of political violence.[70] The first possibility we have to consider, therefore, is that

---

[68] See, for example, M. Blain, 'On the Genealogy of Terrorism', in Staines (ed.), *Interrogating the War on Terror: Interdisciplinary Perspectives*.

[69] Wight, 'Theorising Terrorism: The State, Structure and History', p. 101.

[70] The notion that 'terrorism' is merely a delegitimizing tool used to discredit oppositional political violence, however, does not explain why more 'positive' labels are used for some forms of this violence (such as guerrilla warfare). A common distinction made is that terrorism targets civilians whereas guerrilla warfare does not (although, of course, guerrilla organizations have used the method of terrorism). I shall, however, go on to argue that combatants and non-civilians can

there is nothing distinctive about terrorism compared with other forms of political violence.[71]

If we try and take a step further than this in theorizing what terrorism is (beyond merely being a derogatory label) a second possibility, then, is that it can perhaps be categorized as simply a lower level of political violence. Terrorism can thus be seen as simply at the lower end of the scale or, as many have suggested, as 'the weapon of the weak' (although one could argue that terrorism is not just carried out by the weak). This perspective again does not view terrorism as *qualitatively* different to other forms and so, as with the labelling perspective above, it would leave us with little to theorize about in relation to any distinctiveness about terrorism.

Notwithstanding these two perspectives (terrorism as merely a label and/or a lower level of political violence), the author will endeavour to argue for a third possibility—*that there is something distinctive about terrorism that is worth theorizing about*, that it is wholly unsatisfactory, for example, to simply define or describe terrorism as 'you know it when you see it' or, equally vaguely, that '[w]hat looks, smells and kills like terrorism is terrorism'.[72] Schmid and Jongman, in their seminal contribution, argued that:

> even a 'minimum of theory' requires some consensus about what to theorize about...The search for a universalist definition of terrorism is one which scientists cannot give up. Without some solution to the definitional problem...there can be no uniform data collection and no responsible theory building on terrorism.[73]

In summary, when considering the prospects for defining terrorism, one could perhaps, then, consider three possible avenues: (i) that 'terrorism' is and always has been merely a derogatory *label* for violence that is in actual fact no different to other forms of political violence (and so there is nothing further to discuss concerning any distinctiveness about it); (ii) that our theoretical endeavour to establish what terrorism is may be limited to simply categorizing it as a lower level of violence that, again, is not *qualitatively* different to other forms of political violence; or (iii) that there *is* something qualitatively distinctive about terrorism that we can theorize about.

After the 9/11 attacks, the London 7/7 bombings, the 2004 Madrid attacks, the Bali bombings (2002 and 2005), the Moscow theatre siege (2002), and the Beslan school siege (2004) the idea that there is little to differentiate terrorism

---

also be victims of terrorism and therefore that civilian or non-combatant targeting, although common to many acts of terrorism, should not be *definitional* of the phenomenon.

[71] This paragraph and the following two paragraphs have been reprinted with the permission of Taylor and Francis LLC (see note 2).

[72] Jeremy Greenstock, (former) British Ambassador to the United Nations, cited in Schmid, 'Terrorism: The Definitional Problem', p. 375.

[73] Schmid and Jongman, *Political Terrorism*, p. 3.

from other forms of political violence may seem like an absurd one—that these attacks surely do illustrate that terrorism is a particularly brutal and 'extranormal' mode of political violence that is different to all others. As such, for most, the first two propositions above may be easily dismissed, for a powerful argument is that terrorism is characterized by attacks on civilians in peacetime environments (common to all of the attacks above). Yet, others have argued that terrorism is merely another form of warfare and that by comparison conventional warfare has escaped lightly for all of its own destructive acts against civilians.[74] Silke, for example, questioning the notion that terrorists are devoid of morality, asks:

> how different is the terrorist's ethics from that of a soldier at war? Are the convictions that justify leaving a car bomb in a public street qualitatively different from those used by an airman dropping bombs on a city 10,000 feet below? . . . It seems that for most, warfare is a dirty business in respectable drapings, while terrorism is a dirty business in equally dirty drapings. For those seeking a definition of terrorism, it could be argued that the majority have been blinded by appearances.[75]

Is it really the case, therefore, that 'terrorism' is simply violence that we do not like (or more precisely, whose cause we disagree with), and against which 'terrorism' provides a powerful, emotive, and convenient label, all in an attempt to put other more 'legitimate' forms of political violence on a higher moral plane by comparison? Is terrorism, therefore, the word used to describe *illegal* political violence that is beyond the realms of what is seen as 'legitimate' and acceptable use of 'force' by lawfully constituted states? If this is the case then what is the distinction to be made between terrorism and other forms of illegal political violence, such as guerrilla warfare? Silke, however, cautions against viewing terrorism as a 'distinct entity':

> Terrorist tactics are merely a sub-set within the larger domain of guerrilla tactics. Terrorism is not something distinctly separate. Severe limits in resources and manpower often preclude groups from using anything but terrorist tactics, thus leaving them isolated and identifiable. And because such restricted groups exist, there is a tendency to believe that terrorism as a distinct entity also exists. But this is a dangerous conclusion to make. It plays into the hands of those eager to maintain and strengthen the purgative nature of the term, and ultimately it misleads researchers into believing they are dealing with something extraordinary and very different to what is at hand.[76]

This prompts us to consider the extent to which terrorism can therefore be conceptualized or defined as 'extranormal'. For example, as Silke's argument

---

[74] See Silke, 'Terrorism and the Blind Men's Elephant'.
[75] Silke, 'Terrorism and the Blind Men's Elephant', pp. 23–4.
[76] Silke, 'Terrorism and the Blind Men's Elephant', pp. 25–6.

suggests, are terrorism's supposed 'extranormal' features not also evident in other forms of political violence (not least in warfare in general)? Is it therefore the case that 'terrorism' is used to stigmatize violence that is in actual fact no different to these other forms? Wilkinson, conversely, argues that terrorism *is* a distinctive phenomenon and that '[i]t is a common mistake to equate terrorism with guerrilla warfare in general. Political terrorism proper through the use of bombing, assassinations, massacres, kidnaps and hijacks can and does occur without benefit of guerrilla war... Terrorism is employed as a weapon of psychological warfare.'[77]

In this book I will endeavour to argue *that there is something qualitatively distinctive about terrorism*—but that this distinctiveness for the purposes of a *general* definition does not lie in civilian and/or non-combatant targeting. In keeping with conventional academic wisdom, and common to all terrorism, for this author *the core essence of terrorism is its primary intent to generate a psychological impact beyond the immediate victims*. Terrorism, then, is the use or threat of violence or force with the primary purpose of generating a psychological impact beyond the immediate victims for a political motive. In theory, then, *anybody* can become a victim of terrorism providing he, she, or they serve their purpose as 'message generator(s)' to a broader group or audience. Acts of terrorism, therefore, can, and have been, carried out against 'combatants', providing the intent of such acts is to generate a psychological impact beyond the immediate victims to a broader group, whether this broader group is limited to a wider military body, a government, and/or its civilian population (hence, rather than suggesting that terrorism is *either* a distinctive phenomenon of its own *or* merely another form of warfare, I will suggest in the following that both can be true—that terrorism is a distinctive phenomenon that can also be used as a weapon of war).

Thus, civilian targeting (exemplified in the attacks of 9/11, 7/7, Madrid, Bali, Moscow, and Beslan) is but *one form of terrorism* rather than definitional of the concept as a whole. Certainly, however, if psychological impact is the primary purpose of terrorism, one has to acknowledge that civilian and/or non-combatant targeting is more likely to achieve this effect—but, in the attempt to construct a *general* definition of terrorism, such targeting is not, in my view, a *definitive* feature that applies to all cases of terrorism.

One can entirely appreciate, from a prescriptive and International Humanitarian Law perspective, why there have been attempts by the international community (consistent with international norms relating to the protection of civilians in conflict) to define acts of terrorism as acts of violence against civilians or non-combatants, and thereby try to generate agreement on a

---

[77] P. Wilkinson, quoted in Schmid, 'The Definition of Terrorism', p. 112.

definition of terrorism at least on this basis. For example, in 2005, the then Secretary-General of the United Nations called 'for a definition of terrorism which would make it clear that...any action constitutes terrorism if it is intended to cause death or serious bodily harm to civilians or non-combatants'.[78] He had earlier argued that '[i]f there is one universal principle that all peoples can agree on, surely it is this.'[79] While very few would argue with this on moral grounds, I would suggest that the integrity of a general definition of terrorism should not be compromised by the imperative to respond to *this particular form of terrorism*.

The proposition that civilian targeting should not be definitional of terrorism is by no means new. Indeed, most of the definitions of terrorism in Easson and Schmid's compilation of over 250 do not explicitly include civilians or non-combatants as targets.[80] Nor would the emphasis here on the psychological dimension as being indispensable to terrorism come as any great surprise to those who are familiar with the literature on the subject—with terrorism the direct victims are not the main targets of the 'terrorist message'. One can also suggest, thirdly, that conventional academic wisdom concurs with the view that, when conceptualizing terrorism, it is best seen as a particular method of political violence rather than as being inherent to any particular cause or ideology. And these are three core assumptions upon which much of the following arguments will rest.

Adopting these assumptions, in particular the notion that combatants can be victims of terrorism, has significant implications for the definitional debate. For example, they do not sit comfortably with the idea that terrorism can be defined as 'the peacetime equivalent of a war crime', a proposition (derived from an International Humanitarian Law perspective) that has garnered serious consideration. While the *physical manifestation* of (the form of) terrorism that targets civilians in peacetime may well be the equivalent of a war crime, the thesis is undermined if one holds to the view that ('unprotected')

---

[78] United Nations, *In Larger Freedom: Towards Development, Security and Human Rights for All*, Chapter 3 ('Freedom from Fear'), United Nations, p. 26, available at: <http://www.unmillenniumproject.org/documents/Inlargerfreedom.pdf> (last accessed 27 November 2014).

[79] United Nations, Press Release SG/SM/7977 GA9920, 'Secretary-General, Addressing Assembly on Terrorism, Calls for "Immediate, Far-Reaching Changes" in UN Response to Terror', 1 October 2001, available at: <http://www.un.org/en/terrorism/sg-statements.asp> (last accessed 27 November 2014).

[80] A brief survey of Easson and Schmid's 250 definitions of terrorism appears to endorse the view that terrorism is not just carried out against civilians or non-combatants. It is perhaps surprising, given the common perception of terrorism as something that is carried out against civilians, that most of the definitions in their compilation do not make explicit reference to civilians or non-combatants as being victims (approximately 70 of them make reference to 'civilian', 'non-combatant', or 'innocent' victims, with about half of these appearing in post 9/11 definitions). There are others that use more general terms, such as 'targeting a population' or a 'group', and there are a few that emphasize the arbitrariness and/or indiscriminate nature of terrorist acts (see Appendix 2.1 to Schmid, 'The Definition of Terrorism').

combatants can be the targets of terrorism, while such 'equivalence' also appears to overlook the indispensable psychological dimension of terrorism (see Chapter 6).

The idea that combatants can be victims of terrorism also has implications for the extent that terrorism should be seen as ineluctably 'extranormal' and, indeed, a further ramification is that there then may be some terrorisms with which one sympathizes (providing they refrain from targeting civilians and non-combatants). The notion that there may be some forms of the phenomenon that one might endorse is not new but it does underpin one particular dilemma that has been apparent in the international response to terrorism— that is the paradoxical approach of at times explicitly declaring a zero-tolerance approach to terrorism in all of 'its forms and manifestations' and yet simultaneously exhibiting an implicit sympathy for some terrorisms—for example those against oppressive regimes and that also refrain from targeting civilians or non-combatants.[81] And it does not serve our purpose to label such violence as something more 'positive' (like 'freedom fighting') simply because we might agree with it—*terrorism it remains* and any attempt to find a more 'amenable' label would only serve to entrench terrorism as a pejorative term (to be used only for 'bad' violence) at the expense of a more neutral approach and attempts to instil some analytical quality into the concept. Responses should arguably (and more honestly) be determined by *which forms* of terrorism one objects to (and which causes one concurs with), rather than declaring a blanket condemnation of all terrorism.

Unlike many policymaking approaches, this book is not therefore concerned with 'moral clarity'[82] that often underpins distinctions between civilian and non-civilian targeting when defining terrorism but *is* concerned with more detached and dispassionate analysis. The two approaches are likely to lead to different conceptual outcomes. For example, as noted above, I would refute the view that '"freedom fighters" [inverted commas added] who attack only combatants ... [cannot then be] ... terrorists'.[83] And if some of these acts are carried out against the military of oppressive regimes then one might indeed sympathize with some 'terrorisms' depending on one's perspective.[84]

---

[81] See, for example, discussion in Carlile, 'The Definition of Terrorism'.

[82] The Policy Working Group on the United Nations and Terrorism, for example, argued that 'The phenomenon of terrorism is complex. This does not, however, imply that it is impossible to adopt moral clarity regarding attacks on civilians' (quoted in Schmid, 'The Definition of Terrorism', p. 56).

[83] W. Enders, cited in A. Schmid, 'Introduction', in Schmid (ed.), *The Routledge Handbook of Terrorism Research*, p. 20.

[84] Shanahan, using a hypothetical case of a terrorist campaign in pre-Second World War Germany that sought to undermine Hitler's Nazi regime (not least to prevent his genocidal plans) argues that 'insisting that terrorism is morally wrong by definition precludes even the *logical possibility* of a consequentialist moral justification of this group's acts' (T. Shanahan,

The Structure of the Book

This book will be structured as follows. Chapter 2 will further outline the importance of defining terrorism in the policymaking environment, particularly in the context of the manipulation of the concept and the recent 'Global War on Terror'. It will also present the academic case for continuing to endeavour to conceptualize terrorism in order to strengthen the theoretical foundation of terrorism studies. It makes the case that, in order to study terrorism (including 'terrorist' case studies), it is imperative to establish what is understood by 'terrorism' and what its parameters are.

Chapter 3 will outline the evolution of the definitional debate to date from the policymaking perspective, from the attempt in the 1930s by the League of Nations to address the issue to the contemporary efforts of its successor, the United Nations. The difficulties and obstacles in achieving a universally agreed definition, particularly the persistence of the 'one person's terrorist is another's freedom fighter' mantra (mostly in the context of the conflicts in the Middle East and Kashmir), has historically led to the inclination of the United Nations to address the physical manifestations of terrorism (through its Conventions against certain 'terrorist' acts) rather than to capture what terrorism means. Chapter 4 will draw on academic perspectives on the meaning and purpose of terrorism—and in particular will emphasize the notion of terrorism as a form of violent communication.

In the endeavour to identify what is distinctive about terrorism three assumptions are proposed in Chapter 5 when approaching the definitional issue. The first of these is that *there is no such thing as an act of violence that is inherently in and of itself an act of terrorism*. It is only when one endows layers of meaning upon the act that one can then determine whether or not such an act constitutes terrorism. This renders any lists of types of terrorist attacks (i.e. hostage takings, hijackings, bombings, suicide bombings, car or truck bombings, shootings, and so on) unhelpful in getting us any closer to capturing 'what terrorism is'. The second assumption, as I have noted above, is that, for definitional purposes, *terrorism is best conceptualized as a particular method of political violence that is not inherent to any particular perpetrator, ideology, or cause*. By way of clarification, the *method* here referred to does not allude to the type of violence but to the *primary purpose* behind the act of violence which is to generate a psychological impact beyond the immediate victims. The third assumption, again as noted above, is that *terrorism can be carried out against anybody*, including combatants, providing they serve as sufficient 'message generators'.

'Betraying a Certain Corruption of Mind: How (and How Not) to Define "Terrorism"', *Critical Studies on Terrorism*, Vol. 3, No. 2, 2010 (version accessed through 'Athens' with no page numbers)).

While Chapter 5 will also assess the implications of these assumptions, Chapter 6 will focus on the consequences of the third assumption—that combatants and non-civilians can also be victims of terrorism. In particular it will critique both the proposition that terrorism can be defined as the peacetime equivalent of a war crime and the notion that terrorism can be *conceptualized* as an 'extranormal' form of political violence. In the endeavour to treat 'terrorism' as an analytical concept (rather than as an emotional or pejorative term) the chapter will then consider the possibility of terrorism that one might sympathize with or endorse. In light of the discussion thus far, Chapter 7 will then deduce what should *not* be regarded as terrorism, before addressing the fundamental problem of empirically proving what is terrorism and what is not—how, for example, can one prove the intent or purpose behind an act of violence that will allow us to determine whether or not it can qualify as an act of terrorism?

Chapter 8 attempts to draw distinctions between terrorism, non-state terrorism, state terrorism, state-sponsored terrorism, political terror and state terror, arguing in particular that although political terror (in particular state terror) and terrorism are often used interchangeably they are different phenomena. Moving beyond, and developing further, the discussion in Chapter 5, Chapter 9 assesses other components that could or should be considered for inclusion in a definition of terrorism. Finally, Chapter 10 concludes by offering the author's own conceptualization of terrorism.

2

The Importance of an Agreed Definition of Terrorism

The Subjective Use of 'Terrorism' and 'Terror'

Terrorism was catapulted into the consciousness of the international community in a dramatic and profound way on 11 September 2001. At that time terrorism was, of course, not a novel phenomenon but many heralded the terrorist threat presented by Al Qaeda as new and unprecedented.[1] Policymakers rushed to muster responses to the global adversary that had proven itself capable of perpetrating mass casualties at the heart of the world's most powerful democracy. President George W. Bush declared that 'enemies of freedom committed an act of war against our country' and that 'all of this was brought upon us in a single day, and night fell on a different world, a world where freedom itself is under attack'.[2] Therefore 'whether we bring our enemies to justice or bring justice to our enemies, justice will be done' and 'our war on terror begins with Al Qaida, but it does not end there. It will not end until every terrorist group of global reach has been found, stopped, and defeated.'[3]

The proclamation of the 'war on terror' was followed by the US led invasion of Afghanistan after the Taliban regime had failed to deliver Osama bin Laden. Not only was this 'war' declared against 'every terrorist group of global reach' but terrorism and rogue states were increasingly conflated as part of the same problem. Indeed, the parameters of the 'war on terror' had clearly widened to add weight to the justification for the invasion of Iraq: 'today, the *gravest danger in the war on terror*, the gravest danger facing America and the world,

---

[1] For a discussion on the extent that this 'new' terrorism is actually new see Chapter 3 in Crenshaw, *Explaining Terrorism: Causes, Processes and Consequences*.

[2] *Guardian*, G. W. Bush, 20 September 2001, text of speech available at: <http://www.guardian.co.uk/world/2001/sep/21/september11.usa13> (last accessed 27 November 2014).

[3] *Guardian*, G. W. Bush, 20 September 2001, text of speech.

is outlaw regimes that seek and possess nuclear, chemical, and biological weapons' (italics added).[4]

The presentation of the struggle in bipolar terms, where 'every nation, in every region, now has a decision to make' and where 'either you are with us, or you are with the terrorists',[5] helped to prevent a more nuanced and sophisticated approach to resolving the many different 'terrorisms', particularly those that had local and nationalist goals. Virginia Held argued in 2004 that the United States was:

> asserting that to hold anything else than that all terrorism is the same is to undermine the 'moral clarity' needed to pursue the war on terrorism. U.S. neo-conservatives, Christian fundamentalists, and the Israeli Right are especially intent on arguing that the terrorism carried out by Palestinians is the same as the terrorism carried out by Osama bin Laden and the Al Qaeda network, agreeing with Israeli prime minister Ariel Sharon that 'terrorism is terrorism is terrorism anywhere in the world.'[6]

And Crenshaw noted that:

> If policy makers can rely on a set of simple assumptions about terrorism, they need not concern themselves with understanding a contradictory and confusing reality... They rely on metaphors, narratives, and analogies that make sense of what might otherwise be difficult to comprehend.[7]

The term 'terror' can, of course, refer to all manner of things. There is no doubt, for example, that stalkers can inflict 'terror' on their victims but the 'war on terror' did not presumably target stalkers. Bank robbers can 'terrorize' bank cashiers along with any civilians caught up in the drama but one assumes that these were not the focus of the war on terror. The use of the word 'terror', especially without reference to any political motivation, is very vague indeed. Yet, even if one assumed that *political* terror, or terrorism,[8] was the target of this 'war' there are still problems. Fundamentally, how can one declare a war on a method? For 'terrorism is not an enemy. It is a tactic.'[9] William Odom, former head of the US National Security Agency, further argued that:

---

[4] CNN, transcript of George Bush State of the Union Address, 29 January 2003, available at: <http://edition.cnn.com/2003/ALLPOLITICS/01/28/sotu.transcript/> (last accessed 27 November 2014).

[5] *Guardian*, G. W. Bush, 20 September 2001, text of speech.

[6] V. Held, 'Terrorism and War', *The Journal of Ethics*, Vol. 8, 2004, pp. 59–60.

[7] Crenshaw, *Explaining Terrorism: Causes, Processes and Consequences*, p. 64.

[8] I prefer to draw a distinction between political terror (including state terror) and terrorism (see Chapters 4 and 8).

[9] W. Odom (former head of the US National Security Agency), 'American Hegemony: How to Use It, How to Lose It', p. 10, available at: <http://www.middlebury.edu/media/view/214721/original/OdomPaper.pdf> (last accessed 27 November 2014).

Because the United States itself has a long record of supporting terrorists and using terrorist tactics, the slogans of today's war on terrorism merely makes the United States look hypocritical to the rest of the world.[10]

If the international community is ultimately to respond effectively to terrorism in the longer term, and if states are to avoid charges of hypocrisy and double standards, then there is a need to conceptualize *and apply* the term more objectively. By refraining from defining terrorism according to perceived state or national interests, or 'in the service of power', there might then be potential for a more comprehensive, neutral, honest, and analytical approach to the concept of terrorism that might, in turn, help to prevent the term being batted to and fro in an endless game of name-calling against one's adversaries.

It is not the intention here to provide a comprehensive critique of the war on terror[11] but perhaps most relevant to our discussion is an important question that needs to be asked: who in this global war could decide who was terrorist and who was not, or what was terrorism or not? Crenshaw again noted that the:

'global war on terror' raised familiar and longstanding concerns about labelling and stereotyping opponents as well as puzzlement about just what and who the enemy was. How could the United States go to war against a method of violence (terrorism) or an emotional state (terror)?[12]

Terrorist 'labelling' and 'stereotyping' and the subjective application (and non-application) of the term has, of course, as Crenshaw indicates, not just been evident since 9/11. In the 1970s Syria made it clear that it was witnessing struggles for national liberation in the Middle East (from groups such as the Palestine Liberation Organization) and not terrorist campaigns as characterized by many in the West. In the context of the ideological struggle of the Cold War, the Soviet Union viewed what many saw as left-wing revolutionary terrorism as worthy liberation struggles, while the Reagan administration in the United States openly endorsed as 'the moral equals of our founding fathers' the Nicaraguan Contras who were said to have committed horrific 'terrorist' acts.[13]

The international community, then, has found it difficult to agree upon a definition because it has all too often depended upon who the perpetrators are. The potential for 'terrorism' as an analytical concept that can be applied

---

[10] Odom, 'American Hegemony: How to Use It, How to Lose It', p. 10.

[11] For this see, for example, Staines (ed.), *Interrogating the War on Terror: Interdisciplinary Perspectives*; S. Hauerwas and F. Lentricchia (eds.), *Dissent From the Homeland: Essays after September 11* (Durham, NC: Duke University Press, 2003); English, *Terrorism: How to Respond*, pp. 104–7.

[12] Crenshaw, *Explaining Terrorism: Causes, Processes and Consequences*, p. 2.

[13] Schmid and Jongman, *Political Terrorism*, p. 17.

universally has been limited because, in the battle for legitimacy, it has predominantly been exploited and deployed as a subjective and pejorative label that has often been applied to those who are fighting for a cause one disagrees with. Hence, the old and rather depressingly persistent adage that 'one person's terrorist is another's freedom fighter'. This mantra could be both illuminating and frustrating. It is illuminating if we concede that there really is nothing unique or qualitatively distinctive about terrorism compared with other forms of political violence, and that it is merely a derogatory label, in which case the terrorist/freedom fighter dichotomy tells us all we need to know—that, from this perspective, terrorism really is simply violence perpetrated by your ideological enemies.

It is frustrating, however, if one does see terrorism as an analytically distinct and unique form of political violence, and as a very particular *method* of violence, regardless of its perpetrators or the cause. Whether or not one is a 'freedom fighter' or a 'terrorist', if the method of terrorism is employed then surely an act of terrorism it remains, regardless of the ideology, cause, or identity of the perpetrator. Any serious attempt to conceptualize terrorism, then, if one does accept that it is a distinctive form of political violence, must detach it as a method from the cause or ultimate goal of the perpetrators, other than that this goal must be a political one.

As I have argued in Chapter 1, there are many reasons for refocusing on the definition of terrorism. One of them is to counter the selective exploitation of the term in the policymaking environment—where the concept may be deployed to justify dubious 'counter-terrorism' agendas. The Policy Working Group on the United Nations and Terrorism, for example, cautioned that:

> The rubric of counter-terrorism can be used to justify acts in support of political agendas, such as the consolidation of political power, elimination of political opponents, inhibition of legitimate dissent and/or suppression of resistance to military occupation. Labelling opponents or adversaries as terrorists offers a time-tested technique to de-legitimize and demonize them. The United Nations should beware of offering, or being perceived to be offering, a blanket or automatic endorsement of all measures taken in the name of counter-terrorism.[14]

However sceptical one might be, if at all, of the motivations for counter-terrorism, whether one should *also* question the 'world as . . . [we] . . . find it' and its 'prevailing social and power relationships and the institutions into which they are organized, as the given framework for action' is another matter (for critical theorists, 'counter-terrorism' is driven by 'hegemonic discourses'

---

[14] Policy Working Group on the United Nations and Terrorism, quoted in Schmid, 'The Definition of Terrorism', p. 56.

intended to sustain the status quo at the expense of any threats to its political and economic preponderance[15]).

Perhaps a good example of subjective labelling is in the course of the United States' endeavour to support the Northern Alliance in Afghanistan against the Taliban. In the aftermath of 9/11 US Defence Secretary Donald Rumsfeld was quoted as saying that '[t]here are any number of people in Afghanistan—tribes in the south, the northern alliance in the north—that oppose the Taliban ... And clearly we need to recognize the value they bring to this anti-terrorist, anti-Taliban effort and, where appropriate, find ways to assist them.'[16] Yet, the Northern Alliance itself had been noted for committing many acts that might themselves be defined as acts of 'terrorism' or 'terror' (depending on one's definitions). According to Human Rights Watch:

> Abuses committed by factions belonging to the United Front [formerly the North-ern Alliance] have been well documented ... There have ... been reports of abuses in areas held temporarily by United Front factions, including summary executions, burning of houses, and looting, principally targeting ethnic Pashtuns and others suspected of supporting the Taliban ... Several of the executions were reportedly carried out in front of members of the victims' families ... factions conducted a raid in West Kabul, killing and 'disappearing' ethnic Hazara civilians, and committing widespread rape. Estimates of those killed range from about seventy to more than one hundred.[17]

Again depending on what definition of terrorism is used, the United States supported the mujahedeen in their efforts to repel Soviet forces from Afghanistan. The point is that states have habitually practised double standards when deciding who are terrorists and what constitutes terrorism and the absence of a common definition facilitates this.[18] It may well serve strategic interests to sponsor or support terrorism against one's adversaries, and there may be terrorisms that one might sympathize with, but few, if any, policymakers would concede that they are endorsing *terrorism* such is the stigma attached to the term—as such '[g]overnments characteristically define "terrorism" as something only their opponents can commit.'[19]

---

[15] D. Stokes, 'Ideas and Avocados: Ontologising Critical Terrorism Studies', *International Relations*, Volume 23, No. 1, 2009, p. 88.

[16] D. Rumsfeld, quoted in *New York Times*, 'A Nation Challenged: The Rebels; Bush Approves Covert Aid for Taliban Foes', 1 October 2001, available at: <http://www.nytimes.com/2001/10/01/world/a-nation-challenged-the-rebels-bush-approves-covert-aid-for-taliban-foes.html> (last accessed 27 November 2014).

[17] Human Rights Watch, 'Military Assistance to the Afghan Opposition', 5 October 2001, pp. 3–4, available at: <http://www.hrw.org/legacy/backgrounder/asia/afghan-bck1005.pdf> (last accessed 27 November 2014).

[18] Schmid, 'Terrorism: The Definitional Problem', p. 379.

[19] Held, 'Terrorism and War', p. 62.

Yet, subject to the satisfaction of one's criteria, *terrorism it remains* and, to be clear, this is not a judgement as to whether or not it was right to support the Northern Alliance or the Afghan mujahedeen, but rather that one shouldn't seek out more 'positive' descriptors (like 'freedom fighting') for the same activity, that then only serve to confuse analysis as to what terrorism is. While policymakers may have difficulty in applying 'terrorism' more object-ively there is an obligation for academics to strive for a more neutral approach, not only in an endeavour to advance theoretical and analytical understanding to guide research within academia (see section 'Terrorism Research . . . ' below), but also to try and limit any use of the term as the 'rhetorical servant of the established order'.[20]

The above US examples are not intended to detract attention from the subjective use of the term 'terrorism' by, and the activities of, non-democratic states, some of whom have been responsible for widespread campaigns of 'state terror' (see Chapter 8). But if a holistic approach to the definition of terrorism is what is needed, and if such a definition is to be credible and universally endorsed, then the stance of democratic states also merits atten-tion if charges of double standards are to be avoided. Whether in the cases of dictatorships that have intimidated their populations through campaigns of 'state terror', or whether in those instances of states that have supported or sponsored terrorism and/or tolerated acts of terrorism or domestic 'state terror' by their strategic allies, or whether in the course of determining what counts as 'terrorism', one might be forgiven for thinking that some of those in power would rather not be constrained by general agreement on a definition of terrorism (or 'state terror'). Referring to 'powerful countries', one observer has, for example, argued that:

> Defining terrorism and instituting an international legal mechanism to address it would pose a limitation to those powerful countries that currently are privileged to exercise power unilaterally. Absence of an accepted definition and an international legal mechanism to address terrorism provides room for powerful countries to act flexibly based upon their political agenda.[21]

There is, then, a need for the academic community to endeavour to define terrorism independent of the interests of those in power. In fact, to define terrorism from a state perspective paradoxically could provide a disservice to states and the international community, for it is only a more objective (and strategic) approach to the definition that might incidentally best serve and inform state responses in the longer term (that is if states are committed to

---

[20] C. Gearty, 'Terrorism and Morality', *European Human Rights Law Review*, Issue 4, 2003, p. 1.
[21] Acharya, 'War on Terror or Terror Wars: The Problem in Defining Terrorism', pp. 668–9.

countering terrorism unhindered by other strategic priorities, which is by no means certain). This, to reiterate, is not to be in 'the service of power' (by, for example, advocating more strategic approaches that may in the end consolidate existing power structures) but, as much as anything is to prevent the abuse of state power and the manipulation of the 'terrorist' label.

There are, of course, academic perspectives that fall squarely into 'problem solving' in that they often outline the benefits of an agreed definition of terrorism from a policymaking perspective. Schmid summarizes these benefits:

1. Developing an effective international strategy requires agreement on what it is we are dealing with, in other words, we need a definition of terrorism.

2. International mobilization against terrorism...cannot lead to operational results as long as the participants cannot agree on a definition.

3. Without a definition of terrorism, it is impossible to formulate or enforce international agreements against terrorism.

4. Although many countries have signed bilateral and multilateral agreements concerning a variety of crimes, extradition for political offences is often explicitly excluded, and the background of terrorism is always political.

5. The definition of terrorism will be the basis and the operational tool for expanding the international community's ability to combat terrorism.

6. It will enable legislation and specific punishments against those perpetrating, involved in, or supporting terrorism, and will allow the formulation of a codex of laws and international conventions against terrorism, terrorist organizations, states sponsoring terrorism, and economic firms trading with them.

7. At the same time, the definition of terrorism will hamper the attempts of terrorist organizations to obtain public legitimacy, and will erode support among those segments of the population willing to assist them (as opposed to guerrilla activities).

8. Finally, the operative use of the definition of terrorism could motivate terrorist organizations, due to moral or utilitarian considerations, to shift from terrorist activities to alternative courses (such as guerrilla warfare) in order to attain their aims, thus reducing the scope of international terrorism.[22]

Others have also outlined the practical benefits of an agreed definition of terrorism.[23] The concern of this book, however, is to contribute to theory building that might ultimately render the term less open to abuse in the 'real' world. As Levine noted some six years before 9/11, labelling something as

---

[22] Schmid, 'Terrorism: The Definitional Problem', pp. 379–80, adapted from B. Ganor, 'Defining Terrorism: Is One Man's Terrorist Another Man's Freedom Fighter?', *Police Practice and Research*, Volume 3, No. 4, 2002, available at: <http://www.ict.org.il/Article/1123/Defining-Terrorism-Is-One-Mans-Terrorist-Another-Mans-Freedom-Fighter> (last accessed 27 November 2014).

[23] See, for example, European Commission Sixth Framework Programme Project, 'Defining Terrorism' (WP3 Deliverable 4).

terrorism can have 'transformative consequences' and, using the case of the Israeli–Palestine conflict, such labelling 'permits the [Israeli] government to deploy a variety of countermeasures unavailable when dealing with ordinary "criminal" acts' as well as to provide for political opportunism' (in this instance to bolster the case of those who argued for more draconian measures against the PLO).[24]

Terrorism Research and the Search for an Agreed Definition of Terrorism

While this study is written from an academic perspective, academic research and government priorities are, however, often intertwined. As Gunning has argued '[a]cademia does not exist outside the power structures of its day.'[25] To some extent, therefore, it is inevitable that many academic approaches have a 'problem solving' impetus. For those who endeavour to define terrorism the content is often determined by the perspective of the definers. There are, for example, definitions crafted from the perspective of the state, from the perspective of non-state actors, from an academic viewpoint, from a human rights perspective, from a legal perspective, and even from insurance and medical perspectives. The definition below is an example of the latter:

> The intentional use of violence—real or threatened—against one or more non-combatants and/or those services essential for or protective of their health, resulting in adverse health effects in those immediately affected and their community, ranging from a loss of well-being or security to injury, illness, or death.[26]

State definitions often refer to terrorist acts as being unlawful and illegitimate, and refer to terrorism as something carried out by non-state or sub-state groups, often with reference to governments as being the victims of terrorist coercion. It has also been suggested by international and regional organizations that a definition of terrorism is required to protect the interests of the 'international community':

> Given the rising necessity to differentiate terrorism from other forms of political violence in the interest of protecting vital international community interests and values, a coherent definition of terrorism is needed more than ever before in order

---

[24] V. Levine, 'The Logomachy of Terrorism: On the Political Uses and Abuses of Definition', *Terrorism and Political Violence*, Vol. 7, No. 4, 1995, p. 49.
[25] Gunning, 'Babies and Bathwaters: Reflecting on the Pitfalls of Critical Terrorism Studies', p. 239.
[26] J. Arnold et al., 'A Proposed Universal Medical and Public Health Definition of Terrorism', *Prehospital and Disaster Medicine*, Vol. 18, No. 2, available at: <http://journals.cambridge.org/action/displayAbstract?fromPage=online&aid=8227349> (last accessed 27 November 2014).

to harmonize efforts and ensure closer cooperation in combating terrorist activities at the level of the European Union and abroad.[27]

On the issue of state interests and research priorities one respondent to a Schmid questionnaire cautioned that '[t]he challenge to research on terrorism lies in the strong political influences on the conceptualization of terrorism, through official or legal definitions of terrorism by governments, states or international organizations, definitions that are not aimed at guiding research.'[28] Indeed, for Sartori (on the issue of defining concepts in general), there is a distinction to be made between 'definition of meaning and operational definition'.[29] He argued that:

> the definitional requirement for a concept is that its meaning is declared, while operational definitions are required to state the conditions, indeed the operations, by means of which a concept can be verified and, ultimately, measured …operational definitions generally entail a drastic curtailment of meaning for they can only maintain those meanings that comply with the operationist requirement.[30]

Notwithstanding the concern over 'operationist' influences, while terrorism has been a difficult concept for policymakers to grasp, it has also been a highly contested one *within* academia. In the academic realm, 'terrorism studies' is multi-disciplinary with an array of social sciences that can all credibly claim that they have something to contribute to the topic—including, but not limited to, political science, international relations, psychology, philosophy, criminology, economics, war and peace studies, communication studies etc.— thus one can 'interpret terrorism in different frameworks' (for example, as an act of crime, as a political act, as an act of warfare, as an act of [violent] communication, and so on).[31]

Terrorism research in general has certainly had its problems. A lack of a rigorous empirical foundation, a concomitant over-reliance on secondary sources, a high number of transient contributors to the field who briefly drop by with a single contribution before moving on, have all been noted as undermining the quality and validity of terrorism studies.[32] In 1988, in one of the first assessments of the quality of terrorism research, Schmid and

---

[27] European Commission Sixth Framework Programme Project, 'Defining Terrorism' (WP3 Deliverable 4), p. 88.

[28] 'Scandinavian researcher', quoted by Schmid, 'Introduction', in *The Routledge Handbook of Terrorism Research*, p. 28.

[29] G. Sartori, 'Concept Misformation in Comparative Politics', *The American Political Science Review*, Vol. 64, No. 4, December 1970, p. 1045.

[30] Sartori, 'Concept Misformation in Comparative Politics', p. 1045.

[31] Schmid, 'Introduction', in *The Routledge Handbook of Terrorism Research*, pp. 2–3.

[32] See A. Silke, 'The Road Less Travelled: Recent Trends in Terrorism Research', in Silke (ed.), *Research on Terrorism: Trends, Achievements and Failures.*

Jongman's (often quoted) view was that 'there are probably few areas in the social science literature in which so much is written on the basis of so little research'.[33] Much of the writing has been 'impressionistic' and 'superficial',[34] with as much as 80 per cent of the literature 'not research-based in any rigorous sense'.[35] Despite the increase in 'quantity, scope and variety' in terrorism studies post 9/11, 'the level of theoretical development remains inconsistent and uneven and there is still acute need for a solid empirical foundation'.[36]

It is not within the remit of this chapter to provide an overview of the problems and challenges of terrorism research. These issues have been well documented elsewhere.[37] It is, however, concerned with what has arguably been terrorism research's most fundamental problem—its failure to generate a consensus as to what terrorism means. There are many social science concepts where definition may not be seen as an integral endeavour and where such exploits may be seen as of incidental relevance to the 'real world'. As I have argued, this is not the case with terrorism. There are, unfortunately, serious consequences that result from the failure to agree a definition—not least the political abuse of the term to justify ever-shifting and expanding parameters of 'counter-terrorism'.

To reiterate, this work is not concerned with 'problem solving' on behalf of existing power structures in 'dealing' with this 'particular source...of trouble'.[38] Rather, it sets out to approach the definitional problem in as dispassionate, non-emotive, and neutral way as possible. Whether this better informs policymaking is another question. The key point is that a more objective, impartial, and honest approach on the definitional issue should inform policymaking perspectives rather than state priorities informing the conceptual discussion. It is the responsibility of independent academic research to try to achieve this—to conceptualize terrorism in a world where others have run amok with the term, particularly after 9/11. It is then up to governments to decide whether or not to engage with such academic exploits.

This is, of course, not the first time that such an endeavour has been proposed. Schmid and Jongman, in what one might regard as a 'critical'

---

[33] Schmid and Jongman, *Political Terrorism*, p. 179.

[34] Schmid and Jongman, *Political Terrorism*, p. 177.

[35] Schmid and Jongman, *Political Terrorism*, p. 179.

[36] Crenshaw, *Explaining Terrorism: Causes, Processes and Consequences*, p. x.

[37] See Silke (ed.), *Research on Terrorism: Trends, Achievements and Failures*; Silke, 'The Devil You Know: Continuing Problems with Research on Terrorism'; Schmid and Jongman, *Political Terrorism*; M. Ranstorp (ed.), *Mapping Terrorism Research: State of the Art, Gaps and Future Direction* (Abingdon: Routledge, 2007).

[38] R. Cox and T. Sinclair, 'Social Forces, States, and World Orders', in *Approaches to World Order* (Cambridge: Cambridge University Press, 1996), p. 88.

passage in *Political Terrorism*, called for a more neutral approach to the study of terrorism, which they thought was:

> too often...condemnatory, and prescriptive. Even the prescriptive literature is very one-sided: Almost all recommendations on how to cope with terrorism and how to deal with terrorists focus on non-state, mainly left-wing and minority-group opponents. There is a conspicuous absence of literature that addresses itself to the much more serious problem of state terrorism...Ideally, the scientific literature of terrorism should be apolitical and amoral. The research should not take a 'top-down' perspective, looking at the phenomenon of terrorism through the eyes of the power holders; nor should the researcher look at terrorism from a 'revolutionary' or 'progressive' perspective, identifying with one 'just' cause or another...Such a neutral researcher might be less popular with political parties attempting to win allies to bolster their perspective. However, the quality of his [sic] research might improve and ultimately his [sic] prescriptions for dealing with terrorism might be more valuable if they are not built on the ideological foundations of one or another party to the conflict...the absence of...even-handedness is...the chief deficiency of the literature of terrorism.[39]

While cognizant of the view that 'those who claim objectivity are the farthest of all from that scholarly ideal',[40] this book aims to, at least in part, pursue Schmid and Jongman's 'ideal' to be 'apolitical and amoral', and this includes addressing the activity of states (including democratic ones) as well as being ideologically neutral in any conceptual endeavour. For example, even if we ourselves participate in, legitimize, and endorse democracy (however defined), we shouldn't instinctively shirk from using the term terrorism to describe the violence perpetrated by those struggling for a democratic cause compared with those who are not. Terrorism is a method and should be defined independently from the ideological cause in whose name it is carried out.[41] The more one refrains from using the word terrorism because of sympathy with the cause, or the more that one is inclined to use it because of antipathy towards the goals, then the further away we are from enhancing terrorism as an analytical concept.

It is interesting to note that some of the aspirations of prominent so-called 'traditional' or 'orthodox' terrorism researchers echo the sentiments of contemporary 'critical terrorism studies' scholars, indicating that perhaps these

---

[39] Schmid and Jongman, *Political Terrorism*, pp. 179–80.

[40] K. Booth (ed.), *Critical Security Studies and World Politics* (Boulder, CO: Lynne Rienner, 2005), p. 10.

[41] There may be some ideologies where the use of terrorism may be intrinsic to them but these cannot take ownership of terrorism for there are many doctrines that are not inherently violent (or more specifically, not terrorist) despite the fact that terrorism has been employed in their name, and so for *definitional* purposes terrorism should be seen as a particular method of political violence rather than something that is only peculiar to certain belief systems.

'traditional' and 'critical' perspectives are not that far removed from each other. Schmid and Jongman, for example, observed that:

> The role of academic research and writing on terrorism should not, even in democracies, be confined to providing intellectual support to consolidate the rule of those in power. Rather, social scientists should seek to 'speak truth to power' as well as to the 'powerless' and those who identify with and fight for their causes.[42]

Along with the merits of adopting a more 'neutral' approach, Silke outlines the academic benefits of achieving consensus on the meaning of the concept:

> An agreed definition allows the research world to develop shared methods, approaches, benchmarks and appropriate topics for study. Without a definition, the focus of the field is scattered and fragmented, and an unrealistic range of activities, phenomena and actors have been labelled as terrorist.[43]

It therefore seems strange that there has been such scant attention on the definitional issue in research on terrorism.[44] Silke, in his analysis of the main academic terrorism journals in the period 1990–9, found that '[o]f the 490 articles published in the ten-year period, just eight (1.6 per cent) could be regarded as primarily conceptual papers',[45] while in the period 2000–7 'there were only seven articles on definitional aspects'.[46] Another researcher noted in 2007 that '[given] the exceptional salience and policy relevance of this concept, it is surprising to see that over 77% of scholars in leading political science journals who focus on terrorism fail to define it, and many of the remaining 23% offer definitions of their own without paying due consideration to the implications of their conceptual choices.'[47] Why, given the importance of an agreed definition of terrorism and the serious inhibitions of a lack of one, is there such academic paucity on the issue? Silke suggests the following may be the case:

> that there seems to be something of a war-weariness among established researchers over the definitional quagmire. Everyone is by now very familiar with the huge difficulties faced by any attempt to achieve consensus, and, rather than continue to struggle for the nebulous goal of an agreed framework, researchers seem to have

---

[42] Schmid and Jongman, *Political Terrorism*, p. 185.

[43] A. Silke, 'An Introduction to Terrorism Research', in Silke (ed.), *Research on Terrorism: Trends, Achievements and Failures*, p. 4.

[44] This paragraph and the following two paragraphs have been reprinted with the permission of Taylor and Francis LLC from Richards, 'Conceptualizing Terrorism', pp. 215–16.

[45] Silke, 'The Road Less Travelled: Recent Trends in Terrorism Research', p. 207.

[46] M. Ranstorp, 'Mapping Terrorism Studies after 9/11', in Jackson et al. (eds.), *Critical Terrorism Studies*, p. 23.

[47] O. Bogatyrenko, 'Definitional Analysis of Terrorism: Constructing Concepts and Populations for Social Science Research', paper prepared for 2007 meeting of the International Studies Association, February–March 2007, p. 2, cited in Schmid, 'The Definition of Terrorism', p. 90 (footnote 28).

resigned themselves to accepting the current state of uncertainty and to allow everyone to work within their own more limited frameworks.[48]

He goes on to argue that 'the lack of conceptual/definitional agreement is having some damaging impact' and that the field has become 'extremely applied':

> This can be seen not only in the very small number of writers and articles which tackle conceptual issues full-on, but also in other respects. For example, the field is almost entirely focused on issues of immediate, real-world relevance. The papers are about terrorist groups which are currently active, about current or imminent threats, or are focused on regions with recent or current experience of terrorist violence. There is virtually no effort to set terrorism within a broader context...this wider context is almost entirely ignored as terrorism research is driven by a need to provide a short-term, immediate assessment of current groups and threats. Efforts to establish coherent and stable guiding principles have been almost entirely side-lined. This is a serious cause for concern and is an issue which the more committed researchers will hopefully turn increased attention towards.[49]

'Stable and guiding principles' and the quest for greater conceptual development have therefore been at the mercy of the immediate concerns and sometimes knee-jerk reactions of policymakers (and often, therefore, of academics) to the latest terrorist atrocity. There is a real need for a commitment to the conceptual development of terrorism—so that any ultimate conceptualization of terrorism is *sustainable*, and is able to withstand the constant buffeting of the exigencies of the day and of research efforts rather narrowly being 'driven very much by issues of contemporary relevance' of concern to 'western democracies' and the United States.[50] A definition of terrorism should not, for instance, be moulded by whatever the adversary of the day is doing—for example, by including whatever the latest mode of activity that Al Qaeda is engaged with. Rather, acts of violence should be measured and assessed against the definitional criteria that have been established to determine whether or not such acts constitute terrorism.

As the following chapters will attempt to show, any serious effort to conceptualize terrorism is also inherently an endeavour to *understand* the concept, if one indeed accepts that it is a distinctive phenomenon within the spectrum of political violence. Ineluctably, determining what is and what is not terrorism is the starting point that informs the plethora of other

---

[48] Silke, 'The Road Less Travelled: Recent Trends in Terrorism Research', p. 208.
[49] Silke, 'The Road Less Travelled: Recent Trends in Terrorism Research', pp. 208–9.
[50] Silke, 'The Road Less Travelled: Recent Trends in Terrorism Research', p. 210.

terrorism theories.[51] It is the foundation upon which all other theories of terrorism rest. How, for example, can we begin to theorize about the causes of terrorism if we haven't agreed what terrorism is? How can we determine why individuals become terrorists or the reasons why groups employ terrorism if we are unclear about what constitutes terrorism? Similarly, the meaning of terrorism is fundamental to theories of disengagement from terrorism, to theories of how terrorism begins and ends, and indeed to theories of counter-terrorism. All of these theoretical endeavours are surely dependent on what is meant by terrorism in the first place. Defining terrorism, then, importantly and usefully sets the parameters for terrorism research.

While it has been noted that conceptual issues receive scant attention in the terrorism studies literature, there is much greater attention paid to case study research. Case studies are interesting but they are rarely underpinned by sufficient theoretical and conceptual analysis as to what is meant by terrorism. For example, what is 'terrorist' about a particular case study as distinct from insurgency, civil war, guerrilla warfare, illegal violence in general, and so on? What are the different modes of political violence that exist in a terrorist related conflict, for acts of terrorism can take place 'alongside a multitude of other political and criminal acts'?[52] How is terrorism distinguished from other forms of violence within a conflict and how often are serious attempts made to draw these distinctions?[53] Furthermore, what constitutes a 'terrorist organization'?[54] These are important questions for students and scholars of terrorism studies and ones that can only be addressed through the development of a theoretical framework as to what terrorism is. Indeed, in Schmid's survey of expert respondents the 29 terrorism research priorities that were identified (including theories on the causes of, and responses to, terrorism) *are all in some way or another contingent on what one means by 'terrorism'*.[55]

Drawing such distinctions between different forms of political violence is no easy task, perhaps evident in the broad and catch-all titles of two of the main terrorism journals: 'Terrorism and *Political Violence*' and 'Studies in *Conflict* and Terrorism' (italics added). Indeed, warns Crenshaw, '[e]ven the best scholarly intentions may not suffice to distinguish terrorism from protest,

---

[51] For a list of terrorism related theories and 'approaches' see Schmid, 'Introduction', in *The Routledge Handbook of Terrorism Research*, pp. 11–12.

[52] Schmid, 'The Definition of Terrorism', p. 69.

[53] Crenshaw, for example, poses the following questions: '...which elements in the broad spectrum of violence in Ireland since the eighteenth century should rightly be called terrorism? Which revolutionary or counterrevolutionary practices during the eight years of the Algerian war constituted terrorism?' (M. Crenshaw, 'Terrorism in Context', Pennsylvania State University, cited in D. Whittaker (ed.), *The Terrorism Reader* (New York and London: Routledge, 2001), p. 13).

[54] As Crenshaw suggests, 'the term "terrorist organization" is also contentious...Its use can imply that the organization in question uses terrorism exclusively of other means, which is rare' (Crenshaw, *Explaining Terrorism: Causes, Processes and Consequences*, p. 4).

[55] Schmid, 'Introduction', in *The Routledge Handbook of Terrorism Research*, pp. 7–8.

guerrilla warfare, urban guerrilla warfare, subversion, criminal violence, para-militarism, communal violence, or banditry.'[56] Moreover, terrorism is often said to be 'a product of its own time and place' and 'an attractive strategy to a diverse array of groups which have little else in common'[57]—arguably deeming any attempt to pursue a general theory as to what terrorism means as inherently doomed.

But, in summary, there is a real need to identify what the terrorism is in each case as distinct from other forms of political violence, particularly as it is very unusual for terrorism to be used exclusively as a form of struggle.[58] A greater theoretical appreciation as to what terrorism is would inform both the choice of methodological approaches and the identification of case studies, and, indeed, what aspects of the activities of cases constitute terrorism and what parts do not. Finally, defining terrorism is also integral to attempts to compile chronologies and databases of terrorist incidents in order to determine what acts of violence can and cannot be included in such data-gathering exercises.[59]

[56] Crenshaw, 'Terrorism in Context', cited in Whittaker (ed.), *The Terrorism Reader*, p. 12.

[57] International Summit on Democracy, Terrorism and Security, 'Addressing the Causes of Terrorism', Volume 1, 8–11 March 2005, The Club de Madrid Series on Democracy and Terrorism, p. 7, available at: <http://www.clubmadrid.org/img/secciones/Club_de_Madrid_Volume_I_The_Causes_of_Terrorism.pdf> (last accessed 27 November 2014).

[58] See Crenshaw, *Explaining Terrorism: Causes, Processes and Consequences*, p. 4.

[59] See, for example, B. Jenkins, 'The Study of Terrorism: Definitional Problems', in Y. Alexander and J. Gleason (eds.), *Behavioural and Quantitative Perspectives on Terrorism* (New York and Oxford: Pergamon Press, 1981), and Schmid, 'The Definition of Terrorism', p. 49.

3

The Evolution of the Definitional Debate: The Policymaking Perspective

In what has been described as the 'most significant early modern attempt to define terrorism as an international crime'[1] the League of Nations described it as '[a]ll criminal acts directed against a State and intended or calculated to create a state of terror in the minds of particular persons or a group of persons or the general public'.[2] It was a definition, Saul argues, that 'prefigured many of the legal, political, ideological and rhetorical disputes which plagued the international community's attempts to define terrorism in the 50 years after the Second World War'.[3] He argued that these legal disputes that the League anticipated included:

> the political and technical difficulties of definition; the problem of 'freedom fighters' and self-determination; 'state terrorism' and the duty of non-intervention; state criminality and applicability to armed forces; the scope of the political offence exception to extradition; the impact on freedom of expression; and the relationship between terrorism and asylum. The core definition of terrorism adopted by the League in 1937 has proved remarkably durable, influencing approaches to definition in a variety of legal contexts in subsequent years.[4]

Saul's interesting article sheds light on some of the deliberations of the participating states on the League's Committee for the International Repression of Terrorism, many of which echo with contemporary legal dilemmas. In their attempts to define terrorism it was clear that it would be no easy task with the United Kingdom referring to the 'exceptional complexity' of the proposals

---

[1] B. Saul, 'The Legal Response of the League of Nations to Terrorism', *Journal of International Criminal Justice*, Volume 4, Issue 1, 2006, p. 79. Abstract also available at: <http://jicj.oxfordjournals.org/content/4/1/78.abstract> (last accessed 11 December 2014).

[2] Cited in Acharya, 'War on Terror or Terror Wars: The Problem in Defining Terrorism', pp. 657–8.

[3] Saul, 'The Legal Response of the League of Nations to Terrorism', p. 78.

[4] Saul, 'The Legal Response of the League of Nations to Terrorism', p. 79.

and the 'difficulties inherent in the subject', while Belgium's concern that the term 'terrorism' could be abused to condemn any act of violence or rebellion also certainly has strong contemporary resonance.[5] Again echoing very similar but much later dilemmas Czechoslovakia argued that '[t]o avoid the difficulty of definition . . . the Convention should not refer to the ambiguous term "terrorism", but only to objective criminal acts', while '[i]n contrast, Yugoslavia argued for a generic approach to definition, elaborating the common elements of every form of terrorism.'[6] Indeed, 'the threshold question of whether to define terrorism generically or only to prohibit objective criminal acts persisted throughout the drafting.'[7]

With the onset of the Second World War and the dissolution of the League in 1946, its successor, the United Nations, did not revisit the definitional debate until as late as 1972 (after the dramatic attack on the Munich Olympics by the Black September group). One of three sub-committees to the Ad Hoc Committee on International Terrorism was assigned the task of tackling the problem of definition but, as Schmid describes, it met with little success:

> no consensus could be reached. The Non-Aligned Group defined terrorism as acts of violence committed by a group of individuals which endanger human lives and jeopardise fundamental freedoms, the effects of which are not confined to one state. The proposal stressed that this definition would not affect the inalienable right to self-determination of people subjected to colonial and racist regimes. Other states made similar distinctions. Greece, for instance, distinguished terrorism from freedom fighting. France, on the other hand, described in its proposal, international terrorism as a heinous act of barbarism committed on foreign territory. As a result of such divisions, no resolution on the definition of terrorism could be adopted, and after six years the committee was phased out.[8]

Indeed, for some there has been something of a contradictory approach from the United Nations between emphasizing the right to enjoy 'freedom from fear' while at the same time legitimizing struggles for national liberation. Wilkinson, one of the pioneers of terrorism studies in the United Kingdom, wrote of the 'fatal ambivalence' of this approach:

> Thus the UN is seen to be supporting both sides at once in such conflicts. For example, Israel, as a member state, is accorded full 'sovereign equality' and protection of that sovereignty. Simultaneously other member states of the UN can claim that they are fully entitled to arm and support movements dedicated to the

---

[5] Saul, 'The Legal Response of the League of Nations to Terrorism', p. 89.
[6] Saul, 'The Legal Response of the League of Nations to Terrorism', p. 89.
[7] Saul, 'The Legal Response of the League of Nations to Terrorism', p. 89.
[8] Schmid, 'Terrorism: The Definitional Problem', p. 386.

liquidation of Israel, on the grounds that they are merely supporting a legitimate national liberation struggle aimed at self-determination.[9]

Thus, while some have viewed the Palestine Liberation Organization as a terrorist group others have seen its activity as legitimate and in the cause of national liberation. Similarly (and as I have noted in the previous chapter), in the context of the Cold War, the Soviet Union viewed what many saw as left-wing revolutionary terrorism as worthy liberation struggles, while the United States endorsed the Nicaraguan Contras who were said to have committed horrific 'terrorist' acts.[10] Beres argued that the:

> United States and Soviet leaders accepted a narrow, geopolitical definition of terrorism. The United States characterized any insurgent force operating against an allegedly pro-Soviet regime as lawful regardless of the means used in the insurgency. Reciprocally, any activity by an insurgent force operating against a pro-United States regime was automatically characterized as terrorism. The Soviet leaders believed that the United States was using the term 'terrorism' to discredit what the Soviets alleged were legitimate movements for self-determination and associated human rights. Under the Soviet view, insurgency against what the United States freely called authoritarian regimes—for example, the regimes in El Salvador, Guatemala, and Chile—was not terrorism, as the United States had maintained, but national liberation.[11]

Little wonder, then, that the international community has found it difficult to agree upon a definition when it has often depended upon who the perpetrators are or, rather, for what cause they have been fighting. For 'terrorism' or 'terrorist' has often been used as a derogatory label against one's enemies, or, put simply, terrorism has been viewed as 'violence of which we do not approve', or whose cause one disagrees with.[12] Hence, the reason why the old adage 'one person's terrorist is another's freedom fighter' has managed to retain so much purchase and why 'terrorism' has struggled to gain credibility as an analytical concept above the parapet of political rhetoric and name calling.

One could, of course, simply concede that 'terrorism' is after all intrinsically a rhetorical device and nothing more. Alternatively (if we believe that there is something more to terrorism than this), one can argue that focusing on the perpetrator or the goal in this way deflects us from understanding terrorism as a particular *method* of political violence, regardless of what the cause is or who the perpetrator might be, and any attempt to infuse some analytical utility into the term must be mindful of this. And, as Duvall and Stohl have argued, there is a real

---

[9] P. Wilkinson, *Terrorism versus Democracy: The Liberal State Response* (London: Frank Cass, 2002), pp. 189–90.

[10] Schmid and Jongman, *Political Terrorism*, p. 17.

[11] L. R. Beres, 'Meaning of Terrorism: Jurisprudential and Definitional Clarifications', *Vanderbilt Journal of Transnational Law*, Vol. 28, 1995, p. 248.

[12] Schmid and Jongman, *Political Terrorism*, p. 3.

need to increase the analytical power of the concept by emphasizing denotative criteria at the expense of emotive criteria.[13] Only then can one begin to think rather more objectively as to what constitutes terrorism and what does not.

The Olympic movement, as an international endeavour that seeks to promote peace and harmony, was ideally positioned to experience the frustrations, from a policymaking perspective, of the definitional issue as an obstacle to international cooperation against terrorism. Even after the most devastating attack ever to have afflicted the Olympics in Munich 1972 the then Secretary-General of the United Nations, Kurt Waldheim, in his efforts to encourage member states to agree to the need for 'measures to prevent terrorist and other forms of violence which endanger or take human lives or jeopardise fundamental freedoms', was confronted by deep concern from some African and Arab states that those engaged in legitimate national liberation struggles would be classified as terrorists.[14] And Syria shortly afterwards argued that 'the international community is under legal and moral obligation to promote the struggle for liberation and to resist any attempt to depict this struggle as synonymous with terrorism and illegitimate violence.'[15] There has therefore been a stalemate brought about between those that see certain acts of violence as terrorism and those that prefer not to use the term to describe the activities of 'independence movements and the legitimate defence of land under foreign occupation'.[16] This inclination to associate terrorism or 'freedom fighting' with one cause or another, or with one perpetrator or another, again deflects us from understanding terrorism as a method independent from the cause.

A universally agreed definition of terrorism has continued to elude the international community. Even in the immediate aftermath of 9/11, with a 'spirit of compromise' in the air, efforts were thwarted when the Organization of the Islamic Conference (OIC) argued for the exemption of 'national liberation movements fighting foreign occupation such as the Israeli occupation of Palestinian land'.[17] There were also calls for states to be culpable for acts of 'state terrorism'. Rostow argued that:

> First, the OIC wants to exclude acts directed against foreign occupation from the terrorist label. In 2001, the reasons did not need to be declared: the OIC wanted to

---

[13] R. Duvall and M. Stohl, 'Governance by Terror', in M. Stohl (ed.), *The Politics of Terrorism* (New York: Marcel Dekker, 1988), p. 232.

[14] G. Wardlaw, *Political Terrorism* (Cambridge: Cambridge University Press, 1990), Chapter 1: 'The Problem of Defining Terrorism', p. 105.

[15] B. Hoffman, 'Defining Terrorism', in R. Howard and R. Sawyer (eds.), *Terrorism and Counterterrorism: Understanding the New Security Environment, Readings and Interpretations* (New York: McGraw-Hill, 2002), p. 16.

[16] Which was, for example, the view of the Iranian government (cited in M. Dartnell, 'A Legal Inter-Network for Terrorism: Issues of Globalization, Fragmentation and Legitimacy', *Terrorism and Political Violence*, Vol. 4, No. 11, 1999, p. 199).

[17] Schmid, 'Terrorism: The Definitional Problem', p. 388.

exempt terrorism against Israel and terrorism against India over Kashmir. Second, the OIC wanted to brand violations of the laws of war by State military forces as terrorist. This goal is aimed at the Israel Defense Forces. All countries with large armies objected. Violations of the laws of war are war crimes; they are not ipso facto acts of terrorism.[18]

A somewhat different perspective was presented by Zeidan:

> terrorism should not be equated with the legitimate, internationally protected right of peoples to self-determination. To resist occupation is to end the highest form of terrorism, namely, state terrorism. For example, Israel's occupation and partial annexation of lands conquered in 1967 is a violation of international law, specifically Security Council Resolutions 242 and 338, which urge it to end its illegal occupation of Arab territories. Thus, the struggle of Palestinians is as legitimate as the American War of Independence and the French Revolution. The same applies to Israel's illegal occupation of South Lebanon for more than two decades, and its continued occupation of the Lebanese Shebaa Farms. As long as the totality of Lebanese territory has not been liberated, the Lebanese resistance to the Israeli occupation will thus remain a legitimate right in accordance with international law.[19]

Terrorism has thus continued to be associated with particular causes, and, in the context of the Israeli–Palestine conflict in particular, both have committed acts of 'terrorism' depending upon which side one sits. It is in the context of highly charged and polarized conflict environments that terrorism continues to be deployed as a rhetorical device to denounce one's enemies.

Rostow remarked that '[t]he conventional wisdom concludes that the international community will not succeed in this area [of the definition of terrorism] until the conflicts in the Middle East and over Kashmir come to an end',[20] while Schmid noted that '[t]he two main issues that obstruct progress are . . . "state terrorism" and the "struggle for national liberation"—both of them related to the Palestinian question and to the question of Kashmir.'[21] It seems therefore, at least in the international policymaking context, that there is little hope of elevating 'terrorism' as an analytical concept above the parapet of political rhetoric. Such an endeavour seems, in reality, peripheral to the imperative of mobilizing every propaganda and language ploy to discredit the adversary, leaving little room for detached clinical and objective analysis. As Herbst argued:

---

[18] N. Rostow, 'Before and After: The Changed UN Response to Terrorism since September 11th', *Cornell International Law Journal*, Vol. 35, No. 3, 2002, p. 488.

[19] Zeidan, 'Desperately Seeking Definition: The International Community's Quest for Identifying the Specter of Terrorism', p. 493.

[20] Rostow, 'Before and After: The Changed UN Response to Terrorism since September 11th', p. 489.

[21] Schmid, 'Terrorism: The Definitional Problem', p. 389.

Carrying enormous emotional freight, *terrorism* is often used to define reality in order to place one's own group on a high moral plane, condemn the enemy, rally members around a cause...Conveying criminality, illegitimacy, and even madness, the application of *terrorist* shuts the door to discussion about the stigmatized group or with them, while reinforcing the righteousness of the labelers, justifying their agendas and mobilizing their responses.[22]

Once again, therefore, it is perhaps not surprising that the unhelpful mantra of 'one person's terrorist is another's freedom fighter' still has resonance and, if terrorism is merely a label to describe violence that is not qualitatively different to other forms, then this may indeed be a reasonable depiction.[23] But, *if there really is something distinctive about terrorism* then, as Leonard Weinberg observed, the terrorist/freedom fighter dichotomy confuses the goal with the activity.[24] So too, therefore, does the view (apparently articulated by the UN Secretary-General in March 1987 in relation to the Palestine Liberation Organization and the South West Africa People's Organization) that 'sometimes it is difficult to tell where terrorism ends and the struggle for self-determination begins'[25] or when observers pose similar questions (such as: 'where to draw the line between the quest for nationalist identity and an act of terrorism...?'[26]), or when Yasir Arafat declared that:

The difference between the revolutionary and the terrorist lies in the reason for which each fights. For whoever stands by a just cause and fights for the freedom and liberation of his land from the invaders, the settlers and the colonialists, cannot possibly be called a terrorist.[27]

The difference between the terrorist and the non-terrorist *does not* lie in the reason for which one fights, as Arafat claimed. National liberation is a cause and terrorism is a method. Otherwise we are conceding that terrorism really is 'violence that we don't like'[28] (or whose cause we disagree with) and that there is in fact nothing particularly unique or qualitatively distinctive about the phenomenon compared with other forms of political violence. Yet, unfortunately in practice the 'right to self-determination' and terrorism have still not

---

[22] P. Herbst, *Talking Terrorism: A Dictionary of the Loaded Language of Political Violence* (Westport, CT: Greenwood Press, 2003), pp. 163–4 (emphasis in original), cited in Schmid, 'Terrorism: The Definitional Problem', p. 397.

[23] Parts of this paragraph and the following paragraph have been reprinted with the permission of Taylor and Francis LLC from Richards, 'Conceptualizing Terrorism', p. 225.

[24] L. Weinberg, *Global Terrorism: A Beginner's Guide* (London: Oneworld), p. 2.

[25] V. Romanov, 'The United Nations and the Problem of Combating International Terrorism', *Terrorism and Political Violence*, Vol. 2, No. 3, 1990, p. 295.

[26] Acharya, 'War on Terror or Terror Wars: The Problem in Defining Terrorism', p. 656.

[27] Y. Arafat, cited in B. Hoffman, *Inside Terrorism* (New York: Columbia University Press, 1998), p. 26.

[28] As Schmid maintains, the mantra of 'one man's terrorist is another man's freedom fighter' is therefore also an 'open invitation to maintain and perpetuate double standards' (Schmid, 'The Definition of Terrorism', p. 40).

been 'decoupled' and the freedom fighter/terrorist mantra continues to endure.[29]

The main obstacle that has confronted those aspiring to reach an analytical definition of terrorism in the 'real world', then, has been its almost inexorable and subjective use as a derogatory label, whether warranted or not. Indeed, '[t]o some, the term "terrorism" itself might therefore be seen as an obstacle to genuinely dispassionate analysis, given that it is so profoundly loaded and condemnatory'[30] or used 'as a snare and a delusion, a semantic device by which the state and its agents divert attention from their own crimes'.[31]

The challenge then is to adopt a more detached, dispassionate, and analytical approach in order to determine what it is that is particular about terrorism. As Chapter 1 has argued, it may be that the outcome of such an approach may lead one to sympathize with certain 'terrorisms'. Depending on one's perspective in relation to the goal, and providing civilians and non-combatants are not targeted, there may indeed be some terrorisms that one might endorse, but, subject to the satisfaction of one's definitional criteria, *terrorism nonetheless it remains*, and any such determination is not intended as a moral judgement but as the outcome of dispassionate analysis. For the aim here is to elevate terrorism as an analytical concept at the expense of emotive labelling. In the policy-making arena, as Schmid noted in 2004, 'the problem of finding consensus on a universal definition is, at this stage, more a political than a legal or semantic problem'.[32] For detached academics this should not thwart their own endeavours to imbue some analytical quality into the concept of terrorism.

The UN Focus on 'Terrorist Acts'

With universal agreement on any definition of terrorism proving to be elusive the tendency of the United Nations has been to address the physical manifestations of terrorism, such as hijacking, hostage-taking, or 'terrorist' bombings. As the European Commission Sixth Framework Programme Project on defining terrorism noted:

[29] Schmid, 'The Definition of Terrorism', p. 50. For example (p. 92, footnote 57), the Organization of the Islamic Conference argued for the 'exclusion of acts done in the pursuance of liberation struggles' and proposed that 'Peoples' struggle including armed struggle against foreign occupation, aggression, colonialism, and hegemony, aimed at liberation and self-determination in accordance with the principles of international law shall not be considered a terrorist crime.'

[30] English, *Terrorism: How to Respond*, p. 20.

[31] Weinberg et al., 'The Challenges of Conceptualising Terrorism', p. 786.

[32] Schmid, 'Terrorism: The Definitional Problem', p. 390.

[t]hroughout the years, numerous international legal attempts dealing with terrorism mostly avoided the difficulty of drafting a general definition. The chosen path in the multilateral arena was to tackle issue-specific aspects of terrorism.[33]

There are two problems with this approach: firstly, technological advances mean that there are potentially endless *types* of physical attacks that could be carried out that UN Conventions would be hard pressed to keep up with; secondly, and most importantly for this discussion, there is in my view no such thing as an act of violence that is in and of itself inherently terrorist (see Chapter 5) and so compiling lists of types of attacks that are said to be the physical manifestations of terrorism do not help us to capture 'what terrorism is'. For, as I have argued, the essence of terrorism lies in the *intent* behind the act rather than the type of violent act itself. Schmid and Jongman have also argued that '[t]he nature of terrorism is not inherent in the violent act itself. One and the same act . . . can be terrorist or not, depending on intention and circumstance.'[34]

Not surprisingly the majority of the Conventions, which include addressing hijacking, nuclear material protection, maritime security, fixed platform safety, terrorist bombings, and terrorist financing, do not discuss the definitional issue at length. The 1999 International Convention for the Suppression of the Financing of Terrorism, regarded at the time as the Convention that shed most light on the definitional issue, did, however, refer to a terrorist act as:

intended to cause death or serious bodily injury to a civilian, or to any other person not taking an active part in the hostilities in a situation of armed conflict, when the purpose of such act, by its nature or context, is to intimidate a population, or to compel a government or an international organization to do or to abstain from doing any act.[35]

The 2005 Protocol to the Convention for the Suppression of Unlawful Acts against the Safety of Maritime Navigation also identified a 'terrorist' offence '[w]hen the purpose of the act, by its nature or context, is to intimidate a population, or to compel a government or an international organization to do or to abstain from doing any act',[36] while both the 1997 International Convention for the Suppression of Terrorist Bombings and the 2005 International

---

[33] European Commission Sixth Framework Programme Project, 'Defining Terrorism' (WP3 Deliverable 4), p. 4.

[34] Schmid and Jongman, *Political Terrorism* [1988], p. 101, cited in Jackson, 'The Core Commitments of Critical Terrorism Studies', p. 247.

[35] Available at: <http://www.un.org/en/terrorism/instruments.shtml> (last accessed 27 November 2014).

[36] Available at: <https://www.unodc.org/tldb/en/2005_Protocol2Convention_Maritime%20Navigation.html> (last accessed 27 November 2014).

45

LIBRARY, UNIVERSITY OF CHESTER

Convention for the Suppression of Acts of Nuclear Terrorism refer to terrorism as:

> criminal acts within the scope of this Convention, in particular where they are intended or calculated to provoke a state of terror in the general public or in a group of persons or particular persons, [and] are under no circumstances justifiable by considerations of a political, philosophical, ideological, racial, ethnic, religious or other similar nature and are punished by penalties consistent with their grave nature.[37]

Nevertheless, the Conventions generally steered clear of any serious engagement with the definitional debate. As Rostow acknowledges, '[t]he goal was to create a basis for universal jurisdiction over, and condemnation and criminalization of, the types of crimes that terrorists commit, but not terrorism per se.'[38]

The 2008 European Commission Sixth Framework Programme Project on 'Defining Terrorism' noted that 'at the regional level, in some cases, consensus was reached on a general definition' through, for example, the SAARC[39] Regional Convention on the Suppression of Terrorism, the Arab Convention on the Suppression of Terrorism, the Convention of the Organization of the Islamic Conference on Combating International Terrorism, and the OAU Convention on the Prevention and Combating of Terrorism.[40] Interestingly, scrutiny of the latter three Conventions reveals a familiar dilemma: terrorism is defined *but with the exclusion of violence carried out in the cause of national liberation*, which again deviates us from the analytical task of determining what it is that is distinctive about the *activity* of terrorism, regardless of the cause in whose name it is being employed.[41]

---

[37] Both available at: <http://www.un.org/en/terrorism/instruments.shtml> (last accessed 27 November 2014).

[38] Rostow, 'Before and After: The Changed UN Response to Terrorism since September 11th', p. 480. UN Resolution 1566 (2004) did, however, refer to terrorism as

> ...criminal acts, including against civilians, committed with the intent to cause death or serious bodily injury, or taking of hostages, with the purpose to provoke a state of terror in the general public or in a group of persons or particular persons, intimidate a population or compel a government or an international organization to do or to abstain from doing any act, which constitute offences within the scope of and as defined in the international conventions and protocols relating to terrorism, are under no circumstances justifiable by considerations of a political, philosophical, ideological, racial, ethnic, religious or other similar nature...

Available at: <file:///C:/Users/arich_000/Downloads/SC1566.pdf> (last accessed 8 December 2014).

[39] South Asian Association for Regional Cooperation.

[40] European Commission Sixth Framework Programme Project, 'Defining Terrorism' (WP3 Deliverable 4), pp. 89–90.

[41] The Arab Convention on the Suppression of Terrorism, for example, defines terrorism as:

> Any act or threat of violence, whatever its motives or purposes, that occurs in the advancement of an individual or collective criminal agenda and seeking to sow panic

The UN and Civilians/Non-Combatants as Victims in a Definition of Terrorism

Commenting on the continuing elusiveness of a universally agreed definition, Gearty remarked that:

> The difficulties that have blocked emergence of such a final draft (of a general convention on terrorism) have withstood even the crisis atmosphere engendered by the 11 September attacks. The problem with taking a generalised approach to the subject of terrorism (rather than focusing on particular methods of violence, or places in the world) is that it flushes out, in a way that such targeted agreements do not, the underlying but rarely articulated assumption of many state members, namely that subversive violence can in the right circumstances be a legitimate means of achieving political change or of resisting foreign occupation.[42]

> among people, causing fear by harming them, or placing their lives, liberty or security in danger, or seeking to cause damage to the environment or to public or private installations or property or to occupying or seizing them, or seeking to jeopardize a national resource.

But also states that:

> All cases of struggle *by whatever means*, including armed struggle, against foreign occupation and aggression for liberation and self-determination, in accordance with the principles of international law, shall not be regarded as an offence. This provision shall not apply to any act prejudicing the territorial integrity of any Arab State. (Italics added)

One presumes that 'in accordance with the principles of international law' refers to the UN endorsement of struggles for national liberation (Convention available at Council on Foreign Relations website at: <http://www.cfr.org/terrorism-and-the-law/arab-convention-suppression-terrorism-cairo-declaration/p24799> (last accessed 27 November 2014). A similar example is that of the OIC (the Organization of the Islamic Conference was renamed the Organization of Islamic Cooperation in 2011) which states that:

> 'Terrorism' means any act of violence or threat thereof notwithstanding its motives or intentions perpetrated to carry out an individual or collective criminal plan with the aim of terrorizing people or threatening to harm them or imperiling their lives, honor, freedoms, security or rights or exposing the environment or any facility or public or private property to hazards or occupying or seizing them, or endangering a national resource, or international facilities, or threatening the stability, territorial integrity, political unity or sovereignty of independent States.

While one might detect a Palestinian bias (for example, with the inclusion of [presumably Israeli] occupying or seizing of property) the OIC convention also states that:

> Peoples struggle including armed struggle against foreign occupation, aggression, colonialism, and hegemony, aimed at liberation and self-determination in accordance with the principles of international law shall not be considered a terrorist crime. (Convention available at: <http://www.cfr.org/terrorism-and-the-law/convention-organization-islamic-conference-oic-combating-international-terrorism/p24781> (last accessed 27 November 2014))

The OAU Convention's (Article 1) lengthier definition also contains a similar caveat (available at: <https://treaties.un.org/doc/db/Terrorism/OAU-english.pdf> (last accessed 27 November 2014)). These particular definitions and the deliberate distinctions they draw between acts of terrorism and acts that may be carried out in the cause of national liberation (though in 'accordance with the principles of international law', however interpreted) again deviate us from capturing the essence of terrorism as a qualitatively distinctive form of violence, regardless of the cause.

[42] C. Gearty, 'Situating International Human Rights Law in an Age of Counter-Terrorism', April 2008, p. 20. Available at: <http://www.conorgearty.co.uk/pdfs/EU_UN_textFINAL.pdf> (last accessed 27 November 2014).

Such an acknowledgement resonates with the notion that there may be some terrorisms that one might sympathize with, which in turn arguably questions the utility of zero-tolerance approaches to terrorism in all of 'its forms and manifestations' (and which therefore also seems to question any comprehensive convention that is drafted for the purpose of roundly condemning *all* forms of terrorism—see the following discussion and Chapters 5 and 6).

In 2005 Kofi Annan, the then Secretary-General of the UN, endorsed the definition of the United Nations High-Level Panel on Threats, Challenges and Change that defined terrorism as 'intended to cause death or serious bodily harm to civilians or non-combatants'.[43] He argued for a definition that:

> would make it clear that any action constitutes terrorism if it is intended to cause death or serious bodily harm to civilians or non-combatants, with the purpose of intimidating a population or compelling a Government or an international organization to do or abstain from doing any act. I believe this proposal has clear moral force, and I strongly urge world leaders to unite behind it, with a view to adopting the comprehensive convention as soon as possible.[44]

This understanding of terrorism as attacks on civilians and non-combatants is in keeping with international norms to do with the protection of these categories of persons in conflict. This moral impulse and the concern with *this particular form of terrorism*, however, should not, in my view, compromise attempts to reach a *general* definition of terrorism.[45]

At the policymaking level, one can appreciate endeavours to persuade the international community to at least agree that attacks on civilians should be deplored, and that agreement on a definition could be based around this, but if the essence of terrorism is to primarily generate a psychological impact beyond the immediate victims then this impact can be generated through attacks against combatants as well as civilians and non-combatant (whether intended to have a wider impact against a civilian population or a broader military group). Therefore, terrorism, providing its victims and objects of attack serve as sufficient 'message generators', can potentially be carried out against anyone (see the third assumption in Chapter 5).

If terrorism is *not* defined as limited to the targeting of civilians or non-combatants there may, as I have argued, be some 'terrorisms' that one might sympathize with, calling into question the utility of 'zero-tolerance' approaches

---

[43] United Nations High-Level Panel on Threats, Challenges and Change, Report: 'A More Secure World: Our Shared Responsibility', 2 December 2004, p. 52.

[44] United Nations, *In Larger Freedom: Towards Development, Security and Human Rights for All*, Chapter 3 ('Freedom from Fear'), p. 26.

[45] In other words a definition that also includes the possibility that combatants can be victims of terrorism.

to all terrorism.[46] In October 1995, for example, the UN Security Council 'adopted a decision to condemn terrorism in all its forms and manifestations irrespective of who resorted to it, the first unconditional condemnation of international terrorism in the 40-year UN history, whoever the perpetrator, and—one may assume—whatever the motive'.[47] The UN has continued to condemn terrorism 'in all its forms and manifestations since'.[48] The problem is that along with this approach often lies a simultaneous and implicit recognition that terrorism might in some circumstances be justified (as Gearty suggests above).

A European Commission report noted that:

> the prevailing literature and reports from NGOs point to the potential disintegration effects of terrorism on the freedoms, rights and liberties that also serve as the basis of the Charter of Fundamental Rights of the European Union.[49]

But what about acts of terrorism that do not target civilians (or non-combatants) but are carried out *in defence or pursuit of* 'freedoms, rights and liberties'? As Saul has remarked:

> if terrorism is indeed characterized as a crime against democracy, it begs the historically intractable question of whether terrorist acts directed to subverting non-democratic regimes, or against those which trample human rights, remain permissible. It is notable that some . . . UN resolutions refer to terrorism as 'destabilizing legitimately constituted Governments', implying that terrorism is not objectionable against *illegitimate* governments, particularly those oppressing self-determination movements.[50]

Nor, once again, should any acts of terrorism in support of 'freedoms, rights and liberties' be expediently called something else like 'freedom fighting' which again would only serve to blur analytical clarity. For example, if there is general agreement that the Beslan school siege in Moscow was a particularly

---

[46] Even if one defines terrorism as targeting civilians Schmid offers a hypothetical example of where there might be a case of 'good terrorism', where the seizure of the family of a genocidal dictator might be undertaken in order to prevent further genocide (depending on how one defines civilians), (Schmid, 'The Definition of Terrorism', p. 95 (footnote 101)).

[47] Romanov, 'The United Nations and the Problem of Combating International Terrorism', p. 297.

[48] See, for example, United Nations, 'UN Action to Counter Terrorism', available at: <http://www.un.org/terrorism/> (last accessed 27 November 2014). In 2005, UN officials were apparently divided 'over whether the term should be defined so that it featured only the element of terrorism, or the version of terrorism that focused on "evil men with dark intent" taking actions against others. Used in this way terrorism could never be a positive force used against a ruthless government, for instance, by "freedom fighters"' (H. O'Hair, R. Heath, K. Ayotte, and G. Ledlow (eds.), *Terrorism: Communication and Rhetorical Perspectives* (Cresskill, NJ: Hampton Press, 2008, p. 7)).

[49] European Commission Sixth Framework Programme Project, 'Defining Terrorism' (WP3 Deliverable 4), p. 89.

[50] Saul, 'Defining Terrorism to Protect Human Rights', p. 195.

brutal act of terrorism (that was unequivocally and roundly condemned) there may simultaneously be sympathy for acts of terrorism that do not target children and civilians and are against 'oppressive' regimes—*but they are both nevertheless acts of terrorism*, providing the primary purpose is to generate a psychological impact beyond the immediate victims (and subject to one's other definitional criteria). A more comprehensive approach to terrorism should account for these different forms.

Because there is an inclination to approach the definition with a view of its wrongfulness, it is easy to understand why labelling something as terrorism is seen as casting moral judgement on it as 'bad'. Therefore, the tendency to use alternative and more 'positive' terms to describe acts of terrorism, such as 'freedom fighting', 'resistance', and 'struggle', itself reinforces terrorism as a superficial and pejorative label at the expense of analytical utility. Hence, to reaffirm, when this author determines that a particular act of violence constitutes an act of terrorism this is not an inherently negative judgement on that act, or as something 'bad' to be countered with 'good'. The concern here is not to cast moral judgement as to whether terrorism is a good thing or a bad thing. From a purpose-based perspective my attempt to conceptualize terrorism takes into account its capacity to target non-civilians, non-combatants, and combatants and, if viewed analytically and dispassionately, not to exclude the possibility that there may be terrorisms that one might sympathize with.

4

The Meaning of Terrorism: Academic Perspectives

Academic perspectives, of course, enjoy the luxury of being detached from the policymaking environment and its need for a comprehensive legal framework for countering terrorism and, in particular, the imperative of protecting civilians and non-combatants from political violence. Schmid posed the question: '[i]s it possible to find an objective and watertight definition that satisfies both legal and scientific criteria?' and concluded that '[s]o far, this goal has been elusive'.[1] While such a convergence seems unlikely for the reasons I have outlined, one can argue that a more objective academic definition can indeed inform the legal effort. There is, of course, no one academic perspective as there is no one state definition. A wide spectrum of academic definitions may at one end reflect the interests of states just as there are those that seek to include (or at least not exclude) the state (including democratic ones) as potential perpetrators of terrorism.

The French Revolution is often referred to as the forebear of modern terrorism but I would suggest, however, that it is an antecedent of *state terror* rather than terrorism. In this author's view terrorism and state terror (or, more broadly, 'political terror') are different phenomena. The latter may entail not just the spreading of fear or terror *but also* the wholesale *physical elimination* of perceived enemies whereas wider psychological impact is the sine qua non of terrorism. State terror can, of course, also have a major psychological impact, and, indeed, at times this may be its primary goal, but even here I would suggest that this also differs from terrorism because, by virtue of its all-pervasiveness and ubiquity, the nature of the fear is qualitatively different—with the dread of a knock on the door in the middle of the night from those who actually hold power. So even the sanctuary of 'staying indoors' is no guarantee of safety whereas with terrorism it is more a case of being in the

---

[1] Schmid, 'Terrorism: The Definitional Problem', p. 395.

wrong place at the wrong time. As Chapter 8 will argue, 'state terror', then, is different both quantitatively and, because of this, qualitatively. It refers to a much larger scale of intimidation and violence, exemplified in Hitler's Germany, Stalin's Russia, and Pol Pot's Cambodia. It is about terrorizing a population into compliance, sometimes with the deaths or 'disappearances' of many thousands from that population.

So, in my view, any reference to the 1789 French Revolution and the 'regime de la terreur' as the forebear of *terrorism* is inaccurate.[2] It is, rather, and for the sake of analytical precision, an ancestor of *state terror*. As Chaliand and Blin put it 'The French Terror served ... as the founding act of modern state terror.'[3] Yet these authors also note that the 1798 dictionary of the Académie française defined *terrorism* as a 'system or regime of terror'.[4] This perhaps partly explains why 'terror' and 'terrorism' are so often used synonymously in the terrorism literature as well as in public and political discourse.[5]

The French Revolution's 'terror' was administered through the ironically named Committee of Public Safety and the Committee of General Security 'which applied the legislation of the Terror, and directed the police and revolutionary justice; in principle, this was the ministry of the Terror'.[6] The core piece of legislation was the 'Law of Suspects' that 'gave wide powers of arrest, and defined "suspects" in very broad terms, giving sweeping powers to the ruling Committees, and making "Terror the order of the day"'.[7] It 'would allow the elimination of all the regime's opponents'.[8] In every sense, then, this was an example of state terror where the primary goal was the elimination of the 'enemies' of the revolution.

When trying to instil some sort of analytical quality into 'terrorism' it is worth considering whether or not the word itself was indeed *invented* as a derogatory term (and therefore whether or not its pejorative nature is in a sense intrinsic to it), or whether its negative connotation has been socially

---

[2] This is not to overlook some references made at the time (in the 1790s) to some of the Revolution's protagonists such as Edmund Burke's reference to 'thousands of those hell hounds called terrorists' (cited in W. Laqueur, *A History of Terrorism* (New Brunswick, NJ: Transaction Publishers, 2001), p. 6) or how Robespierre himself was subsequently accused of terrorism (Schmid, 'The Definition of Terrorism', p. 42).

[3] G. Chaliand and A. Blin, *The History of Terrorism: From Antiquity to Al Qaeda* (Berkeley, Los Angeles, and London: University of California Press, 2007), p. 101.

[4] Chaliand and Blin, *The History of Terrorism: From Antiquity to Al Qaeda*, p. 98.

[5] This is evident from reviewing Easson and Schmid's compilation of 250 definitions of terrorism (Appendix 2.1 in Schmid (ed.), *The Routledge Handbook of Terrorism Research*). Chapter 8 will develop further the contention that political terror (including state terror) and terrorism, though etymologically related, are separate phenomena.

[6] M. Linton, Interview, 'The Terror in the French Revolution', available at: <http://www.port.ac.uk/special/france1815to2003/chapter1/interviews/filetodownload,20545,en.pdf> (last accessed 27 November 2014).

[7] M. Linton, Interview, 'The Terror in the French Revolution'.

[8] Chaliand and Blin, *The History of Terrorism: From Antiquity to Al Qaeda*, p. 107.

constructed over time. Schmid suggests that the affirmative may be the case, at least as far back as the French Revolution—that, in the course of those tumultuous events in late eighteenth-century France, terrorism, as distinct from terror, was indeed a term of derision. Commenting on those who eventually sought to overthrow Robespierre he argued that they:

> could not accuse him of 'terror' without implicating themselves, as most of them had voted to make terror the order of the day. Therefore, they accused him of 'terrorisme', a term that had an illegitimate and repulsive flavour of despotic, arbitrary and excessive violence – a criminal abuse of power.[9]

Michael Blain has argued that '[t]he emergence of terrorism as a concept and political problem was associated with the development of modern liberal democracies' and, using Michel Foucault's concept of subjection, stated that '[t]he invention of a discourse of terrorism was a strategic response to danger, and could be deployed through basic regulatory practices of subjection.'[10] This ties in with contemporary 'critical' approaches that argue that 'the accepted knowledge of the field... functions ideologically to reinforce and reify existing structures of power within society, particularly that of the state.'[11]

Seen in this way, if the term 'terrorism' was simply forged as a means of practising subjection in order to reinforce and perpetuate prevailing power structures, then one might indeed argue that its pejorative nature is 'in its genes', that 'moral opprobrium'[12] is ineluctably intrinsic to the concept. If the discourse of 'terrorism' was generated to serve this purpose then how can one confound centuries of pejorative use from its inception and pretend that we can redeem some kind of analytical quality that it has never had? Is terrorism therefore, after all, violence that we simply do not like or whose cause we disagree with? If it was invented as a pejorative term[13] simply to discredit the violence of adversaries (which was not qualitatively distinctive from other forms of violence) then one could indeed argue that prospects for endowing terrorism with some sort of analytical quality are very limited.

It is this line of thinking that underpins and helps to sustain the freedom fighter/terrorist mantra for the same 'practice of subjection' takes place here: that there is nothing intrinsically different about terrorism, that it is merely the violence perpetrated by those we disagree with, that it is simply violence

---

[9] Schmid, 'The Definition of Terrorism', p. 42.

[10] Blain, 'On the Genealogy of Terrorism', pp. 50–1.

[11] R. Jackson, 'Knowledge, Power and Politics in the Study of Political Terrorism', in Jackson et al. (eds), *Critical Terrorism Studies: A New Research Agenda*, p. 67.

[12] Gearty, *Terror*, p. 6.

[13] This is notwithstanding those rare examples of those who have regarded being a 'terrorist' as a positive thing (see Hoffman, *Inside Terrorism*, p. 29).

that is illegal or seen as illegitimate by the prevailing power holders.[14] And herein lies a fundamental question: *is terrorism simply a label for violence that we disagree with or is there something particular or unique about the phenomenon?* If it is the former, then we are conceding that there is no uniqueness or particularity to capture in any endeavour to define terrorism and that therefore any attempt to do so would indeed be pointless. Notwithstanding any apparent historical and pejorative roots of the concept, the endeavour here, however, is to establish that there *is* something qualitatively distinctive about terrorism compared with other forms of political violence.

The proposition that definitions tend to reflect the interests of the definers is borne out by Schmid's surveys of: (i) states and international organizations, and (ii) academics. Comparing the two sets of definitions, his findings show, perhaps unsurprisingly, that 'the illegal, criminal character of terrorism' appears in 85 per cent of the former definitions but in only 30 per cent of the latter whereas 'the political character of terrorism, which is mentioned in 68 percent of the academic definitions, can be found in only 25 percent of governmental definitions and those of international organizations.'[15] These percentages reflect an inclination by governments to portray terrorism as a criminal activity with a reluctance to acknowledge the political goal.

While developing a universally agreed definition in the policymaking world has proved elusive, terrorism has also been a highly contested concept within academia. It is not just the subjective use of the term and the extent to which states should be included as perpetrators of terrorism that impact upon definitions, but also the enormously contentious deliberations over which components (which are themselves contested concepts) should be included in any conceptualization of the term. One need venture no further than Schmid's research (and Schmid and Jongman's) in particular to appreciate that crafting an agreed academic definition of terrorism is something that appears to be beyond our capability. In what has now become a famous and commonly cited work, Schmid and Jongman's survey of 109 definitions identified 22 'word categories',[16] ranging from '[v]iolence, force' (83.5 per cent) to '[m]ethod of combat, strategy, tactic' (30.5 per cent) to '[c]riminal' (6 per cent), which culminated in an 'academic consensus' definition, the latest version of which has no fewer than 16 elements.[17]

---

[14] This sentence and the previous two paragraphs have been reprinted with the permission of Taylor and Francis LLC from Richards, 'Conceptualizing Terrorism', pp. 219–20.

[15] Schmid, 'Terrorism: The Definitional Problem', p. 407.

[16] See Schmid and Jongman, *Political Terrorism*, p. 5.

[17] The definition is:

Terrorism is an anxiety-inspiring method of repeated violent action, employed by (semi-) clandestine individual, group, or state actors, for idiosyncratic, criminal, or political reasons, whereby—in contrast to assassination—the direct targets of violence are not the main targets. The immediate human victims of violence are generally chosen randomly

Notwithstanding this number of potential components and the difficulties in generating agreement on a definition of the concept, a consensus does appear to have developed in the academic literature of the past four decades as to what the *core essence* of terrorism is—*that it entails the intent to generate a wider psychological impact beyond the immediate victims.* The key to terrorism therefore lies in *the intent or the purpose behind the act* and this is captured in Schmid's observation:[18]

> There is, in our view, a solid conceptual core to terrorism, differentiating from ordinary violence. It consists in the calculated production of a state of extreme fear of injury and death and, secondarily, the exploitation of this emotional reaction to manipulate behaviour.[19]

What is therefore key to a definition of terrorism is that the intent behind the act of violence, or the threatened act of violence, 'is psychological and symbolic, not material'.[20] Hoffman has also argued that terrorism entails:

> the deliberate creation and exploitation of fear through violence or the threat of violence in the pursuit of political change... Terrorism is specifically designed to have far-reaching psychological effects beyond the immediate victim(s) or object of the terrorist attack. It is meant to instil fear within, and thereby intimidate, a wider 'target audience' that might include a rival ethnic or religious group, an entire country, a national government or political party, or public opinion in general.[21]

Central to terrorism, therefore, is the '"organized and systematic attempt to create fear"... that aims at attaining specific political ends (motivation) through the creation of fear, and not through the mere act of violence'.[22] As Jenkins also argued: '[f]ear is the intended effect, not the byproduct, of terrorism',[23] while Greisman, too, aptly contends that:

> it is necessary to... focus on the one quality that gives terrorism its unique place in the catalogue of organized violence. Terrorist acts require an audience, the target is

(targets of opportunity) or selectively (representative or symbolic targets) from a target population, and serve as message generators. Threat- and violence-based communication processes between terrorist (organization), (imperilled) victims, and main targets are used to manipulate the main target (audience(s)), turning it into a target of terror, a target of demands, or a target of attention, depending on whether intimidation, coercion, or propaganda is primarily sought. (Schmid and Jongman, *Political Terrorism*, p. 28)

[18] This section beginning with the Schmid quote and ending with the quote from Jenkins ('... the mere act of violence') has been reprinted with the permission of Taylor and Francis LLC, pp. 221–2 (see note 14).

[19] Schmid and Jongman, *Political Terrorism*, pp. 20–1.

[20] Crenshaw, 'Introduction: Reflections on the Effects of Terrorism', p. 2.

[21] Hoffman, *Inside Terrorism*, pp. 43–4.

[22] European Commission Sixth Framework Programme Project, 'Defining Terrorism' (WP3 Deliverable 4), p. 57. Though a distinction should be made, however, between *the purpose of a specific act* and the broader political goal or motive. The former may be successfully achieved but the latter may not (and, in fact, very rarely is).

[23] B. Jenkins, cited in Schmid and Jongman, *Political Terrorism*, p. 36.

of secondary importance, i.e. those that see the target attacked will become terrorized and this is the real goal of terrorism.[24]

As Chapter 1 has stated, the endeavour here is to generate an understanding and conceptualization of terrorism around this indispensable psychological dimension. Thus, while the broader *motive* of terrorism is political, the intent behind the acts of violence is to generate a wider psychological impact. An act of terrorism is therefore the pebble thrown into the lake with the intention of generating the wider ripples or as Schmid and de Graaf put it 'the skin on a drum beaten to achieve a calculated impact on a wider audience'.[25] The definition of terrorism that I will ultimately propose is therefore a purpose-based one.[26]

What, then, is this broader psychological impact designed to achieve, aside from the ultimate political goal? As Jenkins wrote, the 'primary intent' of terrorism 'is to produce fear and alarm that may serve a variety of purposes'.[27] Historically, in the late nineteenth century, terrorism became known as 'propaganda by the deed' with one such act making more propaganda than a 'thousand pamphlets'.[28] Schmid argues that:

> Terrorism cannot be understood only in terms of violence. It has to be understood primarily in terms of propaganda. Violence and propaganda, however, have much in common. Violence aims at behaviour modification by coercion. Propaganda aims at the same by persuasion. Terrorism can be seen as a combination of the two.[29]

Perhaps most of all, then, terrorism is concerned with the *communication of a message* that would not otherwise be heard (were it not for the violence). As 'propaganda by the deed', terrorism has therefore been viewed as a form of *violent communication* aimed at a broader audience or audiences (who are the real target of the 'terrorist message'). For Gressang, 'the dead among the terrorist's victims are not the core audience, since their death eliminates their ability to act in accordance with the terrorist's wishes. The terrorist's core, or primary, audience is that group or entity *which the terrorist believes* he is "speaking" to.'[30]

---

[24] H. Greisman, quoted in Appendix 2.1 of Schmid (ed.), *The Routledge Handbook of Terrorism Research*, p. 113.

[25] A. Schmid and J. de Graaf, *Insurgent Terrorism and the Western News Media* (Leiden: Centrum Onderzock Meatschappelijke Tegenstelliugen, 1980), p. 7.

[26] For purpose-based typologies of terrorism see Schmid and Jongman, *Political Terrorism*, p. 50.

[27] Jenkins, 'The Study of Terrorism: Definitional Problems', p. 4.

[28] P. Kropotkin, cited in Schmid and de Graaf, *Insurgent Terrorism and the Western News Media*, p. 7.

[29] Schmid and de Graaf, *Insurgent Terrorism and the Western News Media*, p. 14.

[30] D. Gressang IV, 'Audience and Message: Assessing Terrorist WMD Potential', *Terrorism and Political Violence*, Vol. 13, No. 3, 2001, p. 90.

The Brazilian urban guerrilla Carlos Marighela's first principle on the use of terrorism was that '[t]errorist acts should be aimed at the audience, the general public'.[31]

The potential target audiences can perhaps be divided into four broad categories: (1) their supporters and members in order to inspire and increase morale, (2) a broader constituency of perceived potential support from which to try and attract more supporters and members, (3) the international community with the aim of attracting attention and sympathy for their cause, and (4) the defined enemy in order to intimidate and spread fear among the targeted government(s) and broader group or population.[32] In keeping with my perception of terrorism, then, '"the most significant technology is not weapons but direct communication with their multiple audiences" and [this] points to the enhanced role modern media can play in the process.'[33,34]

The Black September attack on the 1972 Munich Olympics perhaps exemplified terrorism's intended psychological impact and its purpose of communicating a message—on this occasion to a global audience. George Habash, the leader of the Popular Front for the Liberation of Palestine, was said to have proclaimed that:

> a bomb in the White House, a mine in the Vatican, the death of Mao Tse-Tung, an earthquake in Paris could not have echoed through the consciousness of every man in the world like the operation at Munich . . . The choice of the Olympics, from the purely propagandist viewpoint, was 100 per cent successful. It was like painting the name of Palestine on a mountain that can be seen from the four corners of the earth.[35]

Without the psychological impact, or the 'shock' value of the violence, this communication would not otherwise have been heard. Terrorism, then, is violent propaganda through which to deliver a message or an advert for a cause that would otherwise never receive such exposure. Osama bin Laden underlined the communication value of the 9/11 attacks when he proclaimed

[31] A. Schmid, 'Frameworks for Conceptualising Terrorism', *Terrorism and Political Violence*, Vol. 17, No. 2, 2004, p. 208.

[32] See also A. Schmid, 'Terrorism and the Media: The Ethics of Publicity', *Terrorism and Political Violence*, Vol. 1, No. 4, 1989, pp. 9–10.

[33] B. Jenkins, quoted in European Commission Sixth Framework Programme Project, 'Defining Terrorism' (WP3 Deliverable 4), p. 19.

[34] It is also worth noting that if terrorism is meant to have a psychological impact on a particular audience or audiences then the degree of intended impact (and/or actual impact) may vary with different ideologies. For example, Hewitt found that there may be less potential for generating support with some ideologies, arguing, for instance, that nationalist terrorists have a high degree of support from an ethnic constituency, while revolutionary terrorists attract a much smaller degree of support, primarily from the educated young (see C. Hewitt, 'Terrorism and Public Opinion', *Terrorism and Political Violence*, Vol. 2, No. 2, 1990).

[35] Cited in P. Taylor, *States of Terror* (London: BBC Books, 1993), p. 6.

that: 'Those young men [the hijackers]... said in deeds, in New York and Washington, speeches that overshadowed all other speeches made everywhere in the world. These speeches are understood by both Arabs and non-Arabs.'[36] For Crenshaw, too, terrorism is an exercise in communication:

> Terrorist violence communicates a political message; its ends go beyond damaging an enemy's material resources. The victims or objects of terrorist attack have little intrinsic value to the terrorist group but represent a larger human audience whose reaction the terrorists seek.[37]

And Schmid further emphasizes the communicative function of terrorism:

> The attacks of September 11, 2001 on the World Trade Center and the Pentagon were meant to impress several target audiences. According to a treatise titled 'The Reality of the New Crusade,' they were meant... 'to inflame the hearts of Muslims against America,' in the hope of 'inspiring thousands of others to this type of operation.' Terrorism, then, must also—and in many cases primarily—be seen as a form of violent communication. An example of this communication function (which is linked to intimidation) is a statement broadcasted by Al Jazeera in early October 2002 in which Aiman Al Zawahiri (No. 2 in Al-Qaeda) said, referring to the attack on German tourists in front of the Jewish Synagogue in Djerba, Tunis, and to the attack on the French oil tanker Limburg off the coast of Yemen: 'The Mujahedeen youth has sent one message to Germany and another to France. Should the dose [of the message, AS] not have been sufficient, we are ready—of course with the help of Allah—to increase the dose.'[38]

Terrorism can therefore also be viewed as a form of 'expressive violence', perhaps with the aim of 'advertising the [terrorist] movement' and its cause.[39] It may be that the objective of the terrorist act is no more ambitious than to serve as a psychological reminder to supporters and adversaries that their struggle remains alive. A good example of this might be the belief of Patrick Pearse (one of the Irish republican leaders of the 1916 Dublin Easter Rising) in the cathartic value of violence and its use as an end in itself. He saw the Easter Rising as a sacrificial act and 'believed in the rejuvenating power of blood'.[40] Indeed, such acts and the creation of martyrs should persevere through generations, he argued, via a process of 'apostolic succession'—the

---

[36] Quoted in European Commission Sixth Framework Programme Project, 'Defining Terrorism' (WP3 Deliverable 4), p. 19.

[37] Crenshaw, *Explaining Terrorism: Causes, Processes and Consequences*, p. 34.

[38] A. Schmid, 'Terrorism as Psychological Warfare', *Democracy and Security*, No. 1, 2005, p. 139, available at: <http://www.tandfonline.com/doi/pdf/10.1080/17419160500322467> (last accessed 27 November 2014).

[39] T. Thornton, 'Terror as a Weapon of Political Agitation', in H. Eckstein (ed.), *Internal War* (Toronto: Collier-Macmillan, 1964), p. 82.

[40] P. Bishop and E. Mallie, *The Provisional IRA* (London: Corgi, 1992), p. 24.

idea that uprisings could act as nationalist *statements* to keep the republican ideal alive.[41] Wardlaw argued that:

> The publicity objectives of the terrorist may be quite varied. In some cases, the terrorist may want to ensure that attention is attracted to a broad cause, in others to specific events or activities. Sometimes the internal dynamics of the group will dictate that it mount an operation merely to demonstrate its ability to continue to function as an effective force.[42]

Indeed, terrorism is often perceived as expressive violence because the message is intended to outweigh the physical impact—'to wound the government's prestige by delivering a moral, not a physical blow' and that '[a]s propaganda of the deed, terrorism demonstrates that the regime can be challenged'.[43] Perhaps a good example of this 'demonstration effect' was the Al Qaeda attack on the USS *Cole* in October 2001 that killed 17 US sailors. In what was known as the 'Al Qaeda recruitment tape' (which was produced six months before 9/11) an oration from bin Laden was repeatedly interspersed with images of the USS *Cole* attack in order to illustrate the 'vulnerability' of the United States—to demonstrate that the superpower *could* be wounded, that 'holy warriors' *could* inflict casualties against the 'crusaders' and indeed that the United States *could* ultimately be defeated.[44] Indeed, the Al Qaeda leader serenely stated that 'rational people have no doubts that America will lose its status as a great power in the new millennium'.[45]

This 'expressive' and 'demonstration' effect may be evident in the *symbolic* nature of terrorist targeting, exemplified in the choice of the iconic targets of US economic and military power of the World Trade Center and the Pentagon respectively, as indeed in the targeting of the British cabinet by the IRA through the Brighton bomb of 1984. It is the symbolic nature of many terrorist targets that underpins further the psychological impact and the 'message' of terrorism.

Terrorism may also aim to demonstrate that it can wield power and to prove that a government or governments are incapable of protecting their citizens.

---

[41] Cited in M. Smith, *Fighting for Ireland: The Military Strategy of the Irish Republican Movement* (London and New York: Routledge, 1995), p. 11.

[42] G. Wardlaw, 'The Nature and Purpose of Terrorism', in A. Thompson (ed.), *Terrorism and the 2000 Olympics* (Canberra: Australian Defense Studies Centre, 1996).

[43] M. Crenshaw, 'The Logic of Terrorism: Terrorist Behaviour as a Product of Strategic Choice', in W. Reich (ed.), *Origins of Terrorism: Psychologies, Ideologies, Theologies, States of Mind* (Cambridge: Cambridge University Press, 1990), pp. 18–19.

[44] Columbia International Affairs online, 'Producing Jihad: The Al Qaeda Recruitment Tape', Reel 3, excerpt 10, available at: <http://www.ciaonet.org/cbr/cbr00/video/excerpts/reel3.html?p> (last accessed 27 November 2014).

[45] Columbia International Affairs online, 'Producing Jihad: The Al Qaeda Recruitment Tape', Reel 2, Excerpt 3, available at: <http://www.ciaonet.org/cbr/cbr00/video/excerpts/reel2.html?i> (last accessed 27 November 2014).

This is exemplified in the right-wing Italian New Order's proclamation that: 'We have wanted to demonstrate to the nation...that we are capable of placing bombs where we want, at any hour, in any spot, where and when it pleases us.'[46] For Thornton, then, '*[d]isorientation* is the objective *par excellence* of the terrorist...the target of the disorientation process is the mass, and the desired response is anxiety...Greatest anxiety will be caused if terrorist attacks fall in an apparently random pattern, are intense and unpredictable.'[47] Writing of 'revolutionary terrorism' in 1972, Crenshaw also suggests its use for 'certain ends', including 'general insecurity and disorientation in the state',[48] while Heath and O'Hair concur that '[w]hether established or other space, terrorists seek to take control and breed uncertainty' and '[u]ncertainty and instability are the playground of terrorism'.[49]

The purpose of breeding disorientation and uncertainty, then, is intended to demoralize the adversary[50] and to undermine the prevailing situation against which terrorism is perpetrated—and to prove that that situation is unsustainable. The IRA's strategy, which was outlined in the group's 'Green Book', was explicit about making 'the Six Counties as at present and for the past several years ungovernable except by colonial military rule' in an effort to prove that Northern Ireland was inherently unsustainable as a political entity.[51]

It might be a reasonable assumption to make, then, that the emphasis on *psychological* over physical impact is a reflection of the relative weakness (in general) of those that use the method of terrorism. For terrorism is often employed as an inexpensive tactic by those with limited resources against a more powerful adversary.[52] In the context of non-state terrorism, Ariel Merari

[46] *L'Espresso*, 11 August 1974, p. 6, cited in N. Leites, 'Understanding the Next Act', *Terrorism: An International Journal*, Vol. 3, 1979, p. 12.

[47] Thornton, 'Terror as a Weapon of Political Agitation', p. 84. Although he does point out that it would be extremely difficult to 'induce mass-disorientation in a society whose members feel a high degree of positive identification with the society and are firmly committed to its values' (also p. 84).

[48] M. Crenshaw, 'The Concept of Revolutionary Terrorism', *The Journal of Conflict Resolution* (pre 1986), Vol. 16, No. 3, 1972, p. 394.

[49] R. Heath and D. O'Hair, 'From the Eyes of the Beholder', in O'Hair et al. (eds.), *Terrorism: Communication and Rhetorical Perspectives*, p. 25.

[50] Crenshaw, 'The Concept of Revolutionary Terrorism', p. 394.

[51] T. Coogan, *The IRA* (London: Fontana/HarperCollins, 1987), p. 693.

[52] This is one of a number of potential reasons that Crenshaw summarizes as to why a strategy of terrorism might be adopted in pursuit of a political goal in preference to alternative modes of political action. They are:

(1) The most basic reason for terrorism is to gain recognition or attention for a cause.
(2) It is often designed to disrupt and discredit the processes of government, demoralizing and increasing insecurity amongst government officials.
(3) It may be designed to create sympathy from one constituency and to create fear in an 'enemy' constituency.
(4) It may be intended to provoke the government into a counter-reaction that increases the publicity for the terrorists' cause and demonstrates that their charges against the regime are well founded.

summarizes why the inferior strength of those organizations that use terrorism lends itself to a strategy of psychological impact rather than material or military gain:

> Essentially, terrorism is a strategy based on psychological impact ... The validity of this generalization rests on the basic conditions of the terrorist struggle. Terrorist groups are small. Their membership ranges from a few persons to several thousands, and the majority number tens to a few hundreds. Even the weakest of governments has a fighting force immensely larger than the terrorist insurgents. Under such circumstances, the insurgents cannot expect to win the struggle in any physical way.[53]

Jenkins concurs that '[s]ince groups that use terrorist tactics are typically small and weak, the violence they practice must be deliberately shocking.'[54] Chaliand and Blin argue that 'by definition' 'terrorist movements ... engage in a form of low-cost struggle with the potential to yield a profit that is inversely proportional to the means invested and, often, the risks taken.'[55] This is not to suggest that terrorism should, *by definition*, be seen as the 'weapon of the weak' but with the relative weakness of many of those actors that employ terrorism it is perhaps logical that political violence in the form of terrorism should aim to have a greater *communicative function*—to enable its perpetrators to 'punch above their weight', to generate a message that would not otherwise have been adequately received or heard through other forms of political action. It can therefore perhaps often be seen as 'a tool [used] by power-deficient and power-seeking groups'.[56]

With the aim of destabilizing the status quo terrorism is often used as an incremental psychological strategy designed to wear down the will of a more

---

(5) Terrorism may serve internal functions of control, discipline, and morale building within the group and may be the result of rivalry with other terrorist groups.

(6) Terrorism is the weapon of the weak and when a group perceives its options as limited, terrorism is attractive because it is a relatively inexpensive and simple alternative, and because its potential reward is high.

(7) It may be adopted because of impatience with time-consuming legal methods of eliciting support for or advertising their cause because they are not capable of, or interested in, mobilizing majority support.

(8) It may be the result of the desire for imminent action, a sense of urgency, or to seize that 'historical moment' of opportunity.

(9) Terrorism may occur as a result of the failure of alternative means to achieve goals (adapted from Crenshaw, 'The Causes of Terrorism', *Comparative Politics*, Vol. 13, No. 4, 1981, pp. 381–9).

[53] A. Merari, 'Terrorism as a Strategy of Insurgency', *Terrorism and Political Violence*, Vol. 5, No. 4, 1993, pp. 231–3.

[54] B. Jenkins, quoted in Appendix 2.1 of Schmid (ed.), *The Routledge Handbook of Terrorism Research*, p. 113.Wardlaw also argues that 'because of their numerical inferiority it is important that terrorist groups indulge in dramatic and shocking violence if they are to be noticed' (Wardlaw, 'The Nature and Purpose of Terrorism').

[55] Chaliand and Blin, *The History of Terrorism: From Antiquity to Al Qaeda*, p. 96.

[56] Heath and O'Hair, 'From the Eyes of the Beholder', p. 18.

powerful adversary. This is perhaps no more evident than in its use in the post Second World War anti-colonial campaigns. The strategy of these movements, for example, wasn't to attempt to defeat the armed forces of the colonial power in open combat (against whom they were hopelessly outnumbered) but was often to convince and to demonstrate to the colonial power and its population at home, through terrorist attacks, that the costs of maintaining its mandatory rule in the colony outweighed the benefits. Perhaps the best example of terrorism that was successfully used in this way was that carried out by the Irgun group which ultimately managed to force a British withdrawal from Palestine. And it is this strategy that 'established a revolutionary model which thereafter was emulated and embraced by both anti-colonial and post-colonial era terrorist groups around the world'.[57] It is also a strategy that the IRA emulated in its attempts to force a British withdrawal from Northern Ireland.

Part of anti-colonial strategy was to provoke government repression or an over-reaction to acts of terrorism in the hope that it would, in theory, increase indigenous support for the insurgents. The theory was for a group 'to achieve its goals not through its acts but through the response to its acts'.[58] As Fromkin maintained, 'failing to understand the strategy of terrorism, the French did not see that it was not the FLN's move, but rather the French countermove, that would determine whether the FLN succeeded or failed.'[59] The strategy of provoking an over-reaction from the state to reveal its true 'oppressive' nature has also been a model that has been emulated by the Basque separatist group ETA. Indeed, Stohl includes 'the provoking of indiscriminate reactions or repression to expose the true nature of the regime or insurgent' as one of the strategic purposes of terrorism.[60]

One might also argue that the 'violent communications' of ISIS[61] (through its beheadings of Western hostages) were deliberately designed to provoke.[62] The BBC reported in September 2014 that, apparently in response to President Obama's refusal to send troops to Iraq, the group were attempting to goad and taunt the United States by broadcasting a video of 'masked executioners standing over kneeling captives', and declaring that: '"Fighting has just begun."'[63] One can perhaps speculate that drawing the United States into

---

[57] Hoffman, *Inside Terrorism*, p. 48.

[58] D. Fromkin, 'The Strategy of Terrorism', in C. Kegley, *International Terrorism: Characteristics, Causes, Controls* (New York: St Martin's Press, 1990), p. 60.

[59] Fromkin, 'The Strategy of Terrorism', p. 61.

[60] Stohl (ed.), *The Politics of Terrorism*, p. 6.

[61] Islamic State in Iraq and the Levant.

[62] One can indeed deduce that these were examples of terrorism—that these acts of violence, and the dissemination of videos that filmed them, were clearly intended to generate a psychological impact beyond the immediate victims.

[63] BBC News online, 'Islamic State crisis: US House approves Obama's Syria Plan', 18 September 2014, available at: <http://www.bbc.co.uk/news/world-us-canada-29248955> (last accessed 1 December 2014).

the conflict with 'boots on the ground' would help ISIS to present its conflict as the world's focal point for attacking the Americans and 'infidels' (and thereby boost its aim of recruiting globally from all those wishing to seize the opportunity of taking on the United States in combat).

Terrorism can therefore be used with the aim of fulfilling a variety of objectives aside from the broad political goal.[64] It can be understood as a form of violent communication and the dissemination potential of the 'terrorist message' to its intended target audience(s) rests on the essence of the phenomenon—which is to generate a wider psychological impact to ensure that this message is heard.[65]

If this is generally understood as the core essence of terrorism, the challenge is then to capture this in one's definition. Schmid, however, shortlists four (from a dozen) reasons as to why it is so difficult to define terrorism:

Because terrorism is a 'contested concept' and political, legal, social science and popular notions of it are often diverging;

Because the definition question is linked to (de-)legitimisation and criminalisation;

Because there are many types of 'terrorism', with different forms and manifestations;

Because the term has undergone changes of meaning in the more than 200 years of existence.[66]

As I have argued, the first two obstacles can at least partly be ameliorated by limiting the emotive use of the term and concomitantly enhancing its analytical potential, notwithstanding different 'domain' perspectives. The third

---

[64] Drake draws our attention to seven categories of strategic objectives that are important to 'terrorist organisations':

(1) Threat Elimination—where any perceived threats to the group (whether people or organisations) are eliminated to ensure that it can pursue its other objectives.

(2) Compliance—where the psychological targets of the group acquiesce with the group (i.e. in order to secure logistical support).

(3) Disorientation—to destroy 'the certainties of everyday life' amongst the target population and to create 'a constant feeling of anxiety'.

(4) Attrition—where continual attacks on targets are designed to gradually erode the will of the target population and the government.

(5) Provocation—to provoke an overreaction from the government in order to alienate more people from it.

(6) Advertisement—where the terrorist group seeks to give publicity to its cause.

(7) Endorsement—where a group aims to get the approval of the constituency it represents or claims to represent for its actions (C. Drake, *Terrorists' Target Selection* (Basingstoke: Macmillan, 1998), pp. 39–42).

[65] It is worth recalling a part of Schmid's academic consensus definition: 'Threat- and violence-based communication processes between terrorist (organization), (imperilled) victims, and main targets are used to manipulate the main target (audience(s)), turning it into a *target of terror*, a *target of demands*, or a *target of attention*, depending on whether intimidation, coercion, or propaganda is primarily sought' (original author's italics) (Schmid, 'The Definition of Terrorism', p. 61). Whether the audience(s) is a target of terror, demands, or attention (to intimidate, coerce, or publicize respectively) they all rest on generating a psychological impact beyond the immediate victims.

[66] Schmid, 'Terrorism: The Definitional Problem', p. 395.

obstacle is that there are many different terrorisms—that '[d]epending on where you live, different forms of terrorism are the dominant ones—a fact that tends to shape one's perception of all other forms of terrorism, given the selectivity of our perceptions',[67] or, as one panel of experts noted, 'terrorism is a product of its own place and time'.[68] While terrorism in this sense is often seen as unique to its own particular environment, the challenge is then to determine what form a *general* definition of terrorism should take—one that is sufficiently broad enough to include all forms of terrorism.

The fourth obstacle—the changing meaning of terrorism—is also pertinent to this discussion and in particular the extent to which any conceptualization of terrorism can be sustainable or have any degree of longevity. What is interesting in Schmid's own historical trajectory, however, is that he plots this 'changing meaning' according to the various *perpetrators* of 'terrorism' or 'terror' rather than highlighting any explicit changes in how the phenomenon or *activity* itself has been perceived over time.[69]

Nevertheless, one has to consider the extent that one's definition of terrorism is resilient enough to survive the periodic proclamations of so-called 'new terrorism'. For example, right-wing terrorism was said to be the 'new terrorism' in the early 1980s (though this did not ultimately materialize), while the emergence of the contemporary terrorist threat in the form of Al Qaeda has also spawned a 'new terrorism' discourse, and debates over the extent that Al Qaeda has challenged 'traditional' understandings of the concept.[70] One can argue, however, that, while the manifestations of terrorism may have evolved (particularly in the context of technological advances), the core essence of terrorism has not changed—that is the intent to generate a psychological impact beyond the immediate victims. If the act of violence, or the threat of violence, is not intended to achieve this impact then it is not terrorism.

Being 'Critical'

There are, of course, from a political and legal perspective, powerful reasons for defining terrorism and there have been numerous attempts by policymakers, lawmakers, and academics to do so from this 'problem solving'

---

[67] Schmid, 'Terrorism: The Definitional Problem', p. 398.

[68] J. Post, International Summit on Democracy, Terrorism and Security, The Causes of Terrorism, March 8–11 2005, The Club de Madrid Series on Democracy and Terrorism, p. 7.

[69] Schmid, 'Terrorism: The Definitional Problem', p. 398. Hoffman, in his passage on 'The Changing Meaning of Terrorism' also largely plots these changes in meaning according to the type of perpetrator—revolutionary, anarchist, totalitarian ('terror' in the 1930s), revolutionary again (anti-colonial), and nationalist (Hoffman, *Inside Terrorism*, Chapter 1: 'Defining Terrorism').

[70] For a discussion on this see Crenshaw, *Explaining Terrorism: Causes, Processes and Consequences*, Chapter 3.

perspective. Academic contributions need not, however, be prescriptive in this sense. It is surely possible to observe the world as it is without necessarily *endorsing* the status quo and its prevailing power structures, and to view the phenomenon of terrorism dispassionately—both without a 'problem solving' approach but also without interrogating existing structures. What is suggested, then, is an approach that is neither a problem solving one that reduces 'academic responsibility to a technical exercise of risk governance or management',[71] nor one that is, conversely, underpinned by a critique of the system that constantly challenges the legitimacy of the prevailing order.

And being 'critical' in this sense is nothing new. As I have noted in Chapter 2, Schmid and Jongman, in a 'critical' passage, called for a more neutral approach to the study of terrorism.[72] The point is that to study terrorism dispassionately *without critiquing existing power structures* does not necessarily mean that one is 'problem solving' in service of the status quo. One might argue that using the term 'terrorism' itself implies a problem solving approach (given the widespread pejorative use of the concept), but to avoid doing so would permanently consign 'terrorism' to nothing more than a subjective label of derision or a 'useful insult', rather than to elevate it as an analytical concept. It is in pursuing the latter that the challenge of depicting terrorism as a separate and unique phenomenon lies. The next chapter proposes the adoption of three preliminary assumptions when approaching the definitional debate.

---

[71] Jarvis, 'The Spaces and Faces of Critical Terrorism Studies', p. 15.
[72] Schmid and Jongman, *Political Terrorism*, pp. 179–80.

5

Three Preliminary Assumptions When Approaching the Conceptualization of Terrorism

The Social Construction of 'Terrorism'

In any discussion on the definition of terrorism perhaps the first step is to acknowledge that terrorism is first and foremost a social construct and not a 'brute fact'.[1] Jackson argued that 'terrorism is not a causally coherent, free-standing phenomenon which can be defined in terms of characteristics inherent to the violence itself. It lacks a clear ontological status—which actually makes an objective definition impossible.'[2] Schmid has also cautioned that 'we have to realize that there is no intrinsic essence to the concept of terrorism—it is a man-made construct.'[3] This presents us with a problem—that, because it is 'ontologically unstable and lacking any concrete essence', it is therefore indeed inherently incapable of an objective definition.[4] Hence from this perspective one could argue that terrorism can be whatever one claims it to be, that nobody has the right to assert what terrorism is and what it is not, that in fact those that claim that its meaning has been abused are just as guilty as the 'abusers' for implicitly making some kind of knowledge claim as to what terrorism is.

As I have argued in Chapter 1, however, this does not mean that we should refrain from attempting to define or conceptualize terrorism, for every social science concept is socially constructed—such as crime, legitimacy, politics, insurgency, war, and so on—and, like terrorism, none of them are 'brute facts'.

---

[1] Jackson et al., *Terrorism: A Critical Introduction*, p. 119.
[2] R. Jackson, 'An Argument for Terrorism', *Perspectives on Terrorism*, Vol. 2, No. 2, January 2008, available at: <http://www.terrorismanalysts.com/pt/articles/issues/PTv2i2.pdf> (last accessed 27 November 2014).
[3] Schmid, 'Terrorism: The Definitional Problem', p. 384.
[4] Jackson et al., *Terrorism: A Critical Introduction*, p. 120.

We should not, therefore, be reticent about trying to conceptualize terrorism just as much as we shouldn't refrain from defining social science concepts in general.

Indeed, the development of (socially constructed) norms and values is a vital part of human development, and, within their particular discourses, conceptual clarity (or lack of) can have significant real-life consequences. A good example is the phenomenon of 'crime'. The meaning of crime is socially constructed. It is what humans want it to mean and it is not a 'fact'. As we know, there are practices that may have been considered crimes centuries ago but are not now, and vice versa (such as slavery). There may be forms that are considered crimes in one state but not in another (such as attitudes to homosexuality). There are therefore human, cultural, temporal, and geographical dimensions in the social construction of crime. It is also then inevitably the case that laws that are designed to combat crimes are also socially constructed (as indeed is 'the state' that creates the laws). Yet it is, in general, socially accepted that the commission of 'crime' is wrong and that societies need to develop systems of rules and laws to prohibit and punish 'criminal' behaviours. Endeavouring to define crime and its parameters is therefore imperative, notwithstanding its social construction.

Similarly, if we want to further develop international regimes, norms, and protocols, such as those related to human rights, how can we do so without some notion of the conceptual parameters of our subject matter (for example, what constitutes 'human rights')? In other words many social science definitions, though inevitably 'constructed', are vital in underpinning the evolution of social norms that are part of human progress and development.[5]

Another important element of social construction concerns the etymology of the word 'terror' and how its derivatives have been 'constructed' to mean different things. Using other examples, to become a vigilante seems somewhat far removed from simply being 'vigilant'. In the last decade the concept of 'radicalization' in the United Kingdom has been used to describe a serious threat to domestic security, a very different connotation to, for example, political parties that boast of having 'radical' manifestos. The point is that derivatives do not necessarily carry the same meanings as their etymons. Similarly, in my view, 'terror' and 'terrorism' should not be used interchangeably. While it is fair to say, once again, that these distinctions are socially constructed the following will argue that 'terror', 'political terror', and 'state terror' are distinct phenomena from terrorism (see Chapter 8) while state terrorism, state-sponsored terrorism, and non-state terrorism are all sub-categories of terrorism—

---

[5] This is not to say, of course, that conceptual endeavours cannot also be exploited to sustain what might also be considered harmful discourses—for example, in this context, terrorism might simply be defined in a way that facilitates the discrediting of political opposition groups.

and the way that they are conceptualized (or the lack of any serious attempt to define them) can have significant real-life consequences.

Beyond these etymological issues and the 'ontological instability' of terrorism is a further layer of social construction—that terrorism has been viewed as a pejorative label that has been subjectively applied to one's enemies. Because its meaning has been so difficult to capture in any analytical sense, the term has often been used as a 'useful insult'.[6] For example, some critical perspectives have argued that terrorism knowledge has been constructed to serve the interests of existing power structures—that terrorism has been understood, defined, and studied in the interests of the status quo, that the 'problem' of terrorism has been conceptualized and framed in a way that delegitimizes non-state actors who use violence, while at the same time reinforcing and reifying the legitimacy of states and their own use of violence. In support of a critical studies agenda Jarvis wrote:

> the problem-solving approach to the study of terrorism is normatively problematic in reducing academic responsibility to a technical exercise of risk governance or management. At best, such a reduction militates against any notion of critical enquiry aimed at contesting or destabilizing the status quo: of 'saying the unsayable' in Booth's...terminology. At worst, it simply reifies a tired and unstable inside/outside dichotomy that legitimizes the state's continued monopoly on violence. Either way, the continued structuring of the mainstream literature around the above debates fails to offer any meaningful participatory role for engaged, active scholarship.
>
> In sum, although characterized by considerable diversity, the terrorism studies literature suffers from key analytical and normative limitations. Analytically, the preference for a narrow essentialist framework not only neglects the processes of terrorism's construction, it also reduces the space available for discussing the (il) legitimacy of particular violences. Normatively, the preference for producing policy-relevant, problem-solving research works to detach academic responsibility from any notion of critical enquiry.[7]

This is not altogether a uniquely CTS perspective. As previously observed (in Chapter 2), Schmid and Jongman also 'critically' argued against a terrorism studies agenda that served the interests of the state, which perhaps suggests that the supposed gap between so-called 'orthodox' and CTS approaches is not always so apparent.[8]

[6] Gearty, *Terror*, p. 6.

[7] Jarvis, 'The Spaces and Faces of Critical Terrorism Studies', p. 15.

[8] Although Schmid argues elsewhere that 'While some critical theorists blame Terrorism Studies for the "problem-solving approach", mainstream researchers have no problem with that, arguing that this is entirely legitimate, just as the medical profession studies diseases in order to be able to cure them' (Schmid, 'Introduction', in *The Routledge Handbook of Terrorism Research*, p. 29). This statement appears to misunderstand the point of the 'critical' approach for while the existence of the human being is a *natural*, ineluctable, scientific, and politically neutral fact, the state system is

As noted in Chapter 1, and given the socially constructed nature of terrorism, this work does not (and nor can any work) claim to be speaking 'truth' on the definitional issue. This does not mean to say that there cannot be a universally agreed definition of the concept, even if we acknowledge that such a definition would not be the 'truth' but the culmination of an agreed understanding at any given time. In this context, the challenge is to consider whether there really is something unique or different about terrorism compared with other forms of political violence and their (socially constructed) meanings. And if there is something particular about terrorism, what is it? And how can this particularity be captured in a general definition or conceptualization that applies to all cases of terrorism? As noted in the previous chapter, Schmid and Jongman, notwithstanding their view of terrorism as a 'manmade construct', argued that '[t]here is, in our view, a solid conceptual core to terrorism, differentiating from ordinary violence. It consists in the calculated production of a state of extreme fear of injury and death and, secondarily, the exploitation of this emotional reaction to manipulate behaviour.'[9]

The arguments proposed in this work resonate with this psychological dimension of terrorism and, secondly, with the attempted manipulation of it (Chapter 4). This chapter now proposes three preliminary assumptions when approaching the definition of terrorism.[10]

(1) *There is no such thing as an act of violence that is in and of itself inherently an act of terrorism*

Terrorism's physical manifestation can vary from the use of incendiary devices, to gun attacks, to machete attacks, to a variety of different types of bomb attacks (including suicide bomb attacks), to kidnappings and hostage-takings, to 'mass casualty' attacks on the scale of 9/11, and so on. Therefore the *physical* part of terrorism can be seen as consisting of a range of different methods. The World Incidents Tracking System, for example, codes 'terrorist incidents' as the following: 'armed attack, arson/firebombing, assassination, assault, barricade/hostage, bombing, CBRN, crime, firebombing, hijacking, hoax, kidnapping, near miss/non-attack, other, theft, unknown, and vandalism'.[11]

---

not! Hence the concern with medical treatment for human welfare cannot be compared with solving the ills of the contemporary state system which, of course, is not a given but a man-made social and political construct.

[9] Schmid and Jongman, *Political Terrorism*, pp. 20–1.

[10] Much of the following pages (pp. 68–75) have been reprinted with the permission of Taylor and Francis LLC from Richards, 'Conceptualizing Terrorism', pp. 222–9.

[11] See National Counterterrorism Center (US), 'Annex of Statistical Information', US Department of State, available at: <http://www.state.gov/j/ct/rls/crt/2008/122452.htm> (last accessed 27 November 2014).

None of these acts of violence, however, even those that might be commonly associated with terrorism (such as bombings and hijackings), are in and of themselves inherently terrorist acts. It is only when one adds layers of meaning to the physical act that one can then determine whether or not such an act can be called terrorism. For example, a shooting can be an act of crime, terrorism, or warfare. But once layers of meaning have been imposed upon the act then we can broadly refer to *the method of terrorism* as distinct from the different methods or manifestations of the violence itself. These layers of meaning render terrorism as not just being about violence or the threat of violence and is why *any definition that focuses on the particular acts of violence themselves as integral to terrorism misses the point when it comes to establishing the meaning of the concept.*

The use of examples might help to illustrate the point. A suicide bomb self-detonated in a crowded marketplace might inescapably be labelled an act of terrorism without any further thought-that it 'looks' and 'smells' like terrorism.[12] In theory, however, such an act is still possible without a political motive, thus rendering the act as something other than terrorism. Hypothetically, a disgruntled individual may have carried out the act in revenge against their workplace (or former workplace) or even against a local community.

A car bomb might also be ineluctably associated with terrorism. One exploded in Kent in the United Kingdom in March 2010 and a pregnant woman was badly injured. The incident may have looked like an act of terrorism—a very similar act, for example, to the car bombs that the IRA commonly used to generate a psychological impact and to draw attention to its political cause. The difference is that the Kent car bomb was planted by the victim's husband who was said to be suffering from post-traumatic stress. In other words, even an act of violence that may be commonly seen as synonymous with terrorism (the car bomb) is not necessarily an act of terrorism unless it is imbued with meaning (i.e. a political motive and designed to have a psychological impact beyond the immediate victim(s)).

Acts of terrorism may entail shooting attacks, perhaps best exemplified by the Al Shabaab attack in Nairobi in September 2013, or the November 2008 attack in Mumbai, or by Irish Republican sniper attacks. Again, not all cases of shootings in civilian environments are terrorist. Although Raoul Moat 'terrorized' his community in July 2010 in Northumberland in the United Kingdom after going on the run, his shootings were not acts of terrorism because they lacked a political goal. The same can be said of the actions of a sacked police officer, Rolando Mendoza, in Manila in the Philippines who seized control of a bus and demanded to be reinstated (with a subsequent death toll of eight after

---

[12] Jeremy Greenstock, (former) British Ambassador to the United Nations, cited in Schmid, 'Terrorism: The Definitional Problem', p. 375.

a shoot-out with the authorities). In other words it is wholly inadequate to describe terrorism as 'you know it when you see it', or '[w]hat looks, smells and kills like terrorism is terrorism'.[13]

What about the archetypal acts of terrorism of recent times—how, for example, can one not *immediately* recognize the attacks of 9/11 as acts of terrorism? Again, taken in isolation, each act of violence on 9/11 might not have been an act of terrorism. Any such act might have been carried out by a psychologically disturbed individual, or by those seeking a ransom where crew and passenger resistance may have led to an aircraft crashing, or, considered in isolation, the first crash could have been a tragic accident. Indeed, after this first incident it was by no means clear at that stage that we were witnessing an act of terrorism. In the case of the London bombings of 2007 there were some early indications that an electrical fault might have been the cause. The point is that even in cases of what might subsequently be called archetypal acts of terrorism conclusions as to whether they could be classified as acts of terrorism could not be made immediately. Of course, once layers of meaning were added then it could be confirmed that these were indeed acts of terrorism—that these were deliberate and simultaneous attacks, that they were politically motiv- ated, and that they aimed to generate a massive psychological impact amongst a much broader group than the victims.

The implication of this first assumption is that any lists of 'terrorist acts' or of the physical manifestations of terrorism do not bring us any closer to capturing what terrorism is. Any conjecture, therefore, as to which of the wide range of types of violent acts should constitute terrorism is unnecessary. For example, Weinberg et al. need not have concerned themselves with this when they argued that 'unless we are willing to label as terrorism a very wide range of violent activities, we may be better off finding another governing concept or looking elsewhere for a definition'[14]—for it is the purpose of, and intent behind, the act of violence (and not the type of act itself) that is integral to the phenom- enon and determines whether or not it can be regarded as an act of terrorism.

One could also suggest, therefore, that the United Nations approach of countering certain *acts* as 'terrorist acts' does not assist us in conceptualizing terrorism (though defining terrorism was not its primary intention when drafting its Conventions). Nor do such references as 'Hijacking may be described as a special type of terrorism'[15]—this is because there can, as in the case of other forms of 'terrorist' violence, be non-terrorist hijackings.[16]

---

[13] Greenstock, cited in Schmid, 'Terrorism: The Definitional Problem', p. 375.

[14] Weinberg et al., 'The Challenges of Conceptualising Terrorism', p. 787.

[15] J. Dugard, 'International Terrorism: Problems of Definition', *International Affairs*, Vol. 50, No. 1, 1974, p. 71.

[16] For example, in theory, hijackings can be carried out for non-political reasons, such as for ransom demands.

When focusing on a definition of terrorism, any list of types of violence that are labelled 'terrorist acts' is not then going to be particularly useful in helping us to conceptualize terrorism or in grasping what the essence of terrorism is. As such, the UN and the EU's approach of identifying and addressing 'a wide spectrum of terrorist acts', or French law that specifically names and describes the acts that constitute terrorism,[17] or indeed any such lists,[18] while from a legal perspective may be useful, again serve only to deviate us from this, because terrorism is not inherent to any particular act or type of violence. This perhaps comes as something of a relief because it means that, in the course of our conceptual deliberations, we do not then have to address the emergence of new and different types of acts of violence that may develop along with advances in technology. As Tiefenbrun observes, 'as new forms of technology are created, new forms of terrorist acts are likely to develop', though her suggestion (from a legal perspective) that 'this problem might be countered by enacting an extensive list of specific crimes of terrorism' would again not bring us any closer to capturing what terrorism is.[19, 20]

So, in summary, the first assumption that informs our discussion as to what terrorism is, is that there is no act of violence that can in and of itself inherently be described as an act of terrorism. *Whatever the type of violence chosen* 'the primary intent [of terrorism] . . . is to produce fear and alarm that may serve a variety of purposes'.[21] The essence of terrorism lies in the intent behind the act of violence, and the 'primary intent' of terrorism is to spread fear beyond the immediate victims. If it is not intended to have this wider psychological impact then it is not terrorism.

---

[17] Article 421–1 of the French Criminal Code lists the following acts as terrorist acts: 'Attempted murder, assault, kidnapping, hostage-taking on airplanes, ships, all means of transport, theft, extortion, destructions, and crimes committed during group combat, the production or ownership of weapons of destruction and explosives including the production, sale, import and export of explosives, the acquisition, ownership, transport of illegal explosive substances, the production, ownership, storage, or acquisition of biological or chemical weapons, and money laundering' (cited in Tiefenbrun, 'A Semiotic Approach to a Legal Definition of Terrorism', p. 377).

[18] Bassiouni lists 14 specific acts of terrorism which are: 'aggression, war crimes, crimes against humanity, genocide, apartheid, unlawful human experimentation; torture, slavery and slave-related practices; piracy, and unlawful acts against the safety of maritime navigation; kidnapping of diplomats and other internationally protected persons; taking civilian hostages; serious environmental damage; or serious violation of fundamental human rights' (cited in Tiefenbrun, 'A Semiotic Approach to a Legal Definition of Terrorism', p. 393).

[19] Tiefenbrun, 'A Semiotic Approach to a Legal Definition of Terrorism', p. 365.

[20] While it is not the particular act of violence itself that determines whether or not that act is terrorism, but the intent and purpose behind it, the *seriousness* (however defined) of the act is, however, of relevance to the conceptual discussion. For example, an issue of contention is how serious an act of violence must be to be considered an act of terrorism (see Chapter 9).

[21] B. Jenkins, 'The Study of Terrorism: Definitional Problems', RAND Corporation, December 1980, p. 2, available at: <http://www.rand.org/pubs/papers/2006/P6563.pdf> (last accessed 27 November 2014).

*(2) Terrorism is a particular method used by a wide variety of actors
in pursuit of an equally broad range of ideologies and so perpetrator or
cause based definitions (beyond political motive) are unhelpful*

The notion of terrorism as a method is certainly not new—in fact it was referred to as a 'method of combat' in the *Encyclopaedia of the Social Sciences* in 1936.[22] When I refer to the 'method' of terrorism I am not then alluding to the various types of violence used (i.e. the physical manifestation of terrorism), but to the purpose or intent behind the act of violence, which is to generate a psychological impact beyond the immediate victims. Terrorism, with this indispensable psychological dimension, is a particular method of violence that has been used by a wide variety of actors and requires more than just an act of violence or the threat of violence. A definition does not need to refer to the perpetrator or the cause (other than being political) but it does need to establish the intent behind that act of violence, namely to 'terrorize' (and/or to motivate/mobilize) a wider population.

The utility of viewing terrorism as a method (or a tactic) is that it allows us to implicitly acknowledge that terrorism is not particular to any type of actor for it has been used by a wide variety of actors, not just terrorist organizations. An actor-free definition of terrorism means that no type of perpetrator of terrorism is excluded, be they states, social movements, guerrilla groups, terrorist groups, and so on. In this context, a clearer distinction in terrorism studies 'between "terrorist groups" and groups that deploy terrorism as one of many insurgent and political strategies' is a worthy one to make.[23] As Weinberg rightly observed, the notion that 'one man's terrorist is another man's freedom fighter' is confusing the goal with the activity.[24] So too, therefore, does the view (apparently articulated by the UN Secretary-General in March 1987 in relation to the PLO and SWAPO) that 'sometimes it is difficult to tell where terrorism ends and the struggle for self-determination begins.'[25]

Schmid, in 1983, suggested that 'terrorism is a method of combat in which random or symbolic victims become targets of violence' and aptly makes no reference as to who carries out this 'method of combat',[26] and Cooper rightly argues that we 'can no longer afford the fiction that one person's terrorist is another's freedom fighter. Fighting for freedom may well be his or her purpose, but if the mission is undertaken through the employment of terrorist

---

[22] Schmid and Jongman, *Political Terrorism*, p. 13.

[23] Schmid, 'Introduction', in *The Routledge Handbook of Terrorism Research*, p. 28.

[24] Weinberg, *Global Terrorism: A Beginner's Guide*, p. 2.

[25] Romanov, 'The United Nations and the Problem of Combating International Terrorism', p. 295.

[26] A. Schmid, *Political Terrorism: A Research Guide to Concepts, Theories, Data Bases and Literature* (New Brunswick, NJ: Transaction Books, 1983), p. 111.

means, a terrorist he or she must remain.'[27] Crenshaw also makes the point that 'the identity of the actor [whether state or non-state] does not matter to the specification of the method.'[28]

Any attempt, therefore, in the course of conceptualizing or defining terrorism, to either automatically deny the use of terrorism because of the 'worthiness' of the cause, or indeed, conversely, to conflate terrorism with certain causes one finds unpalatable, obfuscates endeavours to elevate terrorism as an *analytical* concept. Yet, such associations (or non-associations) have proved remarkably (and unhelpfully) resilient. Pillar has also rightly argued that terrorism is something that 'people (or groups, or states) *do*, rather than who they are or what they are trying to achieve' (original author's italics).[29] Terrorism, as a method, should be 'defined by the nature of the act, not by the identity of the perpetrators or the nature of their cause'.[30]

There may have been ideologies that have been interpreted or adapted to explicitly justify the use of terrorism and where terrorism may then become 'ideologically embedded'. It could be argued that this is the case with Al Qaeda and the notion of terrorism and political violence as a doctrinal and religious duty, or indeed with the tradition of 'physical force Irish republicanism'—for example Patrick Pearse's proclamations of the notion of self-sacrificial acts as being a compelling symbol of republican ideology. But such ideologies cannot claim ownership of terrorism—for there are, of course, many nationalist, religious, left wing, right wing, and single issue (anti-abortion, animal rights, environmental) ideologies that are not inherently violent themselves though terrorism has often been employed in their name. It would be wrong, therefore, to confine our conceptualization of terrorism to any particular ideology or ideologies. Rather, it is a method of violence that has at some time or other been perpetrated in the cause of doctrines within all of these categories.

What this way of viewing terrorism enables us to do is to more accurately describe the actors that have often been labelled 'terrorist groups'. For example, the Revolutionary Armed Forces of Colombia (FARC) can more clearly be seen as a guerrilla group that has used terrorist tactics. Hamas can be seen as a social and political movement that has also used the *method* of terrorism. There have been those who claim to be acting on behalf of animal

---

[27] H. H. Cooper, cited in P. Griset and S. Mahan, *Terrorism in Perspective* (Thousand Oaks, CA and London, 2003), p. 59, available at: <http://books.google.co.uk/books?hl=en&lr=&id=YpmZ76zRW2oC&oi=fnd&pg=PR9&dq=defining+terrorism&ots=mN6SlK4htr&sig=YT9v2D6lMm8e-KpHIcszBCfU9mUM#v=onepage&q=defining%20terrorism&f=false> (last accessed 27 November 2014).

[28] Crenshaw, *Explaining Terrorism: Causes, Processes and Consequences*, p. 207.

[29] P. Pillar, 'The Dimensions of Terrorism and Counterterrorism', in Howard and Sawyer (eds.), *Terrorism and Counterterrorism: Understanding the New Security Environment, Readings and Interpretations*, p. 28.

[30] Jenkins, 'The Study of Terrorism: Definitional Problems', pp. 2–3.

rights that have on occasion used terrorist tactics, although it has been argued that most of what animal rights 'extremists' do is not 'terroristic'.[31]

In fact, what becomes apparent is that it is rarely the case that there are what one might call 'pure' 'terrorist organizations'. Crenshaw concurs that it is very unusual for terrorism to be used exclusively as a form of struggle, citing the Abu Nidal group as one of the few possible examples.[32] The so-called Fighting Communist Organizations (FCOs)[33] of the 1970s and 1980s (such as the Red Army Faction, Direct Action, The Red Brigades, and November 17) could arguably be seen as other instances. But, in general, terrorism forms but one part of the political activity of those who carry it out, and in some cases this other activity includes other forms of political violence. Guerrilla movements, such as FARC or the defeated Liberation Tigers of Tamil Eelam (LTTE), as noted above, used traditional guerrilla tactics (such as attacking state forces in the open) as well as acts of terrorism. Crenshaw lists a number of what she calls 'internal wars' (post Second World War) that have been 'accompanied by terrorism' including the 'Philippines, Cyprus, Malaya, Palestine, Tunisia, Morocco, Algeria, Vietnam, [and] Latin America'.[34] From a policymaking perspective, an acknowledgement of such distinctions would facilitate a more differentiated and sophisticated response to those employing the method of terrorism, while it would also better inform the methodologies and choices of 'terrorist' case studies made by scholars studying the phenomenon.

(3) *Acts of terrorism are not just carried out against civilians and non-combatants*

A third assumption that informs my conceptualization of terrorism is that, while acts of terrorism are very often carried out indiscriminately or against civilian or non-combatant targets, civilian or non-combatant targeting should not be *definitional* of terrorism. Indeed, Narodnaya Volya, often cited as one of the most well-known of terrorist antecedents, described its activity as 'the destruction of the most harmful persons in the government' (rather than civilians per se).[35] Feliks Gross, in his study of violence in politics, argued that what he called 'individual terror':

attacked directly, above all, key decision makers or administrators, or acted in lieu of punishment against persons responsible for cruelties and oppression. One of its

[31] As argued by Schmid (personal communication).

[32] Crenshaw, *Explaining Terrorism: Causes, Processes and Consequences*, p. 4.

[33] See Y. Alexander and D. Pluchinsky, *Europe's Red Terrorists: The Fighting Communist Organizations* (London: Frank Cass, 1992).

[34] Crenshaw, 'The Concept of Revolutionary Terrorism', p. 395.

[35] N. Volya, cited in Appendix 2.1 of Schmid (ed.), *The Routledge Handbook of Terrorism Research*, p. 99. See Chapter 9 for a discussion on the meaning of 'civilian' (i.e. who might or might not be included in this category).

functions was retribution and deterrence. The leaders of the organization expected that assassination of an oppressive administrator would deter his successors from inhuman, oppressive acts... Such was the goal of assassination of high German Gestapo officers in Poland during the Second World War... 'Central Terror' which they [Russian revolutionaries] practiced was directed solely against carefully selected major representatives of the Russian autocracy such as the Tsar himself, governors, high police officers. It did not hurt innocent people; it was discriminating.[36]

There are clearly grey areas as to who or what constitutes a 'civilian' target and there are also degrees of 'innocence' (see Chapter 9). I would argue, however, that such distinctions are not relevant to a definition, for terrorism can entail violence against 'any person', as stated in the United Nations' draft comprehensive convention, despite the objections of those who argue for the centrality of civilian or non-combatant targets in the definition.[37] In 1978 Crenshaw also argued that although the victims of terrorism are usually civilian 'they may include the military or the police'.[38]

As noted in Chapter 1, a brief survey of Easson and Schmid's 250 definitions of terrorism appears to endorse the view that terrorism is not just carried out against civilians or non-combatants. Most of the definitions in their compilation do not make explicit reference to civilians or non-combatants as being victims (approximately 70 of them make reference to 'civilian', 'non-combatant', or 'innocent' victims, with about half of these appearing in post 9/11 definitions).[39] In the academic sample of 15 definitions in Schmid and Jongman's study, *none of them* explicitly insist upon *only* civilian or non-combatant targets as being a necessary condition, although, of the 15, Townsend uses the word 'unarmed' (in defining terrorism as 'the use of force by the armed... against the unarmed') and Netanyahu uses 'the innocent' (in his definition of 'the deliberate and systematic murder, maiming, and menacing of the innocent to inspire fear for political ends').[40] The objective of instilling fear into a 'social group' or 'community' or to 'terrorize communities' was noted in three of the definitions, though, of course, this is not the same as being *directly* targeted and the 'social group' or 'communities' being referred to need not be civilian.[41]

Schmid asserts that the 'very core of terrorism' is that '[t]he direct victim of violence (or threat thereof) is different from the ultimate target (audience)',

---

[36] F. Gross, *Violence in Politics: Terror and Political Assassination in Eastern Europe and Russia* (The Hague: Mouton, 1972), p. 10.

[37] See Schmid, 'The Definition of Terrorism', p. 55.

[38] M. Crenshaw, quoted in Appendix 2.1 of Schmid (ed.), *The Routledge Handbook of Terrorism Research*, p. 118.

[39] See Appendix 2.1 of Schmid (ed.), *The Routledge Handbook of Terrorism Research*, pp. 99–157.

[40] Schmid and Jongman, *Political Terrorism*, pp. 34–7.

[41] Schmid and Jongman, *Political Terrorism*, pp. 34–7.

and that '[f]or this reason *anyone* can, in principle, become a victim of terrorism' (italics added).[42] Yet, in the same piece he conversely argued that:

If those opposing terrorism want to maintain the moral high ground, they will have to observe this distinction between the unarmed civilian population and regular or irregular armed forces. However, they should only label as 'terrorism' attacks that deliberately target civilians and non-combatants.[43]

One can't help but sense here some confusion between moral and scientific imperatives in how one conceives of terrorism. There appears to be something of a contradiction (exemplified in Schmid's two differing perspectives above) between the perception of the core essence of terrorism as first and foremost being its intended psychological impact beyond the immediate victims to a wider group (thus providing this is achieved and that the victims serve as sufficient 'message generators', *anybody* can be a victim of terrorism—that terrorism 'may fall upon anyone in a sizable class of persons'[44]), and then, on the contrary, the insistence that victims must be civilian or non-combatant for an act to be called terrorism. If the latter is intrinsic to a definition of terrorism then it is indeed easier to argue that terrorism should always be viewed as immoral, that there can never be 'good' terrorism (even if one agrees with the cause) because, defined in this way, terrorism can only be labelled as such if it is carried out against civilians and non-combatants (however one defines non-combatants—see Chapter 9).

This narrower approach, as I have argued earlier, may, in keeping with international norms, be born of a general desire to protect civilians and 'protected persons' from all forms of political conflict and that this should therefore form the basis of a definition. Contrary to the purpose-based approach this represents a *moral* victim-based approach. It is understandable that there should be a particular concern with those acts of terrorism that are indiscriminate in public places or that deliberately target civilians and non-combatants, and that this concern should be reflected in a definition of the concept, but such moral impulses arguably compromise a more objective (and holistic) approach to the conceptual debate. If we agree that the essence of terrorism lies in its primary intent to generate a psychological impact beyond the immediate victims then, based on this, terrorism can be carried out against both non-combatant and combatant targets. It is then another question as to *which forms of terrorism* (based on target differentiation) should be of more concern to policymakers than others. Were not, for example, many of the 'combatant' targets of the IRA victims of terrorism, providing that the aim was

---

[42] Schmid, 'The Definition of Terrorism', p. 80.
[43] Schmid, 'The Definition of Terrorism', p. 81.
[44] J. Narveson, 'Terrorism and Morality', in R. Frey and C. Morris (eds.), *Violence, Terrorism and Justice* (Cambridge: Cambridge University Press, 1991), p. 119.

to generate a psychological impact beyond the immediate casualties? Terrorism can be carried out against anyone, providing the victims or object of attack serve sufficiently as 'message generators' to a wider group or audience.

In arguing that acts of terrorism can take place against combatants in war, one might consider the example of the 'rogue' Afghan soldiers who turned on NATO troops. If this was a concerted strategy of intimidation against the wider NATO troop body then these can certainly be classified as acts of terrorism. Yet, civilians were not targeted, nor, arguably, did they take place in a peacetime environment. Thus, acts of terrorism are possible within war providing the psychological impact is the primary objective over the physical one.

The cases of the 'rogue shootings' or 'green on blue' attacks in Afghanistan merit closer scrutiny. While it has been argued that most of the attacks have 'nothing to do with the Taliban' and that they tend to be 'rooted in a mixture of personal arguments and cultural misunderstandings' at least some of the attacks have been linked to the Taliban.[45] Indeed, the NATO Secretary-General reportedly argued that the Taliban 'had "played out a strategy" to undermine confidence in the Afghan security forces'.[46] It was widely reported that the green on blue attacks had a broader and negative impact on NATO troop morale—in other words the acts of violence generated a wider psychological impact beyond the immediate victims. Hypothetically, if this psychological impact was the primary and *intended* purpose of the attacks, then one could describe them as acts of terrorism.[47]

If the main purpose of the acts of violence carried out by the resistance movements of the Second World War (in opposition to Nazi rule) was to generate a psychological impact beyond the immediate victims then such acts could also be classified as acts of terrorism against military targets in the context of war, though again what constitutes a 'war environment' is debatable. Terrorism, then, is about the use of violence or the credible threat of violence in order to generate a psychological impact beyond the immediate victims, whether they are civilian (or non-combatant) or not, or whether one sympathizes with the cause or not. As Crenshaw aptly argues, 'we can develop a neutral definition' while also 'retaining the ability to make moral judgments [whether positive or negative] about its use in different political circumstances'.[48]

---

[45] *The Economist*, 'Green-on-Blue blues', 1 September 2012, available at: <http://www.economist.com/node/21561943> (last accessed 27 November 2014).

[46] BBC News online, 'Afghan policeman kills three British soldiers', 2 July 2012, available at: <http://www.bbc.co.uk/news/uk-18670175> (last accessed 27 November 2014).

[47] Indeed, the outcome was to undermine attempts to train the Afghan forces with the United States apparently suspending its training of new recruits to the Afghan police force (BBC News online, 'Afghanistan "rogue" attack: Four US soldiers killed', 16 September 2012, available at: <http://www.bbc.co.uk/news/world-asia-19614911> (last accessed 27 November 2014)).

[48] Crenshaw, 'Introduction: Reflections on the Effects of Terrorism', p. 5.

From my purpose-based perspective there may therefore be some 'terrorisms' that one might sympathize with,[49] and any moral repugnance against some particularly brutal forms of the phenomenon should not deviate us from including the less contemptible (or even noble or laudable) forms from a general definition of the concept as a whole. Of course, what these more palatable forms are is entirely dependent on one's perspective—nevertheless, the possibility needs to be incorporated into, or at least not explicitly excluded from, our conceptualization of terrorism. For many, for example, some forms of terrorism may be justified if they are carried out in pursuit of democracy against oppressive regimes, and if they pass the *jus in bello* test within just war theory that is normally applied to states and their conduct within war (and that is embedded in the international humanitarian law emphasis on protecting civilians and non-combatants in such contexts).

Even if the French resistance did not target civilians when they carried out acts of violence against an oppressive and occupying (Nazi) regime, they nevertheless, subject to the necessary criteria (in particular the intent to generate a psychological impact beyond the immediate victims), *still carried out acts of terrorism*. And once again, any attempt to refrain from using the word 'terrorism' (in favour of more 'positive' labels like 'freedom fighting') simply further reinforces terrorism as a derogatory label at the expense of any prospects it might have for analytical utility. David Anderson, the independent reviewer of UK terrorism legislation (at the time of writing), draws our attention to what would indeed be a fallacious attempt to draw any distinction between terrorism (an activity) and freedom fighting (which refers to a goal):

> Whether directed at our Government or that of Syria, whether an evil attack on civilians or a reaction to extrajudicial murder by the state, terrorism is terrorism. We might wish it otherwise, particularly in relation to national separatist struggles where one would prefer not to take sides. But Parliament in the 2000 Act tried and failed to come up with a workable system for distinguishing freedom-fighters from terrorists, and the Court of Appeal has also, unsurprisingly, declined the invitation to do so.[50]

It is entirely understandable, if regrettable, that in the 'real world' of domestic and international politics 'terrorism' is used selectively given its pejorative connotation in practice, and this is one of the fundamental challenges for

---

[49] The use of 'terrorism' by the resistance movements (against Nazi rule) in the Second World War is often cited as an example.

[50] D. Alexander (Independent Reviewer of Terrorism Legislation), 'The Meaning of Terrorism', Clifford Chance University of Essex Lecture, 13 February 2013, available at: <https://terrorismlegislationreviewer.independent.gov.uk/wp-content/uploads/2013/04/clifford-chance-lecture.pdf> (last accessed 1 December 2014).

more objective academic endeavours in conceptualizing terrorism (and a formidable barrier to 'being heard'). And when such negative connotations become embedded Crenshaw cautions that:

> It is well to remember . . . that the users of political language are not entirely free to shape it; once concepts are constructed and endowed with meaning, they take on a certain autonomy, especially when they are adopted by the news media, disseminated to the public, and integrated into a general context of norms and values.[51]

The implications of arguing that terrorism can be carried out against non-civilians and combatants are discussed further in Chapter 6—not least that it undermines the extent that terrorism can be understood as the peacetime equivalent of a war crime,[52] and it also prompts us to question the extent that terrorism can be conceptualized as an 'extranormal' form of political violence.

Notwithstanding the argument that combatants can be victims of terrorism, one should, however, acknowledge that the intended psychological impact of terrorism is likely to be enhanced by the targeting of civilians.[53] As Gearty remarks, 'A pure terrorist act results in everyone recoiling in horror, with the words "it could have been me" etched on their mind . . . It is, therefore, the indiscriminate nature of its victims which gives the act of terror its powerful impact',[54] and '[i]t is the wanton assault on civilians and non-combatants that provides much of the terror to terrorism.'[55] Terrorist attacks against civilians in peacetime environments, then, are indeed likely to generate greater shock value and psychological impact. Yet, as Shanahan has noted 'although the perceived innocence of victims can enhance the *effectiveness* of some terrorist acts, it should not be part of the *definition* of "terrorism" itself'[56]—for both combatants and non-combatants can be victims of terrorism and definitions of the phenomenon should reflect this. If one is understandably more

---

[51] M. Crenshaw, 'Terrorism in Context', cited in Whittaker (ed.), *The Terrorism Reader*, p. 11.

[52] Such equivalence is in any case undermined by the fact that the intended wider psychological dimension that is indispensable to terrorism is not an essential element for something to be called a war crime.

[53] Apart from civilian targeting, the degree of wider psychological impact from a terrorist attack may be dependent on a number of factors, such as the lethality of the attack (in terms of numbers of casualties) and the context of the attack (such as a public place in peacetime) but also, importantly, on the extent and reach of media coverage. In some contexts media accessibility may be restricted, such as in war or conflict zones (for example, the bitter conflicts in Grozny in Chechnya and Fallujah in Iraq) while editorial decisions to cover (or not) a terrorist event may enhance or curtail wider psychological impact.

[54] Gearty, *Terror*, p. 9.

[55] Schmid, 'The Definition of Terrorism', p. 68. It should be noted that, while acts of terrorism against civilians may be the preferred choice of target, it is also possible that such targets reflect the weakness of terrorist organizations who do not have the capabilities to target government forces or 'well-guarded leaders' (see Crenshaw, 'Introduction: Reflections on the Effects of Terrorism', p. 29).

[56] Shanahan, 'Betraying a Certain Corruption of Mind: How (and How Not) to Define "Terrorism"'.

concerned with acts of terrorism that target civilians and non-combatants than those that do not then one needs to acknowledge that this is but one form of terrorism, rather than determining that civilian and non-combatant targeting be definitional of terrorism as a whole.

* * * * *

In summary, in order to inform the definitional debate I have proposed the following key assumptions—that there is no such thing as an act of violence that is in and of itself inherently terrorist; that terrorism is best conceptualized as a method rather than defined as inherent to any particular ideology or cause; and that terrorism can be carried out against non-civilians and combatants as well as civilians and non-combatants. As I have argued, these assumptions have significant implications for the definitional debate. This is particularly the case with the third assumption, the consequences of which will be further drawn out in Chapter 6, with a particular focus and scrutiny of the following: (i) on the notion of defining terrorism as the peacetime equivalent of a war crime; (ii) on defining terrorism as the use of *extranormal* violence; and (iii) on the possibility of 'good' terrorism. In the context of the arguments made in Chapters 4, 5, and 6 as to what terrorism is, Chapter 7 will then attempt to deduce *what is not* terrorism. Chapter 8 will attempt to draw a distinction between terrorism and state terror while further potential components of a definition will be considered in Chapter 9.

6

Implications of the Assumption that Non-Civilians and Combatants Can Also Be Victims of Terrorism

This chapter will develop further the implications of the third assumption in Chapter 5—that non-civilians and combatants can also be victims of terrorism. It will firstly argue against the notion that terrorism can be conceptualized as the peacetime equivalent of a war crime. It will then suggest that, because not all forms of terrorism are necessarily extranormal, terrorism cannot then be *defined* as such. It will then offer some thoughts on the legal status of terrorism and its (il)legitimacy for the purposes of the conceptual debate, before going on to argue that there may be some terrorisms, as I have conceptualized the phenomenon, that one might sympathize with or endorse.

Conceptualizing Terrorism as the Peacetime Equivalent of a War Crime?

Although the notion that International Humanitarian Law (IHL) 'can provide guidance to the legal approach to terrorism in peacetime' was apparently first contemplated in 1985,[1] Schmid's suggestion of terrorism as the peacetime equivalent of a war crime was proposed in a 1992 report to the UN Crime Prevention Office.[2] The impetus behind this particular way of conceptualizing terrorism is born of the general desire to uphold international norms to do with the protection of civilians and non-combatants—that, for the purposes of agreeing common approaches to terrorism, and whatever else one disagrees about, one can at least surely concur that deliberate attacks against civilians

---

[1] S. Santos, 'Terrorism: Toward a Legal Definition', *The Manila Times*, 5 October 2002, available at: <http://www.i-p-o.org/Manila-Times1.htm> (last accessed 1 December 2014).
[2] Santos, 'Terrorism: Toward a Legal Definition'.

are morally repugnant and that agreement on a definition can at least be generated on this basis.

From an IHL perspective Koechler proposed 'a comprehensive or unified approach' to attacks on civilians both in peace and war time:

In a universal and at the same time unified system of norms—ideally to be created as an extension of existing legal instruments—there should be corresponding sets of rules (a) penalizing deliberate attacks on civilians or civilian infrastructure in war-time (as covered by the Geneva Conventions), and (b) penalizing deliberate attacks on civilians in peacetime (covered by the 12 so far anti-terrorist conventions).[3]

A war crime is described by Article 147 of the fourth Geneva Convention as:

Wilful killing, torture or inhuman treatment, including biological experiments, wilfully causing great suffering or serious injury to body or health, unlawful deportation or transfer or unlawful confinement of a protected person, compelling a protected person to serve in the forces of a hostile Power, or wilfully depriving a protected person of the rights of fair and regular trial prescribed in the present Convention, taking of hostages and extensive destruction and appropriation of property, not justified by military necessity and carried out unlawfully and wantonly.[4]

Although war crimes are often associated with the killing (and sometimes mass killing) of civilians this definition refers to the *broader* category of 'protected persons'. For example, it includes prisoners of war:

The definition of protected persons in paragraph 1 [of General Provisions of Article 4 of Convention IV] is a very broad one which includes members of the armed forces—fit for service, wounded, sick or shipwrecked—who fall into enemy hands. The treatment which such persons are to receive is laid down in special Conventions to which the provision refers. They must be treated as prescribed in the texts which concern them. But if, for some reason, prisoner of war status—to take one example—were denied to them, they would become protected persons under the present Convention.[5]

Protected persons, then, include civilians, those that surrender their arms, members of armed forces 'who fall into enemy hands' (if they are not accorded prisoner of war status), and those combatants who are 'hors de combat'

---

[3] H. Koechler, cited in Santos, 'Terrorism: Toward a Legal Definition'.
[4] Convention (IV) relative to the Protection of Civilian Persons in Time of War, Geneva, 12 August 1949, available at International Committee of the Red Cross website: <https://www.icrc.org/applic/ihl/ihl.nsf/INTRO/380> (last accessed 1 December 2014).
[5] Convention (IV) relative to the Protection of Civilian Persons in Time of War, Geneva, 12 August 1949, Definition of Protected Persons, available at International Committee of the Red Cross website: <http://www.icrc.org/ihl.nsf/COM/380-600007> (last accessed 1 December 2014).

(unable to fight).[6] They do not, of course, include combatants in conflict (who have a right to engage in hostilities).[7]

The first and obvious point to note, then, is that, as I have argued that the victims of terrorism can also be non-civilian or combatant, then, from this perspective, terrorism cannot be defined as the peacetime equivalent of a war crime, simply because combatants are not 'protected' persons. Acts of terrorism within war are therefore not necessarily war crimes, though of course they can be if 'protected' persons are targeted. For example, an attack against a civilian target in Afghanistan may constitute both an act of terrorism and a war crime, whereas a roadside bomb targeting (combatant) NATO troops may be an act of terrorism but not the latter.[8]

Secondly, and more generally, whether against combatants or non-combatants, acts of terrorism can take place within war, hence the use of terrorism is not limited to peacetime environments (and therefore cannot be *defined* as the 'peacetime equivalent'). Thirdly, and arguably the most fundamental problem with defining terrorism as the peacetime equivalent of a war crime, is that it does not account sufficiently for what after all is the essence of terrorism and that is its *psychological* dimension. War crimes may not be at all concerned with generating a psychological impact beyond the immediate victims as their primary goal. As Sproat has argued:

> 'war crimes', such as 'massacres' or 'genocide', 'merely' involve the physical elimination of a particular group of illegitimate targets, and cannot be classified as terrorism because the intention is not to influence the behaviour of others, but merely to destroy the immediate target group or victims.[9]

'Physical elimination' of civilians, then, may well be the main purpose of a war crime, rather than any broader psychological impact.

Can Terrorism Be Conceptualized as Extranormal?

The argument that combatants can also be victims of terrorism has implications for one particular mantra in terrorism studies—that terrorism entails the

---

[6] Additional Protocol 1 to the Geneva Conventions, available at International Committee of the Red Cross website: <http://www.icrc.org/eng/war-and-law/treaties-customary-law/geneva-conventions/index.jsp> (last accessed 1 December 2014).

[7] See Article 43 of the Additional Protocol 1 to the Geneva Conventions.

[8] Both of these hypothetical examples of terrorism, in order to be labelled as such, would, of course, need to satisfy one's definitional criteria, i.e. that their *primary* purpose is to spread fear beyond the immediate victims (i.e. in the case of the second example to the broader troop body or to wider domestic populations of those NATO members involved).

[9] P. Sproat, 'Can the State Commit Acts of Terrorism? An Opinion and Some Qualitative Replies to a Questionnaire', *Terrorism and Political Violence*, Vol. 9, No. 4, 1997, p. 126.

perpetration of *extranormal* violence and that it is this that often distinguishes it from other forms of political violence. In one of the earlier theoretical contributions to the study of terrorism Thornton described the phenomenon as 'a symbolic act designed to influence political behaviour by extranormal means, entailing the use or threat of violence' and that 'terror lies beyond the norms of violent political agitation that are accepted by a given society'.[10] Crenshaw concurs with the view that 'terrorism differs from other instruments of violence in its "extranormality"',[11] while Wardlaw also argued that '[i]t is the extranormal nature of the use of terror that distinguishes it from other forms of political violence'[12] and Schmid, too, writes of the terrorists' 'decidedly extra-normal violence'.[13,14]

Of course, what one regards as 'normal' and 'extranormal' is entirely subjective. After all, paradoxically what might be seen as acceptable, legal, or legitimate violence that complies with 'our norms' might be (and often is) *far more* devastating than what is often regarded as extranormal violence. The impact of 'normal' political violence through, for example, sustained bombing campaigns, is far more destructive than most acts of 'extranormal' terrorist violence.

So what is it that is extranormal about terrorism? Is it the acts themselves, or is it the context in which those acts take place, or is it the specific targets of the violence, or, indeed, does its extranormality lie in its core essence of intending to generate a wider psychological impact beyond the immediate victims? In relation to the first possibility, as I have argued (in Chapter 5) that there is no such thing as an act of violence that is in and of itself inherently an act of terrorism (and so by definition the acts themselves are no more or less extranormal than other forms of political violence), we then have to look beyond the act itself to determine any extranormality.

Perhaps one could suggest that a peacetime environment and/or intended civilian, non-combatant, or indiscriminate targeting is what gives terrorism its extranormal character. Yet, as I have argued that acts of terrorism can take place in a war environment and combatants can be victims of terrorism, then the phenomenon cannot be *defined* as extranormal on these grounds either.[15]

---

[10] Thornton, 'Terror as a Weapon of Political Agitation', pp. 73–6.

[11] Crenshaw, 'The Concept of Revolutionary Terrorism', p. 384.

[12] Wardlaw, *Political Terrorism*, Chapter 1: 'The Problem of Defining Terrorism', p. 10.

[13] Schmid, 'Introduction', in *The Routledge Handbook of Terrorism Research*, p. 19.

[14] The section beginning from 'In one of the earlier contributions...' to the end of this paragraph has been reprinted with the permission of Taylor and Francis LLC from Richards, 'Conceptualizing Terrorism', p. 228.

[15] For many the targeting of civilians and non-combatants is the sine qua non of terrorism and so, defined as such, all acts of terrorism might be seen as extranormal. Citing Walzer, Meisels has argued that: 'For terrorists, the killing of non-combatants is not a regrettable by-product or side effect; innocent victims are not an ' "occupational hazard." ' Instead they are the be all and end all of this form of belligerency. Terrorism ' "breaks across moral limits beyond which no further

While one cannot therefore *conceptualize* or *define* terrorism as such, one could perhaps rather *describe* terrorism as having the capacity to inflict such 'extra-normal' violence, that its extranormality lies in *particular forms* of the phenomenon—i.e. those acts that deliberately target civilians, or those that are indiscriminate in a peacetime environment.

Such attacks would include those on 9/11, the Bali bombings of 2004, and the July 2005 bombings on the London transport system. Waldron argues that: 'Certainly the class of victims is perceived as "extra-normal," in relation to what people regard as the legitimate or ordinary casualties of war.'[16] One could claim that the Beslan school massacre of 2004 was a particularly extra-normal act, entailing as it did the targeting of children in a way that was beyond the comprehension of watching audiences and that was in contravention of 'the powerful norm that non-majority age persons lack intellectual maturity and cannot be held accountable for political policies'.[17] Schmid suggests that:

> The terrorist tendency to see the world only in terms of supporters or opponents tends to eradicate the categories of neutrals and innocents. In other words, innocence is either irrelevant or even a special incentive for targeting, owing to the extra shock value produced by the extra-normal violence of the terrorist.[18]

Some acts of terrorism, however (such as those against combatants in the context of war, or against the military of oppressive states), may not, in fact, be seen as particularly extranormal. One could perhaps argue, then, that the degree of extranormality of terrorism is dependent upon the environment (peacetime/wartime) and the target (civilians/non-civilians).

Thus, parallel with my argument that civilian targeting should not be *definitional* of terrorism, then nor should 'extranormality' be an indispensable part of the concept. As noted above, there are *degrees* of extranormality and, indeed, some acts of terrorism may not even be seen as 'extranormal' at all, depending on one's perspective. This links in with the notion that there may be some terrorisms that one might sympathize with such as (from a democratic perspective) those that refrain from targeting civilians and that are carried out against the military of oppressive regimes. In other words one

---

limitation seems possible, for within the category of civilian and citizen, there isn't any smaller group for which immunity might be claimed...Terrorists anyway make no such claim; they kill anybody"'(T. Meisels, 'The Trouble with Terror: The Apologetics of Terrorism—a Refutation', *Terrorism and Political Violence*, Vol. 18, No. 3, 2006, p. 475, and citing M. Walzer, *Just and Unjust Wars* (Harmondsworth: Penguin, 1977), p. 203).

[16] J. Waldron, 'Terrorism and the Uses of Terror', *The Journal of Ethics*, Vol. 8, 2004, p. 27.

[17] R. Kelly, 'Is Terrorism Always Wrong?', *Perspectives on Terrorism*, Vol. 1, No. 1, 2007, p. 19, available at: <http://www.terrorismanalysts.com/pt/articles/issues/PTv1i1.pdf> (last accessed 27 November 2014).

[18] Schmid, 'The Definition of Terrorism', p. 81.

can suggest that there is a causal relationship between (i) acknowledging that acts of terrorism can take place against non-civilians or combatants, (ii) that not all acts of terrorism are therefore necessarily 'extranormal', and that, (iii) because of these assumptions, in certain circumstances there may be some terrorisms that one might sympathize with.

When we consider the 'extranormality' of terrorism, however, we should be mindful of what democratic states *are* willing to tolerate and what, in cold reality, *our norms actually are*. We may be shocked by the violence perpetrated on 9/11 and 7/7 but how more shocking are these compared with terrorism or terror practised by those who received support from both non-democratic and democratic states during the course of the Cold War and beyond? What unpalatable collaborations have taken place in the name of perceived national interests and security? How often have states (including democratic ones) routinely ignored, endorsed, or even sponsored 'extranormal' terrorism or 'terror' in other countries in pursuit of strategic priorities over and above any universal commitment to democratic norms and values? Stohl once lamented that 'in the interests of national security we must excuse the excesses of authoritarian governments and aid and abet their behaviour regardless of the costs to their own citizens in the interests of U.S. national security.'[19]

States themselves, of course, have the monopoly on the use of violence or 'force' and have been by far the greatest perpetrators of political violence, whether through the two world wars, through other lesser wars, or through campaigns of state terror. In terms of *scale*, terrorism can therefore never be considered extranormal. Yet, even if one uses the targeting of civilians and children as a barometer for the extranormality of terrorism one cannot overlook state culpability for this too. Indeed, English has argued that 'In reality . . . states have targeted civilians repeatedly in orthodox war . . . It is the mixture of state callousness towards civilian victims, and hypocrisy about not admitting what is actually being done by states in so much of war, which actually lends terrorist groups the little credibility which they sometimes do possess.'[20]

Notwithstanding these 'critical' arguments in relation to state culpability, one can suggest that the extranormality of terrorism lies in those forms that deliberately target civilians in a peacetime environment and which arguably elicit the most shock and psychological impact. For Honderich the feeling of shock is heightened because one identifies with the victims more than, say, with soldiers in a war environment—he suggests that we knew the victims of 9/11 'in the sense of knowing them to have been people like ourselves'[21] and

---

[19] M. Stohl, 'National Interests and State Terrorism in International Affairs', *Political Science*, Vol. 36, No. 1, 1984, p. 286.

[20] R. English, *Modern War: A Very Short Introduction* (Oxford: Oxford University Press, 2013), pp. 117–18.

[21] T. Honderich, *After the Terror* (Edinburgh: Edinburgh University Press, 2002), p. 90.

that there was 'a horror owed to entering into the fear of the victims, people in an extreme situation'.[22]

It is also worth considering, in the attempt to determine the distinctiveness of terrorism that applies to all cases of the phenomenon, whether that distinctiveness is itself extranormal. In other words could one argue that the extranormality of terrorism lies in its uniqueness as a phenomenon primarily intended to generate a psychological impact beyond the immediate victims over and above tangible or military gain? As Wardlaw seems to imply, the extranormality of terrorism lies in 'the *design* to create anxiety rather than the "extranormality" of the anxiety ... What differentiates terrorism from other forms of violence is its unexpected nature, its element of surprise and shock. It is this quality which makes terrorism frightening, rather than the physical impact of any incident.'[23] One can argue, however, that 'psychological warfare' and some forms of 'political terror' also share these same objectives (see Chapter 8). Or, alternatively, terrorism might be viewed as extranormal because it aims to disrupt 'societal norms' and the 'normative' structures upon which they are based, though again this cannot apply to all cases of terrorism (such as in the context of war).[24]

In summary, then, nor can the 'extranormality' of terrorism be seen as *definitional* of the concept. While it might be applicable to the form of terrorism that deliberately targets civilians and/or in the context of a peacetime environment, one cannot define terrorism in general as ineluctably extranormal for not all acts of terrorism are necessarily so. For a *general definition* of terrorism all components included should *apply to every act of terrorism*. If there are elements that frequently or even usually apply then there may be merit in accounting for these features either in sub-definitions, or in further elaborations that *describe* the concept rather than being definitive about it.[25]

One final but important caveat needs to be included in any discussion on this issue and that is the impact of the media. What arguably adds to the perception of some forms of terrorism as extranormal is the role of the media in presenting terrorist acts as dramatic and exceptional. Precisely because acts of terrorism very often take place in a context of peacetime it means that such terrorist events are easily and immediately accessible for media outlets to provide blanket coverage. The drama and shocking impact of the terrorist event is then potentially amplified as it reaches the captivated audience who, if the victims are civilian, are prone to identify with them (as Honderich suggests above) with exclamations of 'it could have been me'.

It has been argued, therefore, that the prominence of the media's coverage of terrorist acts 'increases threat perceptions way beyond the reality of the

---

[22] Honderich, *After the Terror*, p. 101.　　[23] Wardlaw, *Political Terrorism*, pp. 10 and 16.
[24] Thornton, 'Terror as a Weapon of Political Agitation', p. 10.
[25] See, for example, Jackson et al., *Terrorism: A Critical Introduction*, pp. 115–18.

danger'.[26] The impact of such coverage is amplified further if the event is a hostage-taking or a hijacking of an aircraft where the drama becomes pro-tracted and where the watching public hangs on every latest development.[27] Hence the '"optical character" of contemporary terrorism' that 'emphasizes the role of the media, which "transmit the powerful images as well as trigger-ing pathological responses to the terrorist event"'.[28] While some acts, particu-larly 'terrorist spectaculars', appear more shocking because they are exposed to full media coverage (hence arguably magnifying their perceived extranorm-ality), some acts of terrorism or 'terror' carried out by states often take place away from the glare of the media, especially in the murky context of war-zones or where the media is state-controlled. Access to conflict zones, such as Grozny or Fallujah, and the exposure of whatever violence was being perpet-rated there, is clearly far less straightforward than it is for (generally accessible) civilian and peacetime environments.

Perhaps the extranormality of terrorism has been further emphasized when its perpetrators have been characterized and depicted in the media as unbal-anced fanatics. Turk wrote that:

Since the nineteenth century caricatures of anarchists in newspapers (deranged, bearded bombers), the established media have encouraged the belief that political violence in opposition to authority is both criminal and crazy . . . Suicidal attacks are similarly pictured as the irrational or obviously misguided acts of uninformed people driven by despair or fanaticism.[29]

This can perhaps again be seen as part of the 'amplifying processes'[30] that enhance the notion of terrorism as something indisputably extranormal. States, naturally enough, in their rhetorical responses to terrorism are also bound to emphasize the extranormal nature of terrorism and so, in short, there may be a number of processes and motivations that could underpin such perceptions of terrorism.

Some Thoughts on the Legal Status of Terrorism, Its Legitimacy and the Possibility of 'Good Terrorism'

As Chapter 2 has argued, the type of definition that is proposed often depends upon who is doing the defining. Some definitions of terrorism, particularly

[26] Schmid, 'The Definition of Terrorism', p. 80.

[27] As with the hijacking of TWA847 (see Hoffman, *Inside Terrorism*, Chapter 5).

[28] J. Der Derian, 'Imaging Terror: Logos, Pathos and Ethos', *Third World Quarterly*, Vol. 26, No. 1, 2005, cited in European Commission Sixth Framework Programme Project, 'Defining Terrorism' (WP3 Deliverable 4).

[29] A. Turk, 'Sociology of Terrorism', *Annual Review of Sociology*, Vol. 30, 2004, p. 274.

[30] N. Onuf, 'Making Terror/ism', *International Relations*, Vol. 23, No. 1, 2009, p. 60.

from a state perspective, refer to it as a non-state activity and as being 'unlawful' and/or 'illegitimate', and to governments as being the victims of coercion. For example, the US Federal Bureau of Investigation defines terrorism as:

> the unlawful use of force or violence against persons or property to intimidate or coerce a government, the civilian population, or segment thereof, in furtherance of political or social objectives.[31]

In other words it is fair to suggest that many state-centric definitions of terrorism primarily see the phenomenon as something that non-state actors do against governments and their populations. Doubtless, reference to terrorism as a non-state activity and inclusion of the words 'unlawful', 'illegal', and 'illegitimate' in state definitions of terrorism are intended to make clear the distinction between the 'illegitimate and unlawful violence' of non-state actors compared to the 'legitimate and lawful force' of the state.[32]

Academic definitions, as we have seen in Chapter 4, tend to be more neutral in this regard, with some of them endeavouring to include (or rather not exclude) state culpability while also refraining from explicitly including governments as necessarily being the victims of terrorism. Myers and Stohl, for example, described terrorism as '[t]he purposeful act or threat of violence to create fear and/or compliant behaviour in a victim/or audience of the act or threat'.[33] They argued that:

> It is intentional that this definition does not distinguish among perpetrators who are ingroups and outgroups, state or non-state actors, or legitimate or illegitimate wielders of violence.[34]

An actor-free definition is certainly to be endorsed (for what is essentially a method or a tactic) and, as long as one agrees that states can commit acts of terrorism, then the state as potential perpetrator should not be excluded from it. In other words any reference to terrorism as being a non-state activity or to governments as being its victims and the target of its coercive intent should not be part of a *general* definition (and a definition should apply to *all cases* of the phenomenon).

Also omitted from Myers and Stohl's definition is the legal status of acts of terrorism—that in actual fact, through state force or violence, the state can

---

[31] Available at: <http://www.fbi.gov/albuquerque/about-us/what-we-investigate> (last accessed 1 December 2014).

[32] Although the FBI definition includes 'force' in its definition, the word 'force' tends to have more of a positive connotation than 'violence' when describing political violence.

[33] P. Myers and M. Stohl, 'Terrorism, Identity and Group Boundaries', in H. Giles, S. Reid, and J. Harwood (eds.), *The Dynamics of Intergroup Communication* (New York: Peter Lang, 2010), p. 142. This definition, however, is so broad that it could arguably include acts of conventional warfare (including what some might call psychological warfare) and one could certainly argue that it also includes acts of 'political terror' or 'state terror' as distinct from terrorism (see Chapter 8).

[34] Myers and Stohl, 'Terrorism, Identity and Group Boundaries', p. 142.

itself be culpable for terrorism even if it happens to be legal or even if they are 'legitimate...wielders of violence', and a more neutral definition should therefore exclude the words 'unlawful', 'illegal', or 'illegitimate'. Although this author would use the term 'state terror' for much of what others refer to as state terrorism, one certainly shouldn't doubt the capacity of states to legally terrorize.

Notwithstanding these 'critical' arguments, and from an entirely different perspective, I have argued that terrorism cannot in any case be conceptualized as illegal or unlawful—premised on my contention that acts of terrorism can also be legal acts of warfare. In the case of roadside bombs that are intended to have a wider psychological impact against a broader troop body (or indeed against a population 'at home') as their primary objective, then they could be described as acts of terrorism but not a war crime, assuming that there is still a war context and that the victims are active combatants and not 'protected' persons. As I have conceived of terrorism, if the attack on the USS *Cole* had taken place in a war environment it could presumably have been seen as both an act of terrorism and an act of legal warfare. As such, terrorism cannot be defined or conceptualized as ineluctably illegal in a *general* definition of the concept. Indeed, the issue as to 'whether the definition of terrorism should be read as excluding **acts which occur in armed conflict and are lawful according to the laws of war**' (bold italics from original author) was considered by the current (at the time of writing) reviewer of UK terrorism legislation.[35]

In summary, the illegal/legal threshold does not necessarily correlate with what is and isn't terrorism respectively, and so it does not help us in determining what constitutes an act of terrorism for the purpose of a definition of terrorism, which, to reiterate, must apply to all cases. If terrorism is defined as intending to achieve a psychological impact beyond the immediate victims then it is perfectly plausible that such acts that primarily seek this effect can take place against combatants with the primary purpose of spreading fear amongst a broader group of armed combatants, or indeed against a wider civilian population (even if it is just combatants that are physically targeted).

The same is true for political 'terror'.[36] State terror against a regime's own populations may be domestically legal, if not internationally. Legal terror was seen by a member of the Russian revolutionary vanguard (1917–18) as:

[35] Alexander, 'The Meaning of Terrorism'. He states that 'Such actions are specifically excluded from the reach of the terrorism laws in Canadian, New Zealand and South African law.'

[36] As I have already argued, I believe 'political terror' (including 'state terror') should be regarded as a separate phenomenon from terrorism. While one can recall countless examples of the former, state terrorism as I have conceived of it (and as distinct from state-sponsored terrorism and state terror) is comparatively rare. Examples might include acts of terrorism that may, in theory, occur within a broader campaign of domestic state terror, and/or acts of violence perpetrated surreptitiously by one state against another (subject to the satisfaction of other definitional criteria). The Lockerbie bombing might serve as an example of the latter, though again this

systematic violence from the top down…Terror is a legal blueprint for massive intimidation, compulsion and destruction, directed by power. It is the precise, sophisticated and scrupulously weighted inventory of penalties, punishments and threats employed by the government to induce fear, and which it uses and abuses to compel the people to do its will.[37]

Moreover, states have also certainly carried out 'external state terror' in the context of war, regardless of its legal status. Surely, for example, notwithstanding their legal status at the time, one must indisputably classify the 'terror bombing' of Dresden and the atomic attacks on Hiroshima and Nagasaki as acts of state terror. Although international law has evolved to forbid such acts, even in the contemporary world one should not underestimate the capacity of states to legally terrorize adversaries (through, for example, 'strategic' bombing campaigns or 'shock and awe' tactics), and to exercise what amounts to a form of 'state terror'. Both concepts of terrorism and state terror, then, cannot be viewed as ineluctably illegal and so cannot be *defined* as such.

Notwithstanding state perspectives that may seek to project the 'inherent wrongfulness' of terrorism through their own definitions, inclusion of words such as 'unlawful' or 'illegal' (that may be designed to serve this purpose) do not, in fact, necessarily stigmatize all terrorism as bad. This is premised on the grounds that legitimacy (or illegitimacy) and legality (or illegality) are very different things—if one deems something to be illegal it does not necessarily follow that one considers it to be illegitimate. As Honderich wrote: '[i]llegality is not wrongfulness or immorality—there have been and there are morally terrible laws, corrupt bodies of law, selfish bodies of law. It serves nobody's end for long to confuse what is legal with what is right.'[38] This is an important distinction that may allow us to contemplate and conceptualize a sub-category of terrorism—that of *non-state terrorism in peacetime*—as unlawful (whether domestically, internationally, or both) without necessarily condemning all such forms of terrorism as illegitimate. This distinction accommodates the notion that there could be (and have been) some terrorisms that, although illegal, one might sympathize with.

Once again a definition of terrorism that includes this possibility may be premised on the assumption that terrorist attacks can be perpetrated against combatant targets and, in some circumstances, such acts of terrorism may be seen as legitimate (also depending on one's perspective in relation to the

would be subject to other definitional requirements (most particularly the intent to generate a psychological impact beyond the immediate victims). See also, for example, Merari's consideration of the possibility of 'duel-by-proxy' terrorism between Syria and Iraq in the 1970s (A. Merari, 'A Classification of Terrorist Groups', *Terrorism: An International Journal*, Vol. 1, Nos. 3 and 4, 1978, pp. 344–5).

[37] Quoted in Chaliand and Blin, *The History of Terrorism: From Antiquity to Al Qaeda*, p. 202.

[38] Honderich, *After the Terror*, p. 94.

cause). From a policymaking standpoint it would seem to be important, if there is to be a logical, consistent, and more honest approach to terrorism, that a definition of the concept incorporates, or at least does not exclude, the possibility of 'good' terrorism as well as the 'bad'. This is certainly not a new proposition but it does expose a particular dilemma that has been apparent in the international community's response to terrorism—that is the paradoxical approach of at times explicitly declaring a zero-tolerance approach to terrorism in all of 'its forms and manifestations' and yet simultaneously exhibiting an implicit sympathy for some terrorisms—for example, those against oppressive regimes and that refrain from targeting civilians or non-combatants.[39]

Saul, for example, considers that the international community might regard 'some terrorist-type violence as "illegal but justifiable" . . . where it was committed in the "collective defence of human rights"',[40] and Crenshaw argues that '[w]e would not, for example, have disapproved of the use of terrorism by the Jews against the Nazi regime.'[41] Terrorism might, for instance, from a democratic perspective, be justified if it refrains from targeting civilians (or non-combatants) and is carried out *in defence or pursuit of* the 'freedoms, rights and liberties . . . [that] . . . serve as the basis of the Charter of Fundamental Rights of the European Union'.[42] In this context, one might venture to suggest that terrorism that targets the military of an oppressive regime might therefore be seen as a worthy activity. This more comprehensive (and more objective) approach towards the definition would render zero-tolerance approaches to terrorism as ill-conceived.

Would the United Kingdom and the United States, for example, object if acts of terrorism were carried out against troops loyal to the Assad regime in Syria, or against pro-regime militias such as the notorious Shabiha? Was not some of the activity of the Kosovan Liberation Army, from the 'Western' perspective, an example of 'good terrorism'? The KLA targeted Serbian military and police, often in its early days relying on hit and run targets that were designed to have a wider psychological impact by '[denting] the self-confidence and prestige of the Serbian Military, and [breaking] the myth of their invincibility'.[43] Nor should one use more 'positive' labels, like 'freedom fighting', for the same activity—freedom fighting refers to a goal whereas terrorism is an activity—and, in this author's view, we should refute the view that '"freedom fighters" [inverted commas added] who attack only

---

[39] See, for example, discussion in Carlile, 'The Definition of Terrorism'.

[40] Saul, 'Defining Terrorism to Protect Human Rights', p. 208.

[41] Crenshaw, 'Introduction: Reflections on the Effects of Terrorism', p. 3.

[42] European Commission Sixth Framework Programme Project, 'Defining Terrorism' (WP3 Deliverable 4), p. 89.

[43] K. Mulaj, 'Resisting an Oppressive Regime: The Case of Kosovo Liberation Army', *Studies in Conflict & Terrorism*, Vol. 31, No. 12, 2008, p. 1111.

combatants are not terrorists'.[44] To do so simply further entrenches terrorism as a derogatory label at the expense of analytical utility. The point is not whether we agree or disagree with the use of terrorism (from which zero-tolerance approaches might emanate) but rather *what* terrorism we agree or disagree with. For example, one may sympathize with the use of terrorism if one identifies with the cause and providing civilians are not targeted—*but acts of terrorism they remain.*[45]

A former British Foreign Secretary, David Miliband, argued that there are circumstances where the use of terrorism may be justified,[46] while it can be argued that some modern states have been founded at least partly through the use of terrorism. The Dublin Easter Rising of 1916, *if* one argues that this was an act of terrorism, was an act of political violence that is celebrated by contemporary Irish governments. And, if one includes acts of violence against property as terrorism (again subject to the satisfaction of one's other criteria), then the Boston Tea Party of 1773 (where colonists destroyed shipments of tea in protest against the British Tea Act) could qualify as an act of terrorism, even though Fletcher argues that '[n]o American would be happy about branding the Boston Tea Party an act of terrorist aggression against British property.'[47]

And herein lies the problem—the term is so embedded in public and political discourse with 'moral opprobrium', carries such 'emotional freight',[48] and is habitually used by accusers against the accused that to admit to any endorsement of terrorism carries serious political risks (notwithstanding rare exceptions, such as that of Milliband above). As Crenshaw noted in the last chapter, this is also because 'once concepts are constructed and endowed with meaning...they take on a certain autonomy' and so politicians and 'the users of political language' are to a certain extent constrained in relation to any attempt to reshape how such concepts are used.[49] Notwithstanding political expediency in the application or non-application of the label of 'terrorism', if progress is to made on the definitional issue then one can no longer accuse others of terrorism while shrouding one's own involvement or endorsement

---

[44] W. Enders, cited in Schmid, 'Introduction' to *The Routledge Handbook of Terrorism Research*, p. 20.

[45] Parts of this paragraph and the previous two paragraphs have been reprinted with the permission of Taylor and Francis LLC, pp. 228–9 (see note 14).

[46] D. Miliband, cited in *Daily Mail*: G. Owen, 'David Miliband: there are circumstances in which terrorism can be justifiable', *Mailonline*, 16 August 2009, available at: <http://www.dailymail.co.uk/news/article-1206833/David-Miliband-There-circumstances-terrorism-justifiable.html> (last accessed 27 November 2014).

[47] Fletcher, 'The Indefinable Concept of Terrorism', p. 906.

[48] P. Herbst, Talking Terrorism: A Dictionary of the Loaded Language of Political Violence (Westport, CT: Greenwood Press, 2003), pp. 163–4 (emphasis in original), cited in Schmid, 'Terrorism: The Definitional Problem', p. 397.

[49] Crenshaw, 'Terrorism in Context', Pennsylvania State University, cited in Whittaker (ed.), *The Terrorism Reader*, p. 11.

by labelling it as something more 'positive', such as 'freedom fighting'. A more holistic and honest approach to the conceptual debate would acknowledge that it comes in many forms, most of which one might be opposed to but not necessarily all, and a general definition of terrorism needs to reflect this, or at least not exclude the possibility.

From a legal perspective, Lord Carlile, in his deliberations over the definition of terrorism, noted that:

> Many people have represented to me that it should not be an offence to plot and perpetrate terrorism against oppressive regimes which act in breach of their international obligations, subject to the proviso that civilians and noncombatants are not deliberately targeted or foreseen as victims.[50]

This statement is interesting for three reasons. Firstly, it is explicitly acknowledged (by the 'many people' who made representations to Lord Carlile) that acts of terrorism can be carried out against non-civilians and combatants. Moreover, not only in such circumstances is terrorism seen as legitimate but the calls above urged that it should be legal (internationally) to carry out acts of *terrorism* against such regimes! Finally, it therefore very unusually (but helpfully) concedes that there may be *terrorism* with which one sympathizes without the impulse to search for another more expedient and 'positive' label. In other words terrorism here is (very rarely) not being used as an inherently derogatory term. An 'informal group of Members of Parliament', however, seem to be arguing the opposite when they state that 'actions designed to further international humanitarian law should be excluded from the definition of terrorism'.[51] As Chapter 2 has argued, the more one refrains from using the word terrorism because of sympathy with the cause, or the more that one is inclined to use it because of antipathy towards the goals, then the further away we are from enhancing terrorism as an analytical (and more neutral) concept. Even if one sees such acts as legitimate, and subject to the satisfaction of other definitional criteria, then acts of terrorism they remain.

The point is that a more comprehensive and objective approach to the definitional issue would include instances of terrorism that one might agree with. The more analytical approach that I have argued for in this book, and the way that I have conceptualized terrorism, acknowledges that there may be 'terrorisms' that might, in certain circumstances, be worthy of endorsement or support. One could argue, therefore, that this should be reflected in international approaches to the phenomenon. Any moral repugnance against some forms should not deviate us from including the less contemptible (or even noble) forms from a general definition of the concept as a whole. For

---

[50] Carlile, 'The Definition of Terrorism', p. 43.
[51] Carlile, 'The Definition of Terrorism', p. 43.

example, if the French resistance carried out acts of violence that refrained from targeting civilians against an occupying (Nazi) regime, they nevertheless, subject to the necessary criteria (in particular the intent to generate a psychological impact beyond the immediate victims), *still carried out acts of terrorism* in contravention of the prevailing (Nazi) legal order.

Judgements, then, as to whether or not an act constitutes terrorism should be cross-referenced against an agreed set of independent criteria and not on grounds of ideological affiliation or sympathy. The distinction that what may be seen as legitimate may be illegal and vice versa is an important one to make because *illegal* terrorism, depending on one's perspective, may be justified in some circumstances. There have, for example, been numerous instances of unjust regimes against whom, depending on one's perspective, one might regard acts of illegal terrorism as nevertheless legitimate and justified. In other words, if agreement on a definition of terrorism is ever to be reached, then it must be conceded that friends and foes alike can, and have, committed acts of terrorism. This is not a moral judgement but, to reiterate, is the outcome of dispassionate analysis untainted by ideological allegiance. Of course, *which* cases of terrorism one opposes or condones may well be ideologically determined.

* * * * *

In summary, then, the above has discussed three implications of the assumption that anybody (including combatants) can be victims of terrorism. Terrorism cannot therefore be viewed as the peacetime equivalent of a war crime as combatants are not 'protected' persons. Moreover, such an 'equivalence' is undermined by the fact that generating a psychological impact beyond the immediate victims is not a necessary prerequisite for something to be called a 'war crime' whereas it is for an act of terrorism. It is possible, however, to argue that the *physical manifestation* of terrorism in peacetime may deem it to be the equivalent of a war crime (though this wouldn't be the case if one included acts of violence against property in a definition of terrorism). A second implication is that terrorism cannot be defined as extranormal as there are some forms that may not necessarily be so, not least acts of terrorism against combatants in the context of war. Finally, if combatants or the military of oppressive regimes are targeted then it is possible, from a democratic perspective, that there may be terrorisms that one agrees with (and one should not search for a different label for the same activity simply because one agrees with the cause). Related to this, the distinction between legality and legitimacy is an important one to make because acts of terrorism that may be technically illegal might nevertheless be seen as legitimate.

7

What Is Not Terrorism

If one argues that the essence of terrorism lies in its intent to generate a psychological impact beyond the immediate victims upon a broader group or population then one must presumably accept that any act of violence for political purposes that is *not* designed to have this impact cannot be labelled terrorism. This chapter will consider activity that may have commonly been labelled terrorism (including ancillary activities) but that, in light of the discussion thus far, should be excluded from a definition of the phenomenon. As I have argued that combatants can be victims of terrorism, it will then attempt to draw a distinction between acts of terrorism within war and other acts of (conventional) warfare, for surely all acts of political violence are messages of sorts and are intended to generate at least some degree of psychological impact. Finally, the chapter will discuss a fundamental problem in determining what constitutes an act of terrorism as I (and indeed many others) have conceptualized it: how can one *prove* intent or purpose (or measure the degree of *intended* psychological impact) behind an act of political violence in order to be able to determine that it is indeed an act of terrorism? I will argue *that this is where the real subjectivity as to what constitutes terrorism lies, or at least where it should lie, rather than in the perpetrator-based 'terrorism versus freedom fighter' mantra.*

Acts of Non-Terrorist Political Violence

What if acts of violence are carried out as a means of leverage in support of specific demands, such as the release of prisoners, or to secure a ransom, or to secure safe passage from a hijacking situation (securing 'specific concessions' is one of Stohl's four purposes of terrorism[1])? These are very concrete and

---

[1] M. Stohl, 'Demystifying Terrorism: The Myths and Realities of Contemporary Political Terrorism', in Stohl (ed.), *The Politics of Terrorism*, p. 4.

tangible objectives that are distinct from the broad political goal and are arguably separate from any intent to generate a wider psychological impact. Yet, conversely, one could equally argue that the realization of even these very specific objectives, as with the objectives discussed in Chapter 4, rests on generating this psychological impact. Determining the degree of *intended* psychological impact is, of course, very difficult, if not impossible (see section 'The Empirical Problem: Proving Intent' later in this chapter). One could certainly argue, however, that a hostage-taking or a hijacking, for example, could be intended to serve both objectives of generating wider psychological impact (not least to advertise a cause) and *also* securing specific concessions, hence the notion of 'integrated' purposes behind an act of violence.[2]

To what extent, then, can what might be called ancillary activities be considered terrorism? For example, are bank robberies that are carried out as the means to financially sustain terrorism to be understood as acts of terrorism themselves? They certainly, one assumes, terrorize those directly affected and there exists the ultimate political goal (ostensibly at least). Such acts, it is assumed, however, are not intended themselves to have a wider psychological impact over and above the tangible and specific objective of resourcing the particular organization, and as such one can determine that they are not acts of terrorism. Indeed, for the same reason one can argue that none of the plethora of financing (of terrorism) activities (including extortion) that might themselves entail the use of violence or the threat of violence can be labelled terrorism. The violence attached to attempts to resource terrorist organizations, for example, might be more akin to ordinary criminality or organized crime.

What about acts of violence that are designed to have very practical utility, such as the bombing of, or an assault on, an inconveniently placed checkpoint? If the tangible outcome of a disrupted enemy checkpoint is the primary objective (over and above any psychological dimension) then neither can this be classified as an act of terrorism. Yet it seems apparent that acts of violence are often labelled terrorism even if they are not intended to spread fear (or where any psychological impact is incidental) but are merely intended to have physical and tangible utility. Even within terrorist campaigns, then, are *all* attacks 'message generators'? Or are some limited to having just a practical purpose, whilst other (perhaps more symbolic) attacks may indeed be intended to communicate a powerful message? On this point Duvall and Stohl have argued that:

---

[2] See R. Alleman, 'Definitional Aspects', *Studies in Conflict and Terrorism*, Vol. 3, Nos. 3–4, 1980. One anonymous reviewer of this work very helpfully noted that, within 'multiple intentions', there may be unconscious intentions behind attacks such as revenge and catharsis.

the compelling agency [of terrorism] is intense fear, not actual physical destructive harm. Thus, excluded from the concept of political terrorism are actions oriented solely or primarily toward the physical harming (e.g. punishment, combat) or elimination (e.g. assassination, genocide) of some target unit. Only included are those oriented primarily toward the inducement of fear.[3]

Related to this, it is unhelpful, then, for our conceptual discussion to label an act of violence as terrorism *simply because it was carried out by a particular actor or adversary*. For example, simply because Al Qaeda, like the word terrorism itself, has come to be regarded with opprobrium one shouldn't fall into the trap of labelling everything it (or those claiming to act on its behalf) does as terrorism, if those acts do not satisfy the criteria that are necessary for an act of violence to be classified as such. This would again lead us into the unhelpful direction of perpetrator-based definitions for what I have argued is essentially a method. For an act of violence to be an act of terrorism there must be the primary intention of generating a psychological impact beyond the immediate victims.

One problem that confronts those aiming to infuse some analytical quality into 'terrorism', then, is that once a group or a network has committed an act of terrorism, or has a reputation for carrying out such acts, then every act of violence they subsequently carry out is also automatically labelled as an act of terrorism. Jenkins wrote in 1981 that '[o]nce a group carries out a terrorist act, it acquires the label "terrorist," a label that tends to stick; and from that point on, everything this group does, *whether intended to produce terror or not*, is also called terrorism'(italics added).[4] Schmid also points to this 'faulty circular reasoning' in that 'once a group has been designated "terrorist", all acts of violence by members of that group are "terrorist"'.[5]

From a policymaking perspective it is perhaps understandable and tempting to view Al Qaeda and its activity as synonymous with terrorism, without troubling oneself with the conceptual niceties or theoretical rigour as to what parts of its activity constitute terrorism and what parts do not. But any such tendency, whether in the case of AQ, ISIS or any other adversaries who have used terrorism, blurs our conception as to what terrorism is. This 'faulty circular reasoning' that Schmid refers to (that acts of violence are labelled terrorism simply by virtue of *who* carried them out) seems to be evident, for example, when commentators argue for a definition of terrorism that includes whatever Al Qaeda's targets have been and are likely to be (regardless of what the intent may be behind the acts of violence),[6] rather than endeavouring to

---

[3] Duvall and Stohl, 'Governance by Terror', p. 183.

[4] Jenkins, 'The Study of Terrorism: Definitional Problems', p. 4.

[5] Schmid, 'The Definition of Terrorism', p. 64.

[6] See Schmid, 'The Definition of Terrorism', p. 67. Whilst this author concurs that acts of terrorism can be carried out against military targets, providing their primary purpose is to

generate a non-perpetrator based definition against which acts of violence should be measured or judged as terrorism or not.

Acts of Revenge as Terrorism?

Viewing terrorism in the way that I propose potentially excludes a significant amount of political violence that may have hitherto been perceived as acts of terrorism. For example, what about those acts of violence that are merely designed to exact revenge, that are not necessarily intended to generate a psychological impact upon a target audience or audiences? Waldron argues that:

> The terrorist act might be intended as punishment or retaliation for some real or imagined offense, and not calculated to achieve anything beyond that ... I am sure many Al Qaeda operatives approach their murderous assignments in this spirit: the U.S. is a great satanic wrongdoer and it simply deserves retribution. Retribution need not be intended to affect (let alone coerce or intimidate) the subsequent conduct of the victim; this, after all, is what distinguishes retributive from consequentialist theories of punishment.[7]

Revenge can, of course, take on an infinite number of forms, both non-violent and violent. There are also many forms of violent revenge, of which terrorism is potentially but one. If terrorism is employed as a weapon of revenge, then, to be called terrorism, it must satisfy one's definitional criteria. Hence, unless such an act of retribution or revenge is primarily designed to generate a psychological blow over physical impact, the impulse to simply 'hit back' and nothing more (i.e. with no particular broader psychological impact intended) would mean that such acts would not sit comfortably with my conceptualization of terrorism. The Lockerbie bombing in December 1988 appeared to be a case of revenge against the United States and has certainly been seen as an *archetypal* example of terrorism.[8] But what was the purpose behind this act of violence? Was there an intended broader psychological impact against the United States leadership and/or its population over and above the physical intent to destroy the aircraft and kill all those on board?[9]

generate a psychological impact beyond the immediate victims and that other identified criteria are also satisfied (see Chapters 9 and 10), the implication in Ross' following comment is that military targets should be included in any definition of terrorism *simply by virtue of the fact that Al Qaeda has targeted them* ('[t]argets are often military (look at al Qaeda's attacks, e.g. on US warships)').

[7] Waldron, 'Terrorism and the Uses of Terror', p. 26.

[8] Possibly in response to the US airstrikes on Libya in 1986 (Operation El Dorado Canyon) which in turn was a response to the bombing of La Belle Discotheque in Berlin ten days earlier in which two American servicemen were killed.

[9] 259 passengers and crew died along with 11 residents of Lockerbie.

One perhaps has to conclude that some acts of violent revenge may be intended to strike a psychological blow while others may be intended to inflict only physical damage, or both—hence some may be classified as acts of terrorism and others not.

Other Acts of Political Violence

The general point is that, for the sake of analytical precision, we should be distinguishing between acts of terrorism (as one defines it) and *other acts of political violence* that do not satisfy the criteria sufficiently to be called terrorism. Hence what do we call acts of violence that have no other motive other than as hopeless but defiant acts of asymmetric warfare driven by optimistic assurances of ultimate victory? Some acts may be more clearly classified as 'terrorist' than others. Terrorist acts, perhaps like the one against the USS *Cole* and those of 9/11, may serve as signifiers, symbols, and propaganda events to underpin and support the supposed *much wider* 'war' between 'Islam and the West', pursued through targeted conflict zones such as the Swat valley in Pakistan, or, in the more recent case of ISIS, in Syria and Iraq—theatres of conflict where the *physical defeat* of the adversary is envisaged (these modes of violence might be more akin to guerrilla warfare, insurgency, or, in some cases, civil war).

Terrorism may therefore be considered to be an auxiliary weapon alongside other (perhaps more 'traditional') modes of political violence. But outside the aforementioned zones of conflict what do we call acts of violence carried out by Al Qaeda that do not satisfy one's definition of terrorism? If we want to generate greater theoretical sophistication as to 'what terrorism is', to reiterate, it is far too blunt to assume that every mode of political violence it uses comes under the rubric of terrorism, simply because Al Qaeda is the perpetrator. Where does the threshold lie between acts of terrorism that are intended to communicate, to symbolize, to spread a psychological impact beyond the immediate victims (and indeed where the immediate victims are not the main target) and other acts of political violence? What do we call acts of violence carried out by those claiming to be acting on behalf of Al Qaeda where the intention is physical harm and destruction and where any psychological impact is unintended or incidental? These are challenging and, as yet, unresolved questions.

For Al Qaeda itself it might be simple—that *all* of its acts of violence are acts of warfare in its global struggle,[10] whereas those tasked with responding to it might label all such acts as terrorism. It is not so simple for those researchers

---

[10] See, for example, G. Kepel and J.-P. Milelli (eds.), *Al Qaeda in its Own Words* (Cambridge, MA and London: Belknap Press of Harvard University Press, 2008).

attempting to establish analytical parameters as to what we mean by terrorism. In an age of increasing asymmetrical and 'intrastate' warfare (and, indeed, after the United States declared a 'war' against terrorism) one has to consider the extent that global and transnational non-state actors can be 'at war'. In the context of the emergence (and focus on) post-Cold War forms of asymmetric warfare, there is a need to determine how terrorism fits in with these contemporary forms, and how one distinguishes terrorism within the broad spectrum of political violence.

Waldron considers 'the possibility that terrorist atrocities may be regarded simply as acts of war and as no more *coercive* in structure or intent than firing a mortar in battle',[11] although in this case, if psychological impact against a broader group is not the intention, then I would suggest that they are not acts of terrorism.[12] Nor, in my view, would acts of violence carried out for the primary purpose of therapeutic benefit be classified as such, as Waldron further considers:

> violent action might be viewed as a form of therapy for the perpetrator, particularly where the perpetrator has suffered for a long time in the ignominy and humiliation of some oppressive form of subordination.[13]

There are, therefore, many forms of asymmetric warfare that do not constitute terrorism. By not labelling them as such, however, is not, of course, to exonerate them just as using the word terrorism in my analysis is not instinctively to condemn.

It is also worth, here, clarifying the difference between terrorism and another form of political violence—that of political assassination. A political assassination is often considered as a separate, though often related, phenomenon. Essentially, the difference between political assassination and terrorism is that with the former the object of attack is of primary concern to the assailant(s) rather than a broader audience. Thornton points out that 'assassinating a public figure to get rid of that person is not terrorism. If it was a symbolic act then it is', while Schmid and Jongman also draw this distinction:

> while both the assassin and the terrorist commit homicide, the intent is different. However, where political murders occur in series and the intimidation of opponents becomes more important than their physical elimination, we are likely to step into the conceptual space of terrorism.[14]

---

[11] Waldron, 'Terrorism and the Uses of Terror', p. 25.

[12] However, just because 'terrorism' as referred to here may not be coercive, it may well be intended to generate a psychological impact for other purposes (such as for advertisement or 'expressive' purposes, or to disorientate in general, or to mobilize a perceived constituency of potential support).

[13] Waldron, 'Terrorism and the Uses of Terror', p. 26.

[14] Schmid and Jongman, *Political Terrorism*, p. 8.

Crelinsten has also rightly argued that:

> many assassinations have no goal other than the removal of the targeted individual. In this case, there is no communication to wider audiences and, according to my definition, no terrorism.[15]

It is, of course, possible for an act of violence to be both a political assassination and an act of terrorism. Schmid suggests that 'from the terrorists' point of view, an assassination can be dual-purpose: eliminate an opponent and scare other members of the opponent's camp.'[16]

One can perhaps argue that this was the case with the assassinations carried out by the European left-wing terrorist organizations of the 1970s and 1980s (sometimes called 'Fighting Communist Organizations'[17]) which, while intended to eliminate prominent figures within the 'oppressive' capitalist and 'imperialist' classes, were also powerful symbolic acts designed to send a message to others who perpetuated the 'unjust' prevailing capitalist order. Similarly, the IRA's political assassination of Ian Gow in July 1990, who was a prominent unionist in the Conservative Party and intimately involved with government policy in Northern Ireland, had a practical value for those who carried it out but it also represented a powerful symbolic act intended to deliver a psychological blow to the wider political status quo as well as the British public. One way of distinguishing terrorism from a political assassination:

> is to insist that for an act to fall within the definition of terrorism, its target group (those being coerced) must be distinct from its immediate victims (those being bombed, shot at, or held hostage). Thus, an act of violence which is aimed only at an immediate victim is not an act of terrorism. The assassination of a head of state, for example, is not an act of terrorism if its purpose is solely that of removing the person from office.[18]

When a political assassination becomes an act of terrorism is perhaps best summed up by the words of an assassin who killed a senior Nazi in Switzerland in February 1936: 'It was the pestilence I aimed at, not the person.'[19]

In the context of the technological revolution and the emergence of the internet and social media, *cyberterrorism* is a relatively recent addition to the terrorism lexicon. For this author, however, 'cyber' only has relevance to terrorism if it is the means used through which to deliberately perpetrate or

---

[15] R. D. Crelinsten, 'Analysing Terrorism and Counter-Terrorism: A Communication Model', *Terrorism and Political Violence*, Vol. 14, No. 2, 2002, p. 86.

[16] Schmid, 'The Definition of Terrorism', p. 64.

[17] See, for example, Alexander and Pluchinsky, *Europe's Red Terrorists, The Fighting Communist Organizations*.

[18] Wardlaw, 'The Nature and Purpose of Terrorism'.

[19] D. Frankfurter, cited in B. Hurwood, *Society and the Assassin: A Background Book on Political Murder* (London: Macmillan, 1970), p. 140.

threaten acts of physical violence with the intention of spreading fear or generating a psychological impact beyond the immediate victims for a political motive. In other words something can only be called cyberterrorism if all the usual criteria for one's conceptualization of terrorism are satisfied in the first place, and so the internet and the 'virtual world' simply becomes the means to threaten or carry out acts of terrorism.

Related to this is whether acts of violence against property should be included in any definition. The United Kingdom Terrorism Act 2000, for example, includes 'serious violence against property' and acts that are 'designed seriously to interfere with or seriously to disrupt an electronic system'.[20] If such acts are intended to spread fear or generate a psychological impact beyond the objects of attack then they can be labelled acts of terrorism. This is also, however, contingent on the 'seriousness' of the acts of violence or damage to property. For example, political graffiti that threatens violence is not in and of itself 'serious' enough to be labelled an act of terrorism.[21] On the other hand an attempt to electronically disrupt air traffic control systems with the intention of threatening or actually killing passengers in flight for the purpose of generating a wider psychological impact and for a political motive would be classified as an act of terrorism.

So, in summary, what is key about terrorism is the intent behind the act of violence. Unless it is designed to have a psychological impact beyond the immediate victims then it is not terrorism. In addition to the objective of generating such impact against an adversary or adversaries, or with the aim of gaining sympathy for a cause from the international community, the intended psychological impact of terrorism can also be aimed at supporters and perceived supporters—perhaps to mobilize or motivate them, or even to convince a constituency that they are willing to go to the greatest lengths for their cause (compared with rivals), and that such sacrifices thereby enhance their claims to be the most dedicated and 'true' representatives of their perceived constituency's grievances. For when we consider the target audiences that acts of terrorism are intended to have a psychological impact upon, there might not just be the intent to intimidate or coerce but also to inspire and motivate, depending on the audience. In this context, when conceptualizing terrorism, *influencing* a broader group rather than the narrower *intimidating* a wider audience might be more appropriate.[22]

---

[20] United Kingdom Terrorism Act 2000, Part 1, Section 1, available at: <http://www.legislation.gov.uk/ukpga/2000/11/section/1> (last accessed 27 November 2014).

[21] The notion as to how serious an act of violence needs to be to be classified as terrorism, including whether or not property should be included as a possible target of terrorism, will be discussed further in Chapter 9.

[22] Contrary to the following policymaking perspective through the deliberations of Lord Carlile, who wrote: 'A[n] . . . issue raised [in relation to the definition of terrorism] concerns the use in the UK legislation of *influence*. International comparison reveals variations on the quality of the

It is said that '[o]ne such [terrorist] act may, in a few days, make more propaganda than a thousand pamphlets ... ',[23] hence the notion of terrorism as 'propaganda by the deed'. It is difficult, however, to envisage *any* act of political violence that is not designed to send some sort of message or to have some degree of psychological impact. So, if one is to persist with a purpose-based definition (that centres around wider psychological intent), and if one is to determine what it is that is distinctive about terrorism, then it is necessary to consider the difference between acts of terrorism and other acts of political violence, not least acts of warfare in general.

Terrorism and Warfare

Rather than thinking of an act of violence as *either* an act of warfare *or* an act of terrorism, one should acknowledge that terrorism can also be a weapon of warfare *within* war, and so in this context it can be understood as one of a number of different modes of warfare. What is it, then, that distinguishes terrorism from other forms in the context of war—for, surely, all acts of political violence are intended to have at least some degree of psychological impact, to send a message of some sort. One can perhaps suggest, however, that the difference between warfare *in general* and terrorism is that those engaged in what one might call more 'conventional' warfare generally seek tangible advantage over psychological impact, that there is more emphasis on physical gain, whether it be in the form of territorial acquisition (or retention) or material harm to the adversary's military or war effort. While terrorism can certainly be used as a weapon of war (perhaps as an auxiliary tactic), it is primarily concerned with generating a psychological impact beyond the immediate victims.

Guerrilla warfare is also primarily concerned with physical gain, though, as I have argued, some guerrilla organizations have also resorted to the method of terrorism. Primoratz makes clear the distinction between political violence in general and terrorism: 'all uses of political violence effect some degree of fear', but in 'terrorism proper, the causing of fear and coercion through fear is *the* objective'.[24] Merari also differentiates terrorism from conventional and

---

intention that is required. The range includes *coerce, compel, intimidate* and *subvert*. In my view there is force in the argument that the "bar" is set rather low by the use of the word *influence* in the definition. Of all the words available that would raise the bar to a more appropriate level, I suggest that *intimidate* has a clear meaning, entirely referable to the most easily understood notions of what terrorism is. It would have the effect too of applying the same standard to government as to the public whose embodiment a government should be. This would be consistent with the *Council of Europe Convention on Terrorism*' (Carlile, 'The Definition of Terrorism', p. 34).

[23] Kropotkin, cited in Schmid, 'Terrorism and the Media: The Ethics of Publicity', p. 542.

[24] I. Primoratz, cited in English, *Terrorism: How to Respond*, p. 5.

guerrilla warfare, arguing that, although 'all forms of warfare have a significant psychological ingredient', wars 'are first and foremost massive collisions of material forces, and they are usually won by the physical elimination of the enemy's ability to resist' while '[g]uerrilla warfare...is [also] primarily a strategy based on a physical encounter.'[25] He concurs that the 'intended impact' of conventional war is physical destruction, of guerrilla warfare is physical attrition, and of terrorism is psychological coercion.[26]

One might argue that, given the degree of physical destruction and loss of life on 9/11, the idea that the physical purpose of terrorism is secondary to its psychological intent is somewhat absurd.[27] Begorre-Bret, for example, considers that such 'mass murder can...be the sign that maybe bombings are now goals in themselves and not messages.'[28] This does not sit comfortably with my conceptualization of terrorism. Despite any temptation to refine my understanding of terrorism accordingly, however, in my view acts that have physical destruction as their primary goal, and indeed any acts of violence where intended psychological impact may be secondary, unintended, or incidental, cannot then be labelled terrorism. So loaded has 'terrorism' become as a pejorative label to be used for the most reprehensible acts that its non-application, especially for major acts of violence, can easily be misconstrued as in some way exonerating such acts—but this would be a serious mistake. What one is striving for here is analytical precision (that neither exonerates nor condemns) and if physical impact is the primary purpose behind acts of violence then one would have to classify it as another form of political violence within the panoply of asymmetrical warfare, rather than terrorism. In keeping with a more dispassionate approach such analytical distinction has no bearing on whether one sees such acts as legitimate or not.

Thus, when Begorre-Bret goes on to suggest that: '[w]hen attacks are aimed at soldiers, judges or a mass of civilians, terrorism is no longer a hermeneutical violence' and that 'the death of these people becomes the first goal, and the delivering of a message is quite secondary',[29] neither, then, would I call these acts of terrorism. Perhaps, given the increased prevalence of intrastate forms of warfare, one might suggest that a form of non-state warfare has increasingly emerged that simply aims to inflict maximum physical damage, that the target itself is the object of attack rather than any wider audience designed to be the 'message recipient'. And such a form is not the same as guerrilla warfare,

---

[25] Merari, 'Terrorism as a Strategy of Insurgency', p. 232.

[26] A. Merari, cited in Schmid, 'Frameworks for Conceptualising Terrorism', p. 206.

[27] In which case, in line with my argument, 9/11 would not be called an act (or acts) of terrorism and that another label would be required.

[28] C. Begorre-Bret, 'The Definition of Terrorism and the Challenge of Relativism', *Cardozo Law Review*, Vol. 27, No. 5, 2005–2006, p. 2001.

[29] Begorre-Bret, 'The Definition of Terrorism and the Challenge of Relativism', p. 2002.

general insurgency, or civil war, because these latter forms are typically waged in the open against their adversary rather than in the form of unexpected acts of violence that strike at home or abroad by those that then disappear from the physical environment.[30] In other words one can argue that a transnational and non-territorial form of violence exists that does not fit into these more traditional categories, but nor, in cases where the psychological impact is not the primary purpose, can they be called terrorism.

Returning to 9/11 one can in any case argue that its psychological impact (though difficult, if not impossible, to measure) has been (and was intended to be) greater even than its profound physical effects. The scale of physical destruction of a terrorist attack may be intended to be colossal precisely because of the desire to generate an *even greater psychological impact*—thus the more devastating the physical attack then the greater the commensurate psychological impact. And one could argue that the psychological impact of 9/11 has indeed far exceeded even its profound physical consequences.[31] Some have suggested, for instance, that the attacks on that day 'to some extent allowed them [the perpetrators] to redefine the American way of life, and for a time to render an entire population less free'.[32] There is, therefore, one has to acknowledge, something of a paradox in arguing that terrorism rests on its ability to generate a wider psychological impact over and above its physical impact when to a large extent the ability to generate such psychological impact may be contingent on inflicting as much physical or tangible damage as possible, such as on the scale of 9/11.

Nevertheless, the psychological dimension is key to terrorism. One might therefore propose the following simple model:

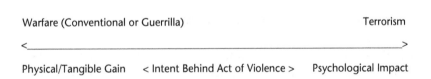

Intent Behind an Act of Political Violence

Warfare (Conventional or Guerrilla)   Terrorism

<_____>

Physical/Tangible Gain   < Intent Behind Act of Violence >   Psychological Impact

---

[30] But not necessarily from the virtual domain—hence the non-territorial concept of 'netwar' where forms of organization (and their strategies and technologies) are attuned to the information age (J. Arquilla and D. Ronfeldt, 'Netwar Revisited: The Fight for the Future Continues', in R. Bunker (ed.), *Networks, Terrorism and Global Insurgency* (Abingdon: Routledge, 2005), p. 8).

[31] Not least because they were carried out in a peacetime environment against civilian and non-combatant targets (assuming that the Pentagon represented a 'non-combatant' target).

[32] C. Miller, J. Matusitz, D. O'Hair, and J. Eckstein, 'The Complexity of Terrorism: Groups, Semiotics, and the Media', in O'Hair et al. (eds.), *Terrorism: Communication and Rhetorical Perspectives*, p. 52.

One could suggest that the further along the physical/tangible intent end of the spectrum we go the less likely it is to be an act of terrorism—and the more likely it is to be conventional or guerrilla warfare, or indeed any act of asymmetrical warfare that is not primarily designed to generate psychological impact—whereas the further along the psychological intent end we go the more likely it is to be an act of terrorism. While this is a very rudimentary model, one of the conceptual problems to be resolved identified by respondents to Schmid's questionnaire was the need for '[f]urther conceptualization and refinement of a "continuum of combat escalation" ranging from terrorism posited at one axis, to full-blown and sustained war at the other axis'.[33] Psychological warfare, however, would also be located at the 'psychological impact' end of the model—and so what difference, if any, is there between psychological warfare and terrorism? In my view, one can plausibly suggest that terrorism can indeed be understood as a form of psychological warfare.[34]

This discussion, and the way that this author and many others have conceptualized terrorism, raises a formidable empirical challenge and one that is rarely acknowledged[35]—how does one establish the intent behind acts of violence that may then help us to determine whether or not we classify them as acts of terrorism? How can one empirically prove that psychological impact is the intended objective over physical goals? It may, of course, be difficult, and perhaps even futile, to attempt to disentangle physical and psychological intent behind an act of violence. Indeed, in my view, and as I have noted at the outset of the chapter, *this is where the real subjectivity lies in the definition of terrorism: who decides or how does one determine whether or not an act of violence constitutes terrorism* or at least where it should lie (as opposed to the subjectivity of the mantra of 'one person's terrorist is another's freedom fighter').This is an issue that this chapter now turns to.

The Empirical Problem: Proving Intent

One of the main purposes of defining terrorism, as I have argued in Chapter 2, is to identify the parameters of the phenomenon which will then enable us to

[33] R. J. Chasdi, cited in Schmid, 'Introduction' to *The Routledge Handbook of Terrorism Research*, p. 28.

[34] Wilkinson, for example, refers to terrorism as being employed as a weapon of psychological warfare (P. Wilkinson, in Appendix 2.1 of Schmid (ed.), *The Routledge Handbook of Terrorism Research*, p. 112). J. Mallin also refers to it as such (p. 114). It is, of course, not the only form of psychological warfare. States may employ psychological warfare in the context of war (a form of 'state terror', see Chapter 8) while the concept may also be employed in non-violent contexts, e.g. rival firms engaging in 'psychological warfare' to gain competitive advantage.

[35] Amongst the few who have acknowledged this are R. De la Roche, 'Toward a Scientific Theory of Terrorism', *Sociological Theory*, Vol. 22, No. 1, 2004, pp. 2–3; Crenshaw, 'Current Research on Terrorism: The Academic Perspective', p. 2; and European Commission Sixth Framework Programme Project, 'Defining Terrorism' (WP3 Deliverable 4), pp. 105–18.

consider whether or not particular acts constitute terrorism or not. Once one has arrived at a definition that one is satisfied with, then it should not be willingly amended according to the exigencies of the day, or after the latest 'terrorist' event, or according to what the modus operandi is of the latest terrorist adversary, or indeed in response to proclamations of the so-called 'new terrorism' that have been heralded more than once in recent decades.[36] Thus, the theory as to 'what terrorism is' should be sustainable and have some degree of 'shelf life', and, whatever definition of terrorism is arrived at, the task is to test each case or act of violence (or threat of violence) to establish whether it constitutes an act of terrorism according to the criteria one has established.

As I have also argued (in Chapter 2), terrorism studies has been beset with a number of problems, not least that it is based on very little empirical research. Theory building on 'what terrorism is' entails identifying criteria that acts need to satisfy in order to be labelled terrorism. The challenge is to empirically establish that these conditions have been met (or not as the case may be), and herein lies a formidable problem for my definition of terrorism. I have argued that the essence of terrorism lies in the *intent* behind the act (or the threat of an act), namely its primary purpose of generating a psychological impact beyond the immediate victims. Intent is key because if the wider psychological impact is unintended or coincidental (but is nevertheless the outcome) then this is not terrorism. Terrorism entails 'the *intention* of generating a wider psychological impact'.[37]

How, then, does one prove intent? In a rare acknowledgement of the difficulty in identifying intent, or even determining the broader motivation (political or otherwise), behind an act of violence de la Roche argued that:

> Because many conceptions of terrorism include elements that are not readily observable, they are difficult to apply to concrete cases of violence. In particular, psychological (subjective) or teleological elements (a means-ends logic) in a definition make it difficult to identify instances of true terrorism. How, for instance, do we know whether a specific case of violence is intended, as Bergesen and Lizardo suggest, 'to obtain a political, religious, or social objective'? While we can observe the expressed grievances of terrorists in their speeches and other pronouncements, how exactly can we ascertain when a violent event has one or more of these ends? How can we know that an act of violence is not something else, such as simple vengeance or retribution? How can we know, for instance, the motives and goals of

---

[36] In the early 1980s the term 'new terrorism' was coined to describe the emergence of right-wing terrorism, while, more contemporaneously, it has been used to characterize 9/11 and the subsequent 'Al Qaeda threat'.

[37] Donna Artz has, for example, argued that rather than 'anxiety-producing', a definition of terrorism should instead include 'intended to cause anxiety' (quoted in Schmid, 'The Definition of Terrorism', p. 71). Ganor has also argued that '[t]he definition of terrorism should refer to the intention of the perpetrator and not to the consequences of the attack, which in many cases are coincidental' (B. Ganor, quoted in Schmid, 'The Definition of Terrorism', p. 57).

those who attacked the World Trade Center in 2001? Surely . . . we never will know exactly how the terrorists viewed their own actions. What resides in the minds of the actors lies beyond the reach of an outside observer. And to impute or to infer these mental elements only introduces uncertainty and complexity into our efforts to distinguish one form of violence from another.[38]

How much of Al Qaeda activity, for example, can we then accurately depict as terrorism according to the criteria that I have laid down? As noted earlier in this chapter, to what extent has the intent behind acts of violence simply been to 'hit back'—where the goal may primarily be tangible or physical and where any psychological impact may be unintended or incidental? If one is to be theoretically rigorous then such distinctions need to be made. Moreover, even if we are able to capture professed intent how do we know if this is the *actual* purpose?[39] Tilly also noted (in relation to terrorism) that 'solid evidence on motivations and intentions rarely becomes available'[40] and that 'the real intent might differ from purported intent'.[41,42]

How can one determine, then, what the intent is behind acts of political violence, and, even if we can agree that the psychological dimension is indispensable, to what extent has terrorist labelling been based merely on the *assumption* that the primary purpose of such acts has been to generate a wider psychological impact? What empirical evidence is there to support such contentions? In the case of the IRA one might cite the repeated mantra that 'we only have to be lucky once', or the 'sniper at work' roadside sign as evidence of the intended psychological impact but, in general, it may be the case that most of what is classified as terrorism is pure conjecture. In this context it seems prudent for the United States 1996 Anti-Terrorism Act to define terrorism as '*apparently* intended to intimidate or coerce' (italics added),[43] though, as I have argued in relation to the inclusion of words like

---

[38] De la Roche, 'Toward a Scientific Theory of Terrorism', pp. 2–3.

[39] The same problem applies, of course, to empirical research in general. For example, how does one know that questions in interviews are being answered truthfully?

[40] C. Tilly, 'Terror, Terrorism, Terrorists', *Sociological Theory*, Vol. 22, No. 1, 2004, p. 7.

[41] Schmid, 'The Definition of Terrorism', p. 83.

[42] There have been studies carried out of the *actual* psychological impact of terrorism but, of course, this is different to *intended* impact (see A.-J. Rapin, 'What is Terrorism?', *Behavioral Sciences of Terrorism and Political Aggression*, Vol. 3, No. 3, 2011; A. Richards, 'Countering the Psychological Impact of Terrorism: Challenges for UK Homeland Security', in A. Silke (ed.), *The Psychology of Counter-Terrorism* (Abingdon: Routledge, 2011), pp. 190–2; Hoffman, *Inside Terrorism*, pp. 148–9). It is also worth noting variations in the type of psychological impact—for example, Rapin, arguing against the idea of a 'single' type of psychological reaction, draws a distinction between a feeling of 'terror' and a feeling of 'anxiety' and how these can manifest themselves in correspondingly different behaviours: 'Terror, in the strict sense of the term, inhibits action and causes panic or flight' whereas anxiety ' "increases overall sensory sensitivity" and is characterized by "risk assessment behaviours" ' (Rapin, 'What is Terrorism?', quoting C. Grillon, ['Models and Mechanisms of Anxiety: Evidence from Startle Studies', *Psychopharmacology*, August 1993], pp. 171–2).

[43] Cited in Tiefenbrun, 'A Semiotic Approach to a Legal Definition of Terrorism', pp. 969–70.

'usually' or 'often', 'apparently' also hardly smacks of being *definitional*. As Gearty has noted, 'numerous caveats and qualifications such as "many", "often", "mainly", "generally" and "usually" are not the words of writers confident about their comprehensiveness [in defining terrorism]'.[44]

The empirical problem of proving intent, however, should not mean that, if we are to retain our commitment to establishing solid theoretical grounds as to what terrorism is, that a definition should be crafted according to what evidence is readily available or observable, contrary to what de la Roche goes on to suggest:

> An ideal definition of terrorism therefore should address only readily observable features of violent behavior, such as whether it is organized, whether it is open or secret, and whether its target is a particular individual, organization, or a mass of strangers.[45]

Rather, in my view, we should hold true to our definition and there should be a focus on the intent or purpose behind the acts of violence (or threat of) in order to establish whether or not they are acts of terrorism. As Crenshaw argues, 'the question of intentions cannot be avoided because assumptions about intentionality are at the root of conceptions of the meaning of violence' even if 'the intentions of political actors, especially clandestine actors, are difficult to know'.[46] Yet, admittedly, if we are not sure about the purpose behind the act then it becomes difficult to confidently attribute the term terrorism to that act—and, as I have argued, this is where the real problem of subjectivity lies in determining what is and what is not an act of terrorism.

The subjective problem of interpreting the purpose behind acts of violence is reflected in legal attempts to define terrorism. For example, the European Union's approach to the definition of terrorism acknowledges the difficulty in proving intent:

> The structure used in the EU definition of terrorism (cf. Article 1, Table 4 of Appendix I) is known in legal research on terrorism as a combination of the subjective and the objective approach. The subjective element refers to the first part of the definition, the intention of the perpetrator... The second part consists of a list of the offences that will, taken together with the intention, be considered as terrorist offences. This sort of listing is often referred to as the objective approach because the classification of whether the offence has occurred or not is quite easy to determine and clearly made explicit within national law. The intention of the perpetrator, however, always contains a subjective element since it has to be interpreted by people. It cannot be proven in and of itself, by pointing to the concrete results... In general, most countries use a combination of the subjective

---

[44] Gearty, *Terror*, p. 14.   [45] De la Roche, 'Toward a Scientific Theory of Terrorism', pp. 2–3.
[46] Crenshaw, 'Current Research on Terrorism: The Academic Perspective', p. 2.

and the objective approach, thereby combining the notion of mens rea, which refers to the intent of the perpetrator, with a specific list of actions, which are the ordinary general criminal offences, in order to derive a definition of terrorism.[47]

The problem of proving intent is further complicated by those acts of violence where no claim is made. Schmid wrote in 2011 that '[a]lmost two-thirds of terrorist acts are no longer claimed—which was not the case when terrorism was "young".'[48] If this is the case then it means that proving intent becomes even more problematic in most instances. If one cannot identify, let alone observe, the perpetrators what chance is there of determining the purpose behind the act, though Hoffman suggests that the absence of any claim could be intended to produce wider fear and apprehension (through not even knowing who the perpetrator is)[49] and Rapoport claims 'that sometimes a message can be delivered without a claim'.[50]

One might argue that the attack on the Boston marathon was clearly designed to shock and spread fear to a wider group than the immediate victims and that it could therefore be described as an act of terrorism, even had the perpetrator been unknown. Yet, in theory, and hypothetically, such an attack could have been carried out for non-political purposes, such as personal revenge hence deeming the acts as something other than terrorism.[51] The situation is complicated further by the possibility of the aforementioned 'integrated' purposes behind an act of violence where, in the case of non-state terrorism, the intent may be to exact specific concessions from the state *as well as* to generate a psychological impact beyond the immediate victims for broader strategic or political goals.[52] And, within what may be a range of purposes, there may be unconscious intentions behind an act of violence such as revenge or catharsis.[53]

The avowed intent behind acts of violence may be clearer in some cases than others. The intent to spread fear beyond the immediate target might include Ayman al-Zawahiri's rallying call that 'with the available means, small

---

[47] European Commission Sixth Framework Programme Project, 'Defining Terrorism' (WP3 Deliverable 4), pp. 105–18.

[48] Schmid, 'Introduction', in *The Routledge Handbook of Terrorism Research*, p. 19.

[49] See B. Hoffman, 'Why Terrorists Don't Claim Credit', *Terrorism and Political Violence*, Vol. 9, No. 1, 1997.

[50] D. Rapoport, 'To Claim or Not to Claim; That is the Question—Always!', *Terrorism and Political Violence*, Vol. 9, No. 1, 1997.

[51] Imagine, for example, the hypothetical, if unlikely, situation of a disgruntled runner seeking revenge for not being entered due to the race being over-subscribed.

[52] Alleman, 'Definitional Aspects'. An example of integrated purposes might be the case of a Taliban bomb attack that was apparently designed to physically eliminate '"cruel judges" who obey Western powers' but was at the same time intended to spread fear and generate a wider psychological impact through warnings of more attacks to come ('Taliban Bomber in Kabul Kills 17 at Supreme Court', Associated Press, 11 June 2013, available at: <http://bigstory.ap.org/article/kabul-police-large-explosion-hits-near-us-embassy> (accessed 19 July 2014)).

[53] This was helpfully pointed out by an anonymous reviewer of this work.

groups could prove to be a frightening horror for the Americans and the Jews',[54] and, as noted in Chapter 4, bin Laden's endorsement of 9/11 first and foremost as an exercise in communication when he apparently spoke of '[t]hose young men' who 'said in deeds, in New York and Washington, speeches that overshadowed other speeches made everywhere else in the world'[55] (he proclaimed after 9/11 that '[t]here is America, full of fear from north to south, from west to east. Thank God for that'[56]), and the right-wing Italian New Order's proclamation that: '[w]e have wanted to demonstrate to the nation...that we are capable of placing bombs where we want, at any hour, in any spot, where and when it pleases us.'[57]

Notwithstanding the difficulties in proving what constitutes terrorism (as I have defined it) we should not change or adapt the meaning of a concept according to what we can prove or what is readily observable. To do so would deflect us from what I (and many others) understand terrorism to be—that it is essentially concerned with the intent to generate a psychological impact beyond the immediate victims.

---

[54] Ayman al-Zawhairi, *Knights Under the Prophet's Banner* (translated and partially condensed by *Al Sharq al-Awsat*), p. 62, cited in G. Ramsay, 'Targeting, Rhetoric, and the Failure of Grassroots Jihad', *Journal of Terrorism Research*, Vol. 3, No. 1, 2012, available at: <http://ojs.st-andrews.ac.uk/index.php/jtr/article/view/415/375> (last accessed 27 November 2014).

[55] *Washington Post*, 'Text: Bin Laden Discusses Attacks on Tape', 13 December 2001, available at: <http://www.washingtonpost.com/wp-srv/nation/specials/attacked/transcripts/binladentext_121301.html> (last accessed 27 November 2014). Also cited in B. Nacos, 'The Terrorist Calculus behind 9-11: A Model for Future Terrorism?', *Studies in Conflict & Terrorism*, Vol. 26, No. 1, 2003.

[56] Cited in Nacos, 'The Terrorist Calculus behind 9-11: A Model for Future Terrorism?', p. 5.

[57] *L'Espresso*, 11 August 1974, p. 6, cited in Leites, 'Understanding the Next Act', p. 12.

8

Drawing a Distinction Between Political 'Terror' and 'Terrorism'

This chapter will attempt to draw a distinction between terrorism and 'political terror', and more specifically between terrorism and 'state terror'. One might argue that in order to do so one should have some idea as to what is actually meant by 'state terror' and how one might distinguish state terror from other forms of state force and violence. This would inevitably be an arbitrary (and rather dubious) exercise for, in truth, surely *all* state violence or force (or the *threat* of the same) against human subjects, whether non-combatant or combatant, whether one sees it as legitimate or not, or whether it is legal or not, terrorizes to varying degrees. This chapter will not, therefore, engage with what would be a forlorn attempt to determine what forms of state violence or force should constitute state terror. It will, however, endeavour to draw a distinction between terrorism and state terror, however widely one might conceive of the latter.

State Terror

Like terrorism, 'political terror' and 'state terror' tend to have negative connotations[1] and as such other labels are often used for what is deemed to be legitimate 'force' exercised by states who have the monopoly on the use of violence. Duvall and Stohl (who prefer to use the term state *terrorism*) wrote that:

> The conceptual problem [of 'state terrorism'] derives from the fact that the state—the institutional-legal foundation of the government—is typically conceived or understood in terms of force and violence...In the state's origin, in its growth, in

---

[1] With the possible exception of the so-called 'terror bombings' of the Second World War.

its present control over its members, and in relation to other states, force is proclaimed to be not only its last resort, but its just principle; not only its special weapon, but its very being (MacIver, 1926, p. 221). Conceptually, the state and force—indeed, violence—are intimately bound up with one another. Since terrorism is a form of violent force, it may be conceptually problematic to speak of state, or government, terrorism. The state is simply being itself, the repository of legitimate physical violence.[2]

The suggestion, then, is that violence, including state terror, is *what states do* but that most state violence is understood as the exercise of 'legitimate force'. It might, for example, be credibly argued that 'conventional' warfare is a form of political terror. As Silke has argued: '[I]t seems that for most, warfare is a dirty business in respectable drapings, while terrorism is a dirty business in equally dirty drapings.'[3] One shouldn't, then, overlook the capacity of states to *legally* terrorize, whether in the context of war, through 'strategic bombing' campaigns, or 'shock and awe' tactics—to strike 'terror' into the hearts of one's enemy.

As we recently commemorated the beginning of the Great War of 1914–18, who can deny that the horrors endured in the trenches on the Western Front amounted to the infliction of state terror by both sides? Or that the intense bombing campaign that was launched against Iraq prior to the land assault in Operation Desert Storm in 1991 was, in truth, the exercise of state terror, as indeed was the bombing of Baghdad before the invasion of Iraq in 2003, and the NATO bombing campaign of Libya in 2011. The point is that it would be delusory to believe that the concept of 'state terror' can only be applied to illegal state violence, or indeed that it is limited to the targeting of civilians. In truth, when states go to war, they are ineluctably engaging in the exercise of state terror, for it is surely the objective of every belligerent to exact every psychological advantage, to *terrorize* in order to demoralize their adversary; that 'conventional warfare', which implies a conflict that is somehow unexceptional, is therefore, in truth, an acceptable form of state terror.

As noted above, the concept of 'state terror' tends to have a negative connotation. Notwithstanding the capacity of states to legally terrorize, this is because it has often been employed as an *organizing concept* to classify state violence that is viewed as illegal or illegitimate, and seen as largely carried out by undemocratic and oppressive regimes against their own populations. It has also, however, been applied beyond national borders in the context of war where a distinction is often made between acts of state terror and warfare in general,[4]

---

[2] Duvall and Stohl, 'Governance by Terror', p. 232.

[3] Silke, 'Terrorism and the Blind Men's Elephant', pp. 23–4.

[4] A distinction between state terror (or state 'terrorism') and warfare in general is implied in the following from Neilson:

> To think seriously about the Palestinian suicide terrorists, we need to fully recognize and take to heart that modern war (perhaps all war) is a very dirty business indeed, where

implied in English's concise account of modern warfare when he argues 'so much of what is done in orthodox warfare itself is inherently terroristic'.[5] However widely one conceives of 'state terror', whether in the form of 'domestic state terror', and/or the extent that one should view the use of state violence beyond national borders as 'terror', the focus of this chapter is to draw a distinction between state terror and terrorism.

On the need to draw an analytical distinction between the two the European Commission Sixth Framework Programme Project on Defining Terrorism argued, 'indiscriminate inclusion of the latter [state terror] under the label of terrorism confuses the discourse'.[6] Silke has also argued that 'while there are similarities between the two [though he uses the term "state *terrorism*" to describe "the terrorist acts of a government toward its own people"], they are ultimately, two entirely different creatures',[7] and English concurs that state 'terrorism' merits separate analysis from non-state terrorism.[8]

Drawing a Distinction Between Terrorism and Political Terror

While 'terror' may share the same etymological roots as terrorism it is, in my view, a different phenomenon. 'Terror', as I have argued in Chapter 4, is not inherently a political phenomenon because its perpetrators do not necessarily have political objectives. Stalkers and snipers can terrorize communities without having a political agenda. 'State terror' *is* a political phenomenon but I prefer to draw a distinction between this and terrorism—both quantitatively and, largely because of this, also qualitatively. While what one means by terror or state terror, like terrorism, is inevitably and ultimately socially constructed, state terror for this author entails a much wider campaign than terrorism because of the substantial resources that are usually available to a state. This in turn generates a very different and potentially all-pervasive type of fear and

---

terrorism, and particularly state terrorism, is utilized routinely by almost all the combatants. Fascist Spain and Italy used it, as did Apartheid South Africa, as did Nazi Germany, as did Japan against China, the Philippines, and Korea. France employed state terrorism in its war with Algeria. The Soviet Union used it against its own population as did China. Israel used it against Lebanon and is using it against the Palestinians. Latin America, Chile, Argentina, Uruguay, Colombia, and Guatemala have used state terrorism. Russia has employed it in Chechnya. And the United States wins the prize for using it. (K. Neilson, 'Commentary: On the Moral Justifiability of Terrorism (State and Other Wise)', *Osgoode Hall Law Journal*, Summer/Fall, 2003, p. 439)

[5] English, *Modern War: A Very Short Introduction*, p. 116.
[6] European Commission Sixth Framework Programme Project, 'Defining Terrorism' (WP3 Deliverable 4), p. 75.
[7] Silke, 'Terrorism and the Blind Men's Elephant', p. 22.
[8] English, *Terrorism: How to Respond*, p. 25.

dread (for example, in cases of domestic 'state terror') as opposed to merely being in the wrong public place at the wrong time (as in the case of terrorism).

Examples of state terror that have been commonly cited are those carried out by Hitler, Stalin (and Lenin before him), Pol Pot, and Mao Zedong of China (the latter was said to have accounted for some 65 million deaths[9]). These cases illustrate a further distinction between terrorism and state terror—that the latter may entail not just the spreading of fear or terror *but also* the wholesale *physical elimination* of perceived enemies. Indeed, physical elimination may be the primary purpose of state terror. In other words, whereas the essence of terrorism lies in its intention to generate a psychological impact beyond the immediate victims, state terror can have the aim of extermination over and above compliance and vice versa.[10,11]

It is not just states that have carried out campaigns of 'political terror'. For example, one could argue that genocide is a form of political terror that need not be committed by a state but could be carried out by one (non-state) group against another.[12] It is also worth noting that guerrilla groups, as well as engaging in guerrilla warfare and at times using the method of terrorism, have also engaged in campaigns of terror. Merari observes that:

> The history of guerrilla warfare also offers ample evidence of systematic victimiza-
> tion of civilians in an attempt to control the population. During its struggle for the
> independence of Algeria, the Front Liberation Nationale (FLN) murdered about
> 16,000 Muslim citizens and kidnapped 50,000 others, who have never been seen
> again; in addition to these figures, an estimated number of 12,000 FLN members
> were killed in internal 'purges'.[13]

Merari also cites the examples of the Vietcong and the Sendero Luminoso as being perpetrators of what one might call political terror, as distinct from terrorism.[14]

---

[9] Chaliand and Blin, *The History of Terrorism: From Antiquity to Al Qaeda*, p. 202.

[10] S. Kalyvas, 'The Paradox of Terrorism in Civil War', *The Journal of Ethics*, Vol. 8, No. 1, 2004, pp. 98–9. See also N. Kalyvas, cited in Schmid, 'The Definition of Terrorism', p. 97. Kalyvas, in the context of civil war, writes of the distinction between terror that aims to enforce compliance in a population and terror that seeks to eliminate.

[11] There is something of a paradox here—that '(state) terror' (a state of mind) is often used to refer to physical activity (elimination of opponents) whereas terrorism (an activity) is conceived of as spreading fear (a mental state) as its main goal, although Walter has suggested that 'terror' can mean both a 'psychic state—extreme fear—and, on the other hand, the thing that terrifies' (E. Walter, in Appendix 2.1 of Schmid (ed.), *The Routledge Handbook of Terrorism Research*, pp. 101–2).

[12] For a brief conceptual discussion on genocide see A. Schmid, 'Repression, State Terrorism, and Genocide: Conceptual Clarifications', in T. Bushnell, V. Shlapentokh, C. Vanderpool, and J. Sundram (eds.), *State Organized Terror* (Boulder, CO: Westview Press, 1991).

[13] Merari, 'Terrorism as a Strategy of Insurgency', pp. 216–17.

[14] Merari, 'Terrorism as a Strategy of Insurgency', pp. 216–17.

Although states can and have carried out acts of terrorism and have spon-sored terrorism (see section 'State Terrorism and State-Sponsored Terrorism' below), state terror is therefore a separate phenomenon and one that has been far more destructive in terms of the loss of human life than terrorism (often because it has not been limited to psychological impact as its main purpose). And by not labelling campaigns of state terror as terrorism is most certainly not to exonerate the state in any way. To reiterate, the aim is to dispassion-ately employ the application or non-application of 'terrorism' as an *analytical* concept and not a pejorative one. Moreover, as I have noted above, one could in any case argue that in practice 'state terror' or 'political terror' has as much negative resonance as 'terrorism' (perhaps exemplified in the proclamation of the 'Global War on *Terror*').

Others have also drawn a distinction between 'terror' and 'terrorism' on the grounds that the former is carried out 'from above' and the latter 'from below'. For Wordemann '[t]error is the inevitable inner force of totalitarian power . . . an expression of established power' whereas '[t]errorism is the use of force to attack the established power of terror or the generally accepted power of the [rule of] law and the laws by means of a broad-based mass uprising or conventional methods.'[15] Hacker also sees terror as 'inflicted from above' and terrorism as 'imposed from below'.[16] In 1974 Crozier, while concluding that terrorism means 'motivated violence for political ends' also stated that 'measures of extreme repression, including torture, used by States to oppress the population or to repress political dissenters, who may or may not be terrorists or guerrillas, are termed "terror"'.[17] Pearlstein too draws a distinction between terror and terrorism, arguing that the former 'may be defined as a specific form of official, governmental intimidation'[18] while Hoffman wrote that:

> state-sanctioned or explicitly ordered acts of *internal* political violence directed mostly against domestic populations—that is, rule by violence and intimidation by those *already* in power against their own citizenry—are generally termed 'terror'.[19]

---

[15] F. Wordemann, quoted in Appendix 2.1 of Schmid (ed.), *The Routledge Handbook of Terrorism Research*, p. 117.

[16] F. Hacker, cited in Appendix 2.1 of Schmid (ed.), *The Routledge Handbook of Terrorism Research*, p. 123.

[17] B. Crozier, 'Aid for Terrorism', in *Annual of Power and Conflict, 1973–4: A Survey of Political Violence and International Influence* (Institute for the Study of Conflict, 1974), p. 4, cited in Schmid and Jongman, *Political Terrorism*, p. 35.

[18] R. M. Pearlstein, *Fatal Future? Transnational Terrorism and the New Global Disorder* (Austin, TX: University of Texas Press, 2004), p. 2.

[19] B. Hoffman, 'Defining Terrorism', in Howard and Sawyer (eds.), *Terrorism and Counterterrorism: Understanding the New Security Environment, Readings and Interpretations*, p. 11.

To reiterate, then, political 'terror' is therefore often understood as something that states carry out against their own domestic populations.

Domestic State Terror

State terror could, in many circumstances, like terrorism, have as its main purpose the spreading of fear or the generation of a psychological impact beyond the immediate victims over and above any physical impact, sometimes exemplified through the choice of symbolic targets. Chaliand and Blin, for example, argued that 'the effectiveness of the [French] Terror depended on its choice of targets rather than on the proliferation of victims'.[20] They cite Robespierre who said that:

> the National Convention must not seek great numbers of the guilty; it must strike at the factional leaders. The punishment of their leaders will terrify the traitors and save the fatherland.[21]

Schmid and Jongman draw our attention to the Soviet NKVD's 'Documents of Terror' which refers to 'enlightened terror' which was apparently 'an improved and refined version of general terror' intended to generate a wide psychological impact upon the masses:

> The only tool which general terror knows and uses is force...[The] tool used by enlightened terror is any means which is able to produce the planned psychological effect...the aim of any action in the system of enlightened terror is to evoke a psychological process and implant and amplify its effects in the consciousness of the resonant mass.[22]

A further conceptual dilemma presents itself here and is one of the major challenges in my attempt to draw a distinction between political terror and terrorism—that is, if there is a campaign of 'state terror' that has as its primary objective the spreading of fear over and above any physical purpose then why can this not instead be called state terrorism? If, for example, one citizen is abducted (or is 'disappeared') from each street with the primary objective of ensuring compliance from the rest of the street does this constitute 'state terror' or 'state terrorism'?

One might plausibly argue that it is a matter of scale—that the psychological impact is much greater and more widespread because it emanates from the power holders rather than the power seekers, that 'terror' better encapsulates

---

[20] Chaliand and Blin, *The History of Terrorism: From Antiquity to Al Qaeda*, p. 102.

[21] Chaliand and Blin, *The History of Terrorism: From Antiquity to Al Qaeda*, p. 102.

[22] Cited in Schmid and Jongman, *Political Terrorism*, p. 24 (also see the caveat in relation to the authenticity of this quote on p. 209).

the more profound and all-pervasive impact of what has been termed at various times *The Terror*, or *la régime de la terreur*, or the *Red Terror*.[23] And because of this difference in scale there is, I would suggest, also a *qualitative* difference—between the fear generated by an act of terrorism (of merely being in 'the wrong place at the wrong time') and the omnipresent fear of state terror where even in the 'comfort' of your own home there may be a sense of impending doom and dread, all the more terrorizing because it comes from those who hold power. In this way, argues Kalyvas, 'the population may be pushed into total passivity and political abdication'.[24]

One senior official involved in the Red Terror from 1917 described 'terror' as the following:

> Terror is systematic violence from the top down...Terror is a legal blueprint for massive intimidation, compulsion and destruction, directed by power...The 'enemy of the revolution' assumes vast proportions when a timorous, mistrustful and isolated minority wields total power. The criterion expands without constraint, gradually embracing the entire country, ultimately applying to all but those who hold power.[25]

This account captures the difference between political terror and terrorism. Rarely, if ever, does terrorism, often as the weapon of the weak rather than the tool of those in power, have such an impact. Chaliand and Blin also describe the potential 'all-pervasiveness' and wider scale of domestic state terror:

> For these people [the peoples of every Soviet province], this meant unremitting dread. Dread of hearing a knock on the door in the middle of the night; dread of disappearing forever. Collectively, the psychological toll was appalling and impossible to quantify. Insecurity, fear, and unpredictability were the order of the day. At work and even at home, suspicion was ubiquitous. The least false step or unguarded word could mean death or the Gulag. No prospect of an end was in sight, nor was faultless behaviour any guarantee of safety...Given the psychological impact on a nation of a terrorist attack that kills a few dozen people, it is not hard to imagine the effects on a country in which everyone knew at least one victim of Stalin's terror: a parent, a relative, a neighbour, or a colleague, if not all of these at the same time.[26]

David Rapoport draws a further distinction between terrorism and state terror—that states do not generally wish to advertise or disclose their methods

---

[23] The Red Terror refers to Lenin's terror of 1917–21 (see Chaliand and Blin, 'Lenin, Stalin, and State Terrorism', in Chaliand and Blin, *The History of Terrorism: From Antiquity to Al Qaeda*, pp. 201–2).

[24] Kalyvas, 'The Paradox of Terrorism in Civil War', p. 104.

[25] I. Steinberg (Soviet 'People's Commissar for Justice'), quoted in Chaliand and Blin, 'Lenin, Stalin, and State Terrorism', pp. 202–3.

[26] Steinberg, quoted in Chaliand and Blin, 'Lenin, Stalin, and State Terrorism', p. 206.

(such as the use of torture or 'disappearances'), even if they still nevertheless want to generate a feeling of omnipresent fear in order to ensure compliance from those who might otherwise become dissenters. He argues that:

> With respect to status, *mutatis mutandis*, the 'stronger' the terrorists are in rela-tion to opponents, the more likely that they will conceal responsibility. This axiom explains why states normally conceal the terror they use against rebels. States possess enormous organizational facilities, every public understands that, and they are normally denied the one argument which seems most likely to justify terror—that the weak are 'entitled' to be desperate...Certainly, exceptions to this general rule of states denying responsibility and/or seeking to pin it on others exist; but even the most casual look at these exceptions under-scores the key point that weakness is a crucial ingredient in encouraging the desire to seek publicity.[27]

In summary, then, where physical elimination is the main purpose of state terror then this differs from terrorism because the latter is primarily concerned with psychological impact. Even where psychological impact is the main object of state terror, however, this also differs from terrorism because, by virtue of its ubiquity, the nature of the fear is qualitatively different where even 'staying indoors' is no guarantee of safety.

External State Terror

Notwithstanding the 'critical' discussion at the outset of this chapter in relation to the extent that state force and violence should be viewed as state terror, history is replete with examples of what might more conventionally, and more narrowly, be understood as state terror in the context of war. Indeed, 'Ancient Rome accepted "terror" as an instrument of state policy, both against foreign enemies and against bad citizens...Exercised on behalf of the community,

---

[27] Rapoport, 'To Claim or Not to Claim; That is the Question—Always!', p. 13. Rapoport cites the following examples:

> The information that Argentine governments made over 12,000 citizens 'disappear' from 1974 to 1980 surprised many when all the gory details finally came out. But the will and ability of governments to conceal their own terror in domestic contexts has always been known. In 1952, for example, a strange chilling piece called 'The Document on Terror' appeared, a work which the CIA says was written by the Soviet NKVD. Its subject was government terror, and it focused on 'enlightened terror', or something better described as terror whose true author is unknown. *Inter alia*, 'The Document' describes how to oblit-erate all traces of an act, how to create cover groups falsely using the name of elements the state wishes to crush and, finally, how to organize 'death squads' (the term itself is more recent) to implement state objectives without making claims even though victims and some circumstances of their fates are clear.

terror acted to "shock and awe" enemies into rapid and permanent capitulation.'[28] Jill Harries describes its ferocity against foreign enemies:

> The expansion by conquest of the Roman Empire was accompanied by scenes of planned and deliberate savagery inflicted on opponents, who had refused to surrender in time. At New Carthage in Spain late in the third century BCE, the Roman general let his troops loose on the citizens, after the town had fallen to assault, 'according to the Roman custom'. They were ordered to kill all living things they encountered, including not only human beings but also dogs and other animals. Such atrocities were policy, designed to ensure that the conquered remained, to use the Roman euphemism, 'pacified'. It was a Roman writer who put into the mouth of a British resistance leader to Rome that they 'made a desert and called it peace'. Under the Republic, generals seeking a triumphal procession were required to produce the heads of 5000 at least of the foe. Terror was not exercised equally on all alike, however. While Caesar resorted to genocide (at second hand) and wholesale mutilation in Gaul in the 50s BCE, the Greeks and other peoples of the 'more civilised' Eastern Mediterranean were dealt with, usually, more diplomatically. It was more acceptable, in other words, to use terror against 'barbarians'.[29]

Ancient Rome, then, practised legal terror and, to ensure compliance, terror had to be publicly displayed: '[t]hose who saw the thousands of followers of the slave leader Spartacus crucified at fixed intervals along the Appian Way in 71 BCE and left to rot in the Italian sun were unlikely to forget the experience. For to be effective in frightening people into being good, terror had to be public.'[30]

Chaliand and Blin document the 'terror' of Ghengis Khan and his Mongol armies, to be carried on by his successor Tamerlane:

> The systematic use of terror against towns was an integral element of Tamerlane's strategic arsenal. When he besieged a city, surrender at the first warning spared its people their lives. Resistance, on the other hand, was brutally punished by the massacre of civilians, often in atrocious circumstances. When the sack of a city was complete, Tamerlane raised pyramids of decapitated heads. In the 1387 taking of Isfahan, a city of about half a million inhabitants, observers estimated the number of dead at 100,000 to 200,000. After the massacre, Tamerlane had some fifty pyramids built, each comprised of thousands of heads. In doing so, Tamerlane hoped to persuade other besieged cities to surrender at first notice.[31]

---

[28] J. Harries, 'Labelling the Terrorist in Ancient Rome', Terrorism: Interdisciplinary Perspectives, CSTPV Seminar Series, University of St Andrews, 10 February 2010.
[29] Harries, 'Labelling the Terrorist in Ancient Rome'.
[30] Harries, 'Labelling the Terrorist in Ancient Rome'.
[31] Chaliand and Blin, The History of Terrorism: From Antiquity to Al Qaeda, p. 87.

This particularly brutal example illustrates some of the key features of 'political terror'—that it can entail either the intention to eliminate the perceived enemy or to terrorize others into submission or both. Again this differs from terrorism in its ubiquitous nature. As Chaliand and Blin put it:

> The example of Tamerlane is a forceful illustration of how a conqueror may use terror to achieve his aims. The conqueror must not only vanquish armies and shatter his enemy's state apparatus but also subdue populations.[32]

Through such conquests, then, political or state terror was very much common to war—'[a]fter decades of fighting, the generals, weary of campaigning, hoped to hasten the process by terrorizing the enemy.'[33]

'External' political terror is not, of course, limited to ancient times. Despite more contemporary state terror often being understood as what governments do to their own people,[34] one can credibly argue that the atomic attacks against Hiroshima and Nagasaki in the Second World War were acts of state terror, designed both to be destructive but also to send a powerful message to Japan's leaders and population that surrender was their only option. These were no less acts of 'state terror' even if they were legal or have been viewed as legitimate now or at the time. Goodin observes that '[t]errorizing civilian populations has long been part of warfare' and that 'the practice of state-on-state terrorism' (or what I would prefer to call external terror), 'was perfected in connection with modern "total war"' through, for example, 'one state terrorizing citizens of another by aerial bombardment'.[35] Indeed, in the context of the Second World War, Western policymakers and war strategists seemed to be quite explicit about the adoption of 'strategic bombing' against civilian populations in order 'to compel governments to surrender'.[36] On the other side of the conflict the German 'Terror Flyer Order' was implemented (which encouraged the lynching of crews in downed aircraft) in order to terrorize allied pilots, while merchant seamen were terrorized (through the killing of shipwrecked crews) 'in order to discourage experienced personnel from making the Atlantic crossing'.[37]

Not that the victims of state terror have necessarily been confined to civilians or non-combatants—as Held suggests using the example of the 'Shock and Awe' phase of the USA's war against Iraq in March 2003.[38] As I have

---

[32] Chaliand and Blin, *The History of Terrorism: From Antiquity to Al Qaeda*, p. 87.

[33] Chaliand and Blin, *The History of Terrorism: From Antiquity to Al Qaeda*, p. 90.

[34] See, for example, Sproat, 'Can the State Commit Acts of Terrorism? An Opinion and Some Qualitative Replies to a Questionnaire', pp. 128–9.

[35] Goodin, *What's Wrong With Terrorism?*, p. 62.

[36] Chaliand and Blin, *The History of Terrorism: From Antiquity to Al Qaeda*, p. 7.

[37] H. Levie, *Terrorism in War: The Law of War Crimes* (New York: Oceana, 1993), cited in Schmid, 'The Definition of Terrorism', p. 91.

[38] Held, 'Terrorism and War', p. 68.

argued in Chapter 6, then, determining whether something is state terror or not does not correlate with the illegal/legal threshold respectively, for there is no questioning the capacity of states to *legally* terrorize adversaries. Finally, one could argue that any form of state military deterrence designed to dissuade, persuade or coerce backed up by military force is a form of state terror. Indeed, through its threat of massive and widespread annihilation, ' "modern deterrence theory" in the context of the Cold War was initially referred to as "the Balance of Terror" '.[39]

The above has attempted to draw a distinction between political or state terror and terrorism. Perhaps the contemporary example of the activity of ISIS serves as a useful example illustrate this distinction. The group's beheadings of Western hostages, I would argue, were acts of terrorism—that there was a political motive, that there was clearly the intent to generate a psychological impact beyond the immediate victims, that the victims were not themselves the main targets of the terrorist message but that they and their deaths served as message generators to its target audiences (the United States, the United Kingdom, the international community, and perhaps its own supporters and perceived constituency of support for recruitment purposes). On the other hand the public hangings and the open display of corpses to ensure that the population under its control is frightened into compliance I would call political terror, that it is the very fact that it is those who govern or rule 'from above' who are the perpetrators that therefore leads to the ubiquitous nature of the terror. And there is no reason why, in theory, a legally constituted state could not carry out both state terror and such acts of terrorism.

State Terrorism and State-Sponsored Terrorism

Because I have suggested that much of what others might term state terrorism I have preferred to call state terror, the former, as I have conceived of it, is comparatively rare. Why, for example, resort to internal state terrorism against a domestic population when the resources and security forces of the state can ensure much more widespread compliance (in the form of state terror)? One could argue that there may be acts of terrorism within a campaign of state terror (though a real challenge is to draw a distinction between the two) and there is no reason why, in theory, a state could not carry out similar acts of terrorism to those of ISIS. While one can suggest that, in theory, acts of terrorism can be committed by states domestically,[40] *external* state terrorism

---

[39] Stohl, 'National Interests and State Terrorism in International Affairs', p. 280.

[40] For example, they may be carried out directly by the state under the guise of a pro-state terrorist group (though *state sponsorship* of such groups may be more common).

is arguably more discernible, though it is, of course, difficult to determine how directly a state might have been involved in the perpetration of an act of external terrorism (the possibility, however, is perhaps reflected in some definitions of terrorism that include '*clandestine* agents' as possible perpetrators[41]). Indeed, for some, state terrorism is what states do abroad while state terror is internal:

> 'state terrorism' and 'state terror'—the former denomination referring to acts of the state institutions outside (direct involvement in the subversive terrorism), the latter to various means of repression of the domestic population.[42]

The 'Lavon Affair' of 1954 could be seen as an example of external state terrorism[43] as indeed could the Lockerbie bombing, subject to the satisfaction of other criteria (see Chapter 7 for a discussion on this).

States have certainly sponsored acts of terrorism. One of the conceptual problems yet to be adequately resolved, according to Schmid's survey of experts, is to define the meaning of state terrorism and to distinguish it from state-sponsored terrorism.[44] For Merari, '[f]oreign states' support of terrorism ... ranges from the passive willingness to allow the presence of terrorists on one's territory or the refusal to extradict [sic] them, to actively equipping terrorists with a variety of weapons.'[45] State-sponsored terrorism occurs, then, when states directly finance, or provide material and tangible assistance to non-state groups or individuals (or indeed other states) for the purpose of carrying out acts of terrorism (if the state carries out the acts themselves then it would amount to state terrorism).

Examples commonly cited for state-sponsored terrorism include Iranian and Syrian sponsorship of Hezbullah (although terrorism has been but one part of the activity of the latter, along with its other 'military' activity, and its social and political dimensions).[46] It also includes the Libyan government's

---

[41] Such as that of the US State Department.

[42] European Commission Sixth Framework Programme Project, 'Defining Terrorism' (WP3 Deliverable 4), p. 79 Although it states (p. 79) that:

> In some cases, it must be conceded that the line between inside / outside, which is crucial for the differentiation between state terror and state terrorism, tends to be rather unclear. Russia's actions in the North Caucasus, Israel's activities in the West Bank or Gaza and Sudan's terrorization of a part of the population via sponsoring the Janjaweed militia can all be, from certain points of view, contested cases. In the last case, the decision would lie not between state terror and state terrorism, but between state terror and state-sponsored terrorism. Yet any typology, it may be argued, produces border cases as it is by necessity, to a certain extent, a theoretical abstraction from the empiric world.

[43] Where Israeli agents and Egyptian Jews planted bombs in Egypt hoping to implicate Egyptian Muslims and to illustrate the incompetence of Egypt's rulers, all in an attempt to prevent the British from leaving the country.

[44] Schmid, 'Introduction' to Schmid (ed.), *The Routledge Handbook of Terrorism Research*, p. 28.

[45] Merari, 'A Classification of Terrorist Groups', p. 343.

[46] For an authoritative account on Hezbullah see J. Palmer Harik, *Hezbollah: The Changing Face of Terrorism* (London: I. B. Tauris, 2005).

shipments of arms to the IRA in the aftermath of the US El Dorado Canyon raid against the country (the UK government permitted the use of British bases for the attack in 1986). If the mujahedeen carried out acts of violence that satisfy one's criteria for them to be called terrorism in their campaign to expel the Soviet Union from Afghanistan, then we can argue that the United States support for such acts can also be classified as state sponsorship of terrorism. Similarly, whether or not one sympathizes with the Syrian 'rebels' in the ongoing conflict (as at the time of writing—late 2014) if they have carried out acts of terrorism then any assistance accorded to them by states for the purpose of carrying out such acts could also be classed as state-sponsored terrorism. To reiterate, these are not moral or pejorative judgements (my concern here is not with whether or not they were justified) but is the outcome of more detached and objective analysis.

* * * * *

In conclusion, a key difference for this author between political terror (including state terror) and terrorism is that while the former might entail *either* the physical elimination of opponents or the spreading of terror to ensure compliance, generating a psychological impact beyond the immediate victims is the sine qua non of terrorism. Where state terror seeks to primarily generate a psychological impact upon a much broader group or population it is different from terrorism in terms of its scale where the resources of the state enable it to exact widespread terror and fear—indeed its quantitative difference itself breeds a qualitative distinction in the nature of the fear that is experienced, with its ubiquitous and all-pervasive presence and the dread of a knock on the door at night. External state terror that seeks to exact psychological impact, too, is of a much wider scale than terrorism, which itself also leads to a qualitative difference in the nature of the fear, exemplified in 'strategic' bombing campaigns and the waging of (state) psychological warfare.

9

Further Potential Components of a Definition of Terrorism

The previous chapters have argued that there are two elements in particular that are fundamental to our understanding of terrorism. Firstly, and in my view this is the core essence of the phenomenon, terrorism entails generating a psychological impact beyond the immediate victims as its primary goal, that the target serves as a message generator to a wider audience which is the real target of attention. Secondly, terrorism should be viewed as a *method* and defined as such (rather than conceptualized as a phenomenon that is inherent to any particular cause, ideology, or perpetrator). As I have previously noted, this is not to suggest that there cannot be cases where the use and endorsement of terrorism may itself be (or become) intrinsic to the doctrine. But a definition should not be confined to these as terrorism has been carried out in pursuit of a wide variety of ideologies and causes, most of which are not themselves inherently terrorist. The implication of perceiving terrorism as a method is that it helps us to steer clear of actor-based definitions that focus on who the perpetrator or what the cause is, and that *confuse analysis of the activity* that one is trying to conceptualize.

These may not be the first or most obvious components for many in any definition of terrorism (such as—commonly—the use or threat of violence or force, or the political motive), but they have been integral in my discussion as to what differentiates terrorism from other forms of political violence. This chapter considers further components that should or potentially could be included in any definition. The formidable nature of this task is probably no better exemplified than in Schmid and Jongman's conscientious efforts to formulate an 'academic consensus' definition which ultimately contained no less than sixteen components!:

> Terrorism is an anxiety-inspiring method of repeated violent action, employed by (semi-) clandestine individual, group or state actors, for idiosyncratic, criminal or

political reasons, whereby—in contrast to assassination—the direct targets of violence are not the main targets. The immediate human victims of violence are generally chosen randomly (targets of opportunity) or selectively (representative or symbolic targets) from a target population, and serve as message generators. Threat- and violence-based communication processes between terrorist (organization), (imperilled) victims, and main targets are used to manipulate the main target (audience(s)), turning it into a target of terror, a target of demands, or a target of attention, depending on whether intimidation, coercion, or propaganda is primarily sought.[1]

It is not the intention here to scrutinize each and every one of these elements. Nevertheless, before finalizing my own conceptualization of terrorism I would like to consider further potential components.

Before this, however, two important points are worth noting. Firstly, if one is endeavouring to *define* a phenomenon then we should be *definitive* and 'determine with precision'.[2] It is therefore arguably not particularly helpful to include components in a definition that 'usually' or 'often' apply—for example, if one defines terrorism 'as *often* targeting civilians', or as '*usually* having a political motive'. The use of such words as 'often', 'usually', or 'predominantly' in relation to any features, then, would mean that these elements cannot then be *definitional* of terrorism. Horgan concurs that 'the definition should not include terms that are "usually" true, suggesting that there are exceptions to the rule',[3] although in response to this Schmid has argued that 'few laws in *social* science are without exception' (original author's italics).[4] Nevertheless, a *definition* of terrorism should apply to all forms and cases of terrorism. Beyond definition, however, it might then be useful to *describe* frequent or predominant (though not definitive) features of terrorism (see Chapter 10).

The second point is that in my endeavour to determine what components should be included in a definition of terrorism one has to concede that these components *are themselves disputed concepts* whose parameters are far from clear (and this is rarely acknowledged by those crafting definitions of terrorism). What, for example, do we understand by the term 'violence'? Does it include poisoning or the contamination of products, or spraying slogans on a wall? Does it include so-called 'structural violence' that encompasses injustices that breed inequality? Also, what are the parameters of 'political', and how do we disentangle the 'political' from the 'economic' or the 'cultural'? Addressing these questions is beyond the remit of this work. Suffice to acknowledge that

---

[1] Schmid and Jongman, *Political Terrorism*, p. 28.
[2] The definition of 'define' in the *Chambers Giant Paperback Dictionary* (Edinburgh: Chambers Harrap Publishers, 1997), p. 270.
[3] J. Horgan, quoted in Schmid, 'The Definition of Terrorism', p. 45.
[4] Schmid, 'The Definition of Terrorism', p. 45.

such concepts that are widely regarded as important components when conceptualizing terrorism are themselves highly contested terms.

Terrorism as the Use of Violence or Force and/or the Threat of Violence or Force

Perhaps one feature above all else that is commonly associated with terrorism is the use of, or the threat of, violence or force. Schmid and Jongman, in their survey of 109 definitions found that the use of the words 'violence' or 'force' appeared in 83.5 per cent of them.[5] It is interesting, given the pejorative use of the term terrorism, that the word 'force' (which is seen as a less emotive term with a more positive connotation than 'violence') is also included in many definitions. There may indeed be some merit in this—if, for example, we are not to exclude terrorism by the state in any general definition, and if we are to circumvent the inevitably complex debate as to the extent that a state's use of force constitutes terrorism, then the word 'force' should also arguably be included.[6] As David Claridge remarked, 'separating acts that are intended to protect from those that are intended to coerce' can be 'an increasingly challenging task' and that the 'area between legitimate use of force and violent abuse' is a murky one.[7]

While both the words 'violence' and 'force' can reasonably be included in any definition of terrorism, there is no universal agreement as to what is meant by violence. The *Oxford English Dictionary* defines violence as 'behaviour involving physical force intended to hurt, damage, or kill someone or something'.[8] Yet, for many, as long as there is the intent or threat to 'hurt, damage, or kill' then many acts that don't actually involve 'physical force' (which is integral to this definition of violence) can nevertheless surely still be classified as terrorism. Hence the proposition that rather than 'violence or the threat of violence' we should instead include more broadly 'harm or the threat of harm'. Shannon makes a convincing case for this:

> Rather, what matters for 'terrorism' is *harm* or the threat of harm … This can be seen by considering cases of terrorism that involve harm but no violence per se. For example, in November 2001, letters containing anthrax spores were mailed to

---

[5] Schmid and Jongman, *Political Terrorism*, p. 5.

[6] There might, for example, be states that have used what they view to be their legal and rightful recourse to employ force that might from others' perspectives be viewed as the *violence* of 'state terrorism' or 'state terror'.

[7] D. Claridge, 'State Terrorism? Applying a Definitional Model', *Terrorism and Political Violence*, Vol. 8, No. 3, 1996, p. 49.

[8] Oxford Dictionaries, available at: <http://www.oxforddictionaries.com/definition/english/violence> (last accessed 27 November 2014).

select US news outlets and members of the US Senate. Five people died and seventeen people fell ill from the spores. The news media, following the US government, uniformly described this as a terrorist act, despite the fact that it involved no violence or force.[9]

While the above instances (and poisoning or contamination in general) may, for some, still constitute a form of *violence* the adoption of the inclusion of 'harm' in a definition of terrorism might also facilitate the inclusion of a further component that one might again argue is harmful but does not entail the exercise of direct physical force—that of 'structural violence'. This has been used to refer to injustices in the global system that have an adverse effect on the lives of others (for example, in the form of inequality and poverty) and who are, as a result, unable to fulfil their basic needs. Honderich, for instance, has argued that '[w]hat is non-violent can be more destructive than violence.'[10]

The notion of structural violence is, however, excluded from my own deliberations as to what constitutes terrorism—for terrorism, like all forms of political violence, is concerned with deliberate and direct physical harm, and/ or its threat, to people and/or property. It is not the by-product of some other greater process or motive, such as global capitalism or economic interest (respectively). Moreover, as Crenshaw argues, the notion of structural violence confuses the condition with the action.[11]

The issue as to whether either 'harm' or 'violence' should be included is a complicated one. 'Violence' evokes stronger passions (and arguably, from a state perspective, facilitates the galvanizing of response). It is also the case that the more prominent cases of 'terrorist spectaculars' are ineluctably *violent*. Yet, if somebody or some group threatens 'harm' as opposed to violence can this not also be terrorism (subject to the satisfaction of other criteria)? Here, however, one is in danger of labelling any 'direct action' that is intended to cause harm as terrorism, including, for example, the daubing of graffiti. This links in to the debate as to how *serious* an act of harm or violence has to be to be considered terrorism, and the extent to which, for example, attacks on property should be included in a definition (see section 'Further Potential Components' below). Notwithstanding the narrow confines of the *OED* definition that limits violence to physical force, I would prefer to view the examples of deliberate poisoning as acts of violence. I would therefore prefer to retain the word 'violence' rather than 'harm' in a definition of terrorism— not least because 'harm' can include an enormous range of (less serious) activity that one wouldn't call terrorism.

---

[9] Shanahan, 'Betraying a Certain Corruption of Mind: How (and How Not) to Define "Terrorism"'.

[10] Honderich, *After the Terror*, p. 100.

[11] Crenshaw, 'Current Research on Terrorism: The Academic Perspective', p. 3.

Terrorism as *Political* Violence

Beyond the core element of the 'use of violence or force and/or the threat of violence or force' terrorism has widely been viewed as being carried out *for a political purpose*. Hoffman, for example, has argued that terrorism is ineluctably political.[12] But does the act of violence have to have a political motivation to be labelled an act of terrorism?[13] Lord Carlile, former reviewer of British counter-terrorism legislation (2001–11), argued that the UK's definition of 1989 'was restricted in terms of intention/design, in that it excluded violence for a religious end, or for a non-political ideological end',[14] implying from his perspective that there can indeed be non-politically motivated terrorism. Schmid has also argued this:

> While there are nonpolitical forms of terrorism (such as criminal or psychopathological terrorism), the political motivation of terrorism is one that is often present and stressed by analysts and even more so by terrorists themselves. Since terrorists generally challenge the monopoly of violence of the state and its ability to protect its citizens, terrorist acts obtain political significance even when the motivation for them is not primarily political but religious, criminal or psychopathological.[15]

For example, if the purpose behind an act of violence is to generate fear beyond the immediate victims, then, according to Schmid, it could be carried out by a psychopath with no political motive, or indeed by criminals engaged in organized crime (even if such acts do ultimately have political ramifications). Thus, from this perspective, one might also need to include economic motivation for acts of terrorism.

In this author's view, however, if an act of violence is carried out by a psychopath with no political motive then this is not an act of terrorism. Nor is an act of violence carried out for private economic gain—for example, in cases of violence or the threat of violence associated with organized crime.[16]

---

[12] Hoffman, *Inside Terrorism*, p. 43.

[13] For example, the title of Grant Wardlaw's book *Political Terrorism* implies that there are other forms of (non-political) terrorism.

[14] Carlile, 'The Definition of Terrorism'.

[15] Schmid, 'Frameworks for Conceptualising Terrorism', p. 200.

[16] Shanahan considers whether the following organized crime example should be viewed as terrorism:

> on 16 November 2008, the Associated Press published an article entitled 'Italy Fights Mob Terror Near Naples'. The Camorra, a Naples crime 'family', was identified as the group responsible for a 'strategy of terror' in the region intended to persuade local businessmen to pay protection money. As a police official in the provincial capital of Caserta explained, the Camorra's rationale for the murders attributed to it, 'You kill one to teach a lesson to 100.' Despite the economically motivated, non-political nature of the murders, the Camorra's acts were nonetheless described as 'terrorism'. Unlike definitions that restrict acts of terrorism to politically motivated attacks, (T[author's own definition]) explains why this designation is not necessarily in error. Although (T) classifies some financially motivated criminal acts as acts of terrorism, it nonetheless excludes most

One might contemplate 'terrorism' that is economically motivated in other ways. A case in point, and subject to the satisfaction of other definitional criteria, might be the activity of the Nigerian group MEND (Movement for the Emancipation of the Niger Delta), who have claimed that they are fighting for the production of oil in the Niger Delta to be brought under local control and away from (Nigerian government-sanctioned) multilateral organizations. Again, however, while there is apparently a significant economic dimension to the sense of MEND grievance here, its acts of violence can be viewed as politically motivated against the policies of the Nigerian government.

One might suggest that an act of terrorism could be carried out by an *individual* through purely religious conviction without any political motive, but even here it is difficult to disentangle political motive from religious, especially if at the 'group level' (on behalf of whom the attack has taken place) there are clear political goals.[17] 'Religiously motivated' terrorism might apply to individuals acting in the name of Al Qaeda but the latter has clear political goals. It has, for example, sought to banish US influence from the Middle East and to overthrow 'puppet' regimes there, while its desire for a caliphate is a territorial and political goal, even if these objectives have been (or have been claimed to be) religiously driven.

What about those religious or millenarian groups who isolate themselves from the rest of society and who foresee the oncoming of the apocalypse, with no apparent concerns for mere politics? Yet, even these groups and their belief systems are in some way a response to the environments (and the political contexts) within which they find themselves. Aum Shinrikyo, which was led by the charismatic Shoko Asahara, like most such groups, was engrossed in 'inevitable', grandiose, and catastrophic prophecies, but its violence was also ineluctably a political attack against the status quo. Indeed, for Asahara a combination of natural *and* political developments represented major warning signals for the future:

> a worsening of the trade friction between the United States and Japan, an increase in defense spending, and abnormalities in the Fuji volcanic region and the Pacific Plate have already proved true . . . If we allow the demonic energy to increase, it will

ordinary criminal assaults against persons, such as murder, robbery, and rape as having the wrong sort of agenda. A mugger who lurks in an alley, selects his victims 'randomly', and threatens to stab them if they don't hand over their valuables, is not committing a terrorist act, both because his victim selection is better described as *opportunistic* than as *strategically indiscriminate*, and because he has no agenda that requires influencing an audience group through the use of strategically indiscriminate harm. (Shanahan, 'Betraying a Certain Corruption of Mind: How (and How Not) to Define "Terrorism"')

[17] The distinction between the motivation of the group and of the individual is an important one to make. See, for example, Gressang IV, 'Audience and Message: Assessing Terrorist WMD Potential', p. 93.

be extremely difficult to prevent the slide towards a nuclear war at the end of the century.[18]

And Aum's aim was to build Shambhala (a kingdom) governed by the god Shiva and it did, indeed, embark on an unsuccessful foray into politics with the formation of its political party (Shinrito, the 'Truth Party') and the running of 25 candidates in the Japanese election of February 1990.[19]

It is difficult, then, to conceive of a religiously motivated attack not also being designed to have some political goal. Is it really the case then that terrorism is 'ineluctably political' as Hoffman has argued?[20] From a policy-making perspective Lord Carlile again seems to suggest otherwise:

> For consistency with the UN Resolution 1566 [2004] and Council of Europe Convention on the Prevention of Terrorism 200332, consideration should be given to the possibility of replacing section 1(1)(c) with the words 'the use or threat is made for the purpose of advancing a political, philosophical, ideological, racial, ethnic, religious or other similar cause'. And: A change of that kind, in addition to the advantage of consistency, would cement into the law clarity that terrorism includes campaigns of terrorist violence motivated by racism.[21]

In particular, Carlile argued that '[r]eligious causes should continue to fall within the definition of terrorist designs.'[22] Primoratz also suggested that there can be non-political terrorism by suggesting that 'the method of coercive intimidation by infliction of violence on innocent persons has been used in non-political contexts: one can speak of religious terrorism (e.g. that of the Hizb Allah) and criminal terrorism (e.g. that of the Mafia).'[23] One could strongly dispute that the 'religious terrorism' of 'Hizb Allah' has taken place in a 'non-political context', while one could argue that the 'criminal terrorism' of the Mafia is more akin to organized crime than terrorism—and that therefore 'coercive intimidation' is not on its own synonymous with terrorism or sufficient to be classified as such.

While I have argued that perpetrator-based definitions are unhelpful, more broadly the type of goal (i.e. political or not) *is key* in classifying whether or not an act of violence constitutes terrorism, subject to other definitional criteria. There may be many acts of violence that intend to generate a psychological impact beyond the victims that, unless they are politically motivated,

---

[18] Brackett, *Holy Terror: Armageddon in Tokyo* (New York: Weatherhill, 1996), p. 70.

[19] Brackett, *Holy Terror: Armageddon in Tokyo*, pp. 76–82.

[20] Hoffman, *Inside Terrorism*, p. 43.

[21] Carlile, 'The Definition of Terrorism', p. 37. Incidentally, the UN Resolution 1566 (2004) stated that acts of 'terrorism' 'are under no circumstances justifiable by considerations of a political, philosophical, ideological, racial, ethnic, religious or other similar nature'.

[22] Carlile, 'The Definition of Terrorism', p. 47.

[23] I. Primoratz, 'What is Terrorism?', *Journal of Applied Philosophy*, Vol. 7, No. 2, 1990, reprinted in Gearty (ed.), *Terrorism*, p. 22.

cannot then in my view be classified as terrorism. Interestingly, Schmid in a list of Key Characteristic Elements of terrorism wrote of 'the *predominantly* political character of the act' but again 'predominantly' suggests that political motive cannot therefore be *definitional* of terrorism.

Nevertheless, whether one also includes 'philosophical, ideological, racial, ethnic, religious', or (rather vaguely) some 'other similar cause' or economic motivation, one could argue that many of these causes have, in one way or another, a political dimension. Racial, ethnic, and religious motivation are all politically related, although 'philosophical' and 'ideological' are so broad and vague as to almost mean anything! Everyone, for example, has their own ideological outlook. Nevertheless, for some it may indeed be sufficient to classify *any act* of violence that intends to spread fear beyond the immediate victims as terrorism regardless of the overall goal. This author ultimately, however, and in concurrence with Hoffman, understands and conceptualizes terrorism as being (in one way or another) *politically* motivated. Some have suggested that the lack of consensus on the definition of terrorism itself 'points to its inescapably political nature'.[24] Schmid rather paradoxically (and rather undefinitively!) argues that '[i]n short, "political" is an element that ought to be included in a definition of terrorism, but non-political terrorism should not be totally ruled out either'![25]

The Targeting of Civilians and Non-Combatants

For those who *define* terrorism as entailing attacks on 'civilians' and/or 'non-combatants', what is meant by these categories, and what their parameters are, is essential in determining what can then be classified as an act of terrorism. One significant benefit of viewing terrorism as entailing attacks on potentially anybody (including combatants) is that, for definitional purposes, and from my own purpose-based perspective, one does not need to draw distinctions between combatant and non-combatant and between civilian and non-civilian. Of course, one can argue that the 'shock value' and psychological impact against a wider audience is likely to be enhanced by those acts of terrorism that take place in a peacetime environment and where civilians are the victims (particularly in democratic environments and a context of a free

---

[24] B. Golder and G. Williams, quoted in Schmid, 'The Definition of Terrorism', p. 78.

[25] Schmid, 'The Definition of Terrorism', p. 78. Perhaps, if one cannot be definitive about the concept before us then we should err on the side of caution by instead *describing* the phenomenon that we are confronted with (in this case by *describing* terrorism as something that is *usually* carried out for a political purpose) (see Chapter 10 and Jackson et al., *Terrorism: A Critical Introduction*, pp. 115–20).

media). And while one can argue that civilian targeting is not definitional of terrorism one can certainly *describe* terrorism as *often* targeting civilians or non-combatants.[26] In this context, it is perhaps worth considering, then, what is understood by the terms civilian/non-civilian, combatant/non-combatant, and the 'innocent'.

Who Constitutes a Civilian and a Non-Combatant?

Determining who or what constitutes a 'civilian' target is not as obvious as it might seem. For example, do civilians include politicians who have key security decision-making roles in the relevant theatre of conflict? Should prison guards be regarded as civilians? Are those who supply and deliver food and equipment to armed forces to be considered any less civilian than others? Are there degrees of innocence and should distinctions be made between categories of civilian[27]—for example between those civilians going about their daily routines in their own homelands prior to the 9/11, London, and Madrid attacks and those engaged in business contracts in post-conflict zones? Are civilians who take up arms still to be considered civilians?

Should settlers in disputed territories always be regarded as civilians? Schmid cites a 'US-based Muslim scholar' who argued the following:

> historically, settlers, while they appear to act like civilians, are often armed and hostile to the indigenous populations of the occupied lands... settlers are often a voice against ending occupations and a voting bloc that gives legitimacy to the occupation, hence constituting direct material support for occupiers.[28]

Even if one can agree as to who or what constitutes a civilian target English provides a paradoxical example as to how, from a victim-based civilian definitional perspective, one and the same attack can be called a terrorist attack or not depending on the victims:

> Imagine an attack on a military target, in which it is very likely that both soldiers and non-soldiers will be hurt or killed by the violence (since cleaners, canteen workers, family members, visitors, passers-by, and others will be in the vicinity of the attack, along with soldiers). Are the injuries and deaths of the non-soldiers in this instance the result of terrorist violence, while the deaths of soldiers are non-terrorist in kind?[29]

---

[26] Again, for the case for *describing* rather than *defining* terrorism see Jackson et al., *Terrorism: A Critical Introduction*, pp. 115–20.

[27] For a discussion on this see, for example, Tiefenbrun, 'A Semiotic Approach to a Legal Definition of Terrorism', p. 363.

[28] Schmid, 'Introduction', in Schmid (ed.), *The Routledge Handbook of Terrorism Research*, p. 21.

[29] English, *Terrorism: How to Respond*, p. 10.

One could, however, argue that it depends upon the *intent* of the perpetrators, and if the intent was to kill soldiers in order to strike a symbolic blow against the military and to generate a psychological impact beyond the immediate victims (whether a broader troop body, a government, or a civilian population) then, according to a civilian victim-based definition, this would not be classified as an act of terrorism.[30]

Beyond civilian targeting, if terrorism is defined as targeting a broader category of non-combatants then who and what constitutes a non-combatant target? Some have suggested that military personnel are non-combatants for as long as they are outside a war zone.[31] But does this mean that armed peacekeeping troops in such zones are combatants? Alternatively, were armed military patrols in Northern Ireland during the Troubles non-combatants? Again, for those who hold to a victim-based approach (that *defines* terrorism as targeting both civilians *and* non-combatants) the distinction between combatant and non-combatant is an important one because it determines whether or not an act of violence then constitutes terrorism.

For the purpose of the United States National Counterterrorism Center World Incidents Tracking System (of terrorist incidents) combatants and non-combatants were defined as the following:

> the term 'combatant' was interpreted to mean military, paramilitary, militia, and police under military command and control, in specific areas or regions where war zones or war-like settings exist . . . Noncombatants therefore included civilians and civilian police and military assets outside of war zones and warlike settings. Diplomatic assets, including personnel, embassies, consulates, and other facilities, were also considered noncombatant targets.[32]

Thus, non-combatant has been used to refer to both civilians and 'military personnel (whether or not armed or on duty) who are not deployed in a war zone or a war-like setting',[33] or 'as unarmed or off-duty military personnel or military units stationed in areas where the armed conflict is absent'.[34] Thus, those who define non-combatant in this way and who conceive of terrorism as ineluctably targeting civilians and non-combatants are able to define acts of

---

[30] The civilian casualties in this example could, however, be said to be the 'known consequences', though known consequences are not the same as deliberate intent and as such should arguably not be included in a definition of terrorism.

[31] Schmid, 'The Definition of Terrorism', p. 46.

[32] National Counterterrorism Center (US), *Country Reports on Terrorism 2005*, Statistical Annex, 7 April 2006, available at: <http://www.state.gov/documents/organization/65489.pdf> (last accessed 27 November 2014).

[33] US State Department, quoted in Schmid, 'The Definition of Terrorism', p. 46.

[34] US Department of State cited in European Commission Sixth Framework Programme Project, 'Defining Terrorism' (WP3 Deliverable 4), p. 25.

violence against military targets in peacetime settings as terrorism, including, for example, the attack on the USS *Cole*.[35]

In the context of the 'principle of discrimination' within just war theory the stipulation is:

> that the only appropriate objects of force in a conflict are combatants—those who are engaged in fighting and are therefore either individually or collectively offering harm to the putative agent of force or to another. All others are to be regarded as noncombatants and excluded from attack...the immunity of noncombatants from attack is the foundational element in our moral thinking...It is this basic moral judgment that ordinary people who are not engaged in any threatening combat operations should not be subject to attack that explains and underlies the moral repugnance we justifiably feel about acts of terrorism.[36]

Yet, even if one can be reasonably clear about who or what constitutes a non-combatant target, there is an alternative view that attacks on military targets in peacetime, even if they are in non-combatant mode, should not, by virtue of the fact they are military targets, be called terrorism. The argument is that those carrying out acts of terrorism are playing by 'the rules of international humanitarian law' by limiting their targets to military ones in general (even if they are in non-combatant mode), and that therefore such acts should not be referred to as terrorist. Schmid, for example, in his list of what *does not* constitute terrorism, and whether or not in the context of war, excludes:

> attacks on military installations, aircraft, navy vessels, barracks which are guarded even when those who attack military installations or personnel are otherwise also engaging in acts of terrorism.[37]

This perspective seems to suggest that acts of violence against at least some non-combatant targets (i.e. military targets in non-combatant mode) should not be called terrorism (either that or that such military targets, whether in peacetime or not, should be viewed as 'combatant'). The view is that the attack on the USS *Cole*, for example, could not then be classified as an act of terrorism.

Boaz Ganor argues against the need for a combatant/non-combatant distinction in defining terrorism (which at least helpfully circumvents the debate as to what counts as 'non-combatant' beyond civilian in peacetime). He suggests that the civilian/non-civilian distinction sets a much clearer 'moral standard':

> the U.S. State Department, for example, has put forward a definition according to which terrorism is the deliberate use of violence against *non-combatants*, whether

---

[35] See discussion and further commentary on the meaning of 'combatant' and 'non-combatant' in Schmid, 'The Definition of Terrorism', pp. 46–8.

[36] D. Rodin, 'Terrorism without Intention', *Ethics*, Vol. 114, No. 4, 2004, pp. 6–7.

[37] Schmid, 'Terrorism: The Definitional Problem', p. 408.

civilian or not. However, this definition of terrorism will not work in practice, as it designates attacks on non-combatant military personnel as terrorism. Despite the natural tendency of those who have been harmed by terrorism to adopt this broad definition, terror organizations and their supporters can justly claim that they cannot be expected to attack only military personnel who are armed and ready for battle. If they were held to such a standard, they would lose the element of surprise and be quickly defeated. By narrowing the definition of terrorism to include only deliberate attacks on civilians, we leave room for a 'fair fight' between guerillas and state armies. Thus we set a clear moral standard that can be accepted not only by Western countries, but also by the Third World and even by some of the terrorist organizations themselves. When such a moral distinction is internationally applied, terrorist organizations will have yet another reason to renounce terrorism in favor of guerilla actions.[38]

There is clearly much debate as to whether or not attacks on military targets in peacetime constitute acts of terrorism. Nevertheless, from my own perspective, and for the purposes of a general definition of terrorism, deliberations as to what constitutes 'civilian' and 'non-combatant' are immaterial. Providing the primary intention is to generate a psychological impact beyond the immediate victims, and subject to other definitional criteria, acts of terrorism can in my view be carried out against *anybody*—whether they be civilians, non-combatants, or combatants.

Further Potential Components

Can Attacks on Property Be Acts of Terrorism?

Should attacks on property be included in a definition of terrorism? To what extent can damage to property truly terrorize and, if such attacks can be called terrorism, how 'serious' does an act of violence have to be before it can be labelled as such? It seems that if such an act is primarily intended to spread fear beyond the immediate object of attack (property or otherwise) then it can be called terrorism. The FBI's definition of terrorism includes attacks on property[39] while the UK Terrorism Act 2000 definition also includes 'serious damage to property' and acts 'designed to interfere with or seriously to disrupt an electronic system'.[40] If one agrees that acts of terrorism may also include attacks on property then this again, of course, further challenges the notion

---

[38] B. Ganor, 'Terrorism: No Prohibition Without Definition', 7 October 2001, available through Google search, no URL address/link on the actual document (last accessed 27 November 2014).

[39] See, for example, FBI Reports and Publications, *Terrorism 2002–2005*, available at: <http://www.fbi.gov/stats-services/publications/terrorism-2002-2005> (last accessed 27 November 2014).

[40] United Kingdom Terrorism Act 2000, available at: <http://www.legislation.gov.uk/ukpga/2000/11/section/1> (last accessed 27 November 2014).

that terrorism is ineluctably about targeting civilians, even if such attacks might be intended to spread fear or intimidate a civilian population.

Lord Carlile suggests the following examples as to how attacks on property can be deemed acts of terrorism:

> So far as offences against property are concerned, I have no doubt that these and threats to damage property should be included in any definition. Damage to property can induce a real sense of terror for the future. There is no difficulty in producing examples. A threat to explode bombs on the London Underground would produce both physical fear and practical difficulty for commuters and severe economic consequences. The bombing of schools at weekends or in the school holidays, accompanied by a threat that future bombings might not be limited to out of school times, would hold the pupils of those schools and everybody else associated with them in a state of terror for a considerable time, even if nothing more happened. The major disruption by damage of the gas or electricity systems of cities and towns would cause a risk to the lives of those exposed to danger by sudden power losses, as well as widespread economic damage to the nation. All these are real examples of terrorism.[41]

A distinction should be made, however, between attacks on property where the intention is *also to kill* (i.e. an attack on the public transport system), or where there are *also threats of violence* against people (i.e. the pupils above), and those where there is no intention to physically harm human beings. In other words can an attack on property with no intent to kill or injure people (and with no threat of this) be called terrorism? The litmus test must surely be whether or not the violence is intended to spread fear and to generate a psychological impact beyond the object of attack. The argument has been made that it is impossible to frighten inanimate objects[42] and that therefore attacks on property cannot be deemed to be terrorism. The essence of terrorism, however, does not lie in the impact it has on the direct object of attack, inanimate or otherwise, but in its capacity to instil a broader psychological impact amongst a wider group, a population or a section of it.

From a policymaking perspective, the concern with including attacks on property is that protests that have violent fringes or that end up in general disorder that entails damage to property might be considered terrorism.[43] The Quakers in Britain, for example, in a memorandum to Lord Carlile, were concerned that criminal damage caused in such instances would erroneously

---

[41] Carlile, 'The Definition of Terrorism', p. 31.

[42] B. Whittaker, 'The Definition of Terrorism', *The Guardian*, 7 May 2001, available at: <http://www.guardian.co.uk/world/2001/may/07/terrorism> (last accessed 27 November 2014).

[43] C. Walter, 'Defining Terrorism in National and International Law', in *Terrorism as a Challenge for National and International Law: Security versus Liberty?* (Berlin: Springer-Verlag, 2004), conference paper version, p. 6, available at: <https://www.unodc.org/tldb/bibliography/Biblio_Int_humanitarian_law_Walter_2003.pdf> (last accessed 27 November 2014).

be considered terrorism,[44] while Schmid has argued that most of the illegal activity that animal rights extremists carry out is not 'terroristic'.[45]

To consider another example, should the actions of seven anti-war activists who broke into a weapons factory in Brighton in the United Kingdom in 2009 and caused significant damage to property (claiming to be preventing Israeli 'war crimes') be seen as terrorism? Incidentally, the judge in this case acquitted all of the accused. The solicitor acting for the defendants was quoted as saying that '[i]t sends a clear indication that sometimes direct action is the only option when all other avenues have failed' and one of the defendants was reported as arguing that '[i]t was the right verdict. During one operation 1,400 people had been killed, 350 children had died, and nobody was willing to take action... Our politicians and the United Nations were not taking action to support the people of Gaza and it was necessary for ordinary people to take action like we did.'[46]

If attacks on property can be acts of terrorism, and if the 'seriousness' of the act is also sufficient for it to be classified as such, then could this therefore be deemed an act of terrorism? The key determining factor is the extent that this incident primarily intended to generate a wider psychological impact and/or wider message to a target audience (or audiences), perhaps in order to publicize a cause. Or if the aim was very much a tangible one—to destroy weapons that the attackers feared would be used in the execution of 'war crimes'—then it would not count as an act of terrorism as I have conceptualized the phenomenon. Thus, I would argue that there is a need to draw a distinction between terrorism and violent protest in general.

How serious does an act of violence have to be to be considered an act of terrorism? Commenting on the Prevention of Terrorism (Temporary Provisions) Act 1989 definition, that terrorism included '... *any* [italics added] use of violence for the purpose of putting the public or any section of the public in fear', Carlile noted that '[t]hough it excluded threats of violence, otherwise it was very broad so far as actions were concerned. Notably, it did not require a *serious* level of violence or *serious* damage or risk to health and safety.'[47] Indeed, acts of political graffiti would presumably not warrant the label of terrorism because it would not meet the 'seriousness' threshold. Yet, like 'usually' or 'often', the inclusion of highly subjective words like 'substantial',

---

[44] Quakers in Britain, 'Memorandum to Lord Carlile's independent review of the definition of terrorism in UK law', available at: <http://www.quaker.org.uk/definition-terrorism-uk-law> (last accessed 27 November 2014).

[45] Schmid, personal communication.

[46] BBC News online, 'Activists cleared over Brighton weapons factory raid', 2 July 2010, available at: <http://www.bbc.co.uk/news/10489356> (last accessed 27 November 2014).

[47] Carlile, 'The Definition of Terrorism', p. 3.

'serious', or 'major' within a definition 'do not contribute to the building of a consensus over what qualifies as an act of terrorism'.[48]

The issue as to whether unintended consequences should also then qualify such acts as terrorism is pertinent here. Should campaigns of sabotage on transport systems that may not necessarily have intended to threaten or kill human life but nevertheless did so (thereby potentially frightening a wider travelling public) be deemed terrorism? Railway lines, for example, have often been the target of such sabotage.[49] In keeping with my general thesis if the aim was to kill, injure, or threaten with the intention of spreading fear amongst the broader travelling public then such attacks can be classified as terrorism. If their aim was simply to damage and disrupt with no intended threat to human safety nor any purpose of spreading wider psychological impact then it cannot. Conversely, even if nobody was harmed and even if there was no wider psychological impact, if the *intended* purpose was to spread fear then it can be considered an act of terrorism. Classifying something as terrorism rests on the intent of the perpetrator rather than the outcome, which may be incidental and unintended.

Do Acts of Violence Have to Be Part of a Campaign to be Called Terrorism?

A further consideration is whether a *single* act of violence (or a single threat of violence) can be viewed as an act of terrorism or whether it has to be part of a campaign to be considered as such.[50] The view of the latter perspective is that in order for it to be terrorism there needs to be a *sustained threat* of violence (not least in order to sustain psychological impact). Badey eloquently makes the case:

> One of the critical underlying characteristics of violence generally classified as terrorism is repetition. The assumption of systematic violence distinguishes terrorism from isolated events or individual violence. While individual acts of violence may resemble terrorism, employ similar methods, evoke similar responses, or meet other definitional criteria, they are not, despite the temptation to use the term, terrorism. Although the general public, the media, and politicians, because of its emotive impact and headline-appeal, freely use the term, one must clearly distinguish between isolated acts of violence which evoke terror and repetitive violence and systematic patterns of violence, called terrorism. Terror is something one feels. Terrorism is the repeated, systematic exploitation of this fear.[51]

---

[48] J. Augusteijn, quoted in Schmid, 'The Definition of Terrorism', p. 53.

[49] See, for example, BBC News online, 'India "Maoist" train attack kills more than 100', 28 May 2010, available at: <http://www.bbc.co.uk/news/10178967> (last accessed 27 November 2014).

[50] For a discussion on this see Wardlaw, *Political Terrorism*, p. 13.

[51] T. Badey, 'Defining International Terrorism: A Pragmatic Approach', *Terrorism and Political Violence*, Vol. 10, No. 1, 1998, p. 93.

Crenshaw concurs that '[i]f the purpose of the act of violence is to create a psychological effect in a watching audience rather than to destroy an asset of military value, and if the attack occurs *in the context of a systematic campaign of similar threatening actions*, then the attack can be presumed to be terrorism' (italics added).[52] Given the purpose of terrorism it is perhaps logical that it resembles a 'systematic campaign' that is constantly posing threats and that involves 'strategies that may have the effect of incremental erosion'.[53] Or, as Schmid puts it, 'to have some chance of being effective, it requires a *campaign* of terrorist attacks' (italics added).[54] This is not a uniform view, however. Paust, for example, has argued that 'terrorism can occur at an instant and by one act'.[55] Indeed, in my view, providing an act of violence satisfies the criteria that have been established, in particular that the intent is to generate a wider psychological impact (which may persist for a period if the *threat* remains, even if there is no further violence), I would concur that it is theoretically possible for even a single act of violence to be classified as terrorism.

Terrorism as an Organizational Phenomenon?

A further contested issue is the extent that an act of violence has to be carried out by an organization or at least by more than one person in order to qualify as terrorism. Hoffman, for example, argues that 'to qualify as terrorism, violence must be perpetrated by some organizational entity.'[56] Wilkinson also suggested that terrorism 'invariably entails' some organizational structure[57] while Walker notes that the UK Reinsurance (Acts of Terrorism Act) Act 1993 'uses the phrase "persons acting on behalf of, or in connection with, any organisation" which eliminates any actions carried out by individuals with eccentric or singular purposes'.[58] It does, of course, depend on what one means by an 'organization'. For example, can an act of violence carried out by an individual who sees themselves as acting on behalf of the 'Animal Liberation Front' but who has no tangible organizational connection then be labelled an act of terrorism? The same question could be asked of acts carried

[52] Crenshaw, *Explaining Terrorism: Causes, Processes and Consequences*, p. 3.

[53] Heath and O'Hair, 'From the Eyes of the Beholder', p. 37.

[54] Schmid, 'The Definition of Terrorism', p. 83.

[55] J. Paust, quoted in Appendix 2.1 in Schmid (ed.), *The Routledge Handbook of Terrorism Research*, p. 115.

[56] Hoffman, *Inside Terrorism*, pp. 42–3, although he later refers to the 'terrorist campaign' of the lone 'Unabomber', who killed three people through sending letter bombs (though he argues that this was 'not terrorism as most commonly understood', p. 155).

[57] P. Wilkinson, *Political Terrorism* (London: Macmillan 1974), pp. 17–18, cited in Sproat, 'Can the State Commit Acts of Terrorism? An Opinion and Some Qualitative Replies to a Questionnaire', p. 124.

[58] C. Walker, *Blackstone's Guide to the Anti-Terrorism Legislation* (Oxford: Oxford University Press, 2002), p. 28.

out by *individuals* who claim to be acting on behalf of Al Qaeda. In fact, in the face of the highly decentralized contemporary terrorist threat one might reconsider whether acts of terrorism, to be labelled as such, really do have to be carried out by an organizational entity or even by more than one person.

In fact, even before the emergence of the Al Qaeda threat, the phenomenon of 'lone-wolf terrorism' was evident through the examples of Theodore Kaczynski (the 'Unabomber'), Timothy McVeigh[59] (responsible for the Oklahoma bombing) and Steve Copeland (the London nail bomber).[60] In the following case of an Egyptian (by the name of Hadayet) who killed two people and injured five, and the ensuing debate as to whether or not it was an act of terrorism (no, if he was a loner, yes if he was part of an organization), Fletcher shares some interesting thoughts as to why terrorism is seen as an organizational phenomenon:

> The assumption of the FBI was that terrorists act as part of a terrorist cell or group. I doubt if this is true about all terrorists in all cases. So far as we know, Timothy McVeigh acted alone, but he was widely described as an American terrorist. Most people I have asked seem to be willing to classify Ted Kaczynski, the Unabomber, as a terrorist...In the Hadayet case we are left with the FBI's intuition that an organizational connection should be considered a critical factor in the analysis of terrorism. But one wonders why organization matters. The reason, I think, is that we have less to fear from solitary actions of loners like Hesham Muhammad Hadayet. Thus we experience terror more deeply when we perceive the individual suicide bomber not as a lone wolf, but as one of many potential agents organized and funded by terrorist handlers...The element of theatre, along with the organizational dimension of terrorism, accounts in part for its destabilizing impact on the public.[61]

The perception here of terrorism as an organizational phenomenon, then, ties in with the notion of terrorism as entailing a *campaign* of violence (with 'many potential agents'), rather than a single act. To reiterate, particularly in the context of the decentralized contemporary form of international terrorism, and the notion of (and arguably the increased prevalence of) 'lone-wolf' terrorism, my view is that terrorism, to be labelled as such, need not be committed by an organizational entity. Having considered further potential elements in this chapter the final chapter will conclude with the author's own conceptualization of terrorism.

---

[59] Although McVeigh was said to have been assisted by at least one accomplice (an individual by the name of Terry Nicholls was also convicted in relation to the Oklahoma bombing).

[60] For a discussion on lone wolf terrorism see R. Spaaij, 'The Enigma of Lone Wolf Terrorism: An Assessment', *Studies in Conflict & Terrorism*, Vol. 33, No. 9, 2010.

[61] Fletcher, 'The Indefinable Concept of Terrorism', pp. 907–9.

10

Conclusion

Terrorism, like all social science concepts, is not a fact but a social construct. And there is no such thing as objectivity—every individual sees the world differently. There are, however, *degrees* of objectivity and one can endeavour to be as neutral and objective as one can be; and so the social construction of terrorism does not mean that we shouldn't try and conceive of such phenomena within our own political and social contexts or indeed that we should not endeavour to explore what *one's own* conception of terrorism is, even if a definition that is 'likely to satisfy all concerned is a virtually impossible task'.[1] This book began by proposing three possible outcomes when assessing the prospects for terrorism as an analytical concept. The first is that there is nothing qualitatively distinctive about terrorism compared to other forms of political violence, the second that it is simply a 'lower level' of political violence (thus a quantitative distinction rather than a qualitative one), and the third is that there *is* something distinctive about 'terrorism' that we can theorize about.

If there is nothing qualitatively distinctive about terrorism, and if our analytical endeavour is restricted to conceding that terrorism is only different from other forms of political violence in terms of scale, then we might have to concede that 'terrorism' really is the preferred label for the violence of those whose goals one disagrees with. Perhaps 'terrorism' is in its 'pre-theory' stage for a very good reason—that there is in fact nothing to theorize about, that terrorism really is, and always has been, a *label* of derision to stigmatize activity that is in fact not qualitatively different to other forms of political violence, that, indeed, terrorism's 'natural home is in polemical, ideological and propagandist contexts'.[2] In this case the old mantra of 'one person's terrorist is another's freedom fighter' might indeed tell us all we need to

---

[1] L. Weinberg and E. Eubank, 'Everything that Descends Must Converge: Terrorism, Globalism and Democracy', in Silke (ed.), *Research on Terrorism: Trends, Achievements and Failures*, p. 91.

[2] J. Coady, cited in J. Teichman, 'How to Define Terrorism', in Gearty (ed.), *Terrorism*, p. 505.

know—that terrorism is a word deployed according to where one's interests lie, rather than a concept that more analytically depicts a distinctive form of political violence.

There are those who would disagree—for many what marks terrorism out as distinctive is the *deliberate* targeting of civilians, often in peacetime environments and it is this that makes terrorism so shocking and extranormal. Indeed, confronted with attacks like those of 9/11 and 7/7, 'societies are clear that terrorism is an especially violent and unethical wrong'.[3] As Laqueur once wrote, a characteristic feature of terrorism is 'the violation of established norms'.[4] States have, of course, also targeted civilians. In the context of war these are now called 'war crimes', hence, in pursuit of a 'unified' approach,[5] the notion of terrorism as 'the peacetime equivalent of a war crime'.

The inclination then, has been to place terrorism within the broader framework of international norms to do with the protection of the 'innocent', 'civilians', or 'non-combatants' and terrorism has thus been defined accordingly. States are obliged to comply with these norms and where they haven't they suffer the indignation of the international community. In other words there is generally a compliance, or at least a pretence of compliance, with these norms of international behaviour whereas those carrying out acts of terrorism deliberately flout them, and that this is what makes terrorism different. From a policymaking perspective, it seems logical that the application of these norms across the board should inform a definition of terrorism—that what marks acts of political violence out as terrorism is the deliberate targeting of civilians or non-combatants.[6]

The problem with this is that while acts of terrorism very often target civilians and non-combatants, this, in my view, is not *definitional* of terrorism, even if this is a predominant form of the phenomenon and even if civilian targeting and its 'shock value' best achieves the core purpose of terrorism—namely, to generate a wider psychological impact *beyond* the immediate physical victims. For, as I have argued, acts of terrorism can also be carried out against non-civilian and combatant targets. If one is searching for any uniqueness in a *general* definition of terrorism (that applies to *all* cases), then, in my view it is not to be found in civilian or non-combatant targeting. Indeed, there are many commonly included components of a definition of terrorism that are not, one could argue, *definitional* of the phenomenon. Thus, instead we may say that terrorism *often* entails the deliberate targeting of civilians. Similarly, while we might describe *many* acts of terrorism as 'extranormal' this, in

---

[3] Gearty (ed.), *Terrorism*, p. xi.
[4] W. Laqueur, *Terrorism* (London: Weidenfeld & Nicolson, 1977), p. 3.
[5] H. Koechler, cited in Santos, 'Terrorism: Toward a Legal Definition'.
[6] This paragraph has been reprinted with the permission of Taylor and Francis LLC from Richards, 'Conceptualizing Terrorism', p. 221.

my view, is again not definitional of terrorism. So one may be left with frequent or even predominant features of many acts of terrorism that are not, ultimately, definitive features. There may from this perspective, therefore, and as some have suggested, be some merit in abandoning the goal of *defining* terrorism and instead limiting our endeavours to *describing* the phenomenon (see p. 150).

If we are endeavouring to *define* terrorism, however, and if we argue that there *is* something different about terrorism that is common *to all acts of terrorism* (and that this is not civilian targeting or a peacetime environment, or indeed extranormal violence), then *what is it* that is qualitatively distinctive about the phenomenon? I ultimately conclude that what makes terrorism different to other forms of political violence is *its primary purpose of generating a wider psychological impact beyond the immediate victims or object of attack.* How then should we ultimately define the phenomenon? It has been said that '[t]he art of making a good definition is to include as few elements as possible but also as many as necessary.'[7] Hence my definition is limited to simply this: *terrorism is a method that entails the use of violence or force or the threat of violence or force with the primary purpose of generating a psychological impact beyond the immediate victims or object of attack for a political motive.* This, in my view is common to *all acts of terrorism*. If the primary aim is not to generate this wider psychological impact then it is not terrorism.

The related concepts of non-state terrorism and state terrorism, as sub-categories of terrorism in general, can therefore be drawn from my general definition above. Hence non-state terrorism can be understood as *a method that entails the use of violence or the threat of violence by non-state actors with the primary purpose of generating a psychological impact beyond the immediate victims or objective of attack for a political motive.* State terrorism, which I have argued is comparatively rare, can similarly be defined as *a method that entails the use of violence or the threat of violence by state actors with the primary purpose of generating a psychological impact beyond the immediate victims or object of attack for a political motive.* This is distinguished from state terror by the fact that it is of a much lower scale—for example, domestic state terror can be defined as *the internal and widespread use of violence or force or the threat of violence or force by states in order to either eliminate perceived opposition groups or to coerce a population into compliance.* State-sponsored terrorism can be defined as *states who knowingly provide assistance, including finance and material resources, to groups or individuals for the purpose of carrying out acts of terrorism.*

---

[7] Schmid, 'The Definition of Terrorism', p. 73. See also Sartori on the challenge of establishing a minimum common denominator when forming concepts (Sartori, 'Concept Misformation in Comparative Politics', p. 1052).

There are many definitions of terrorism in the academic literature that are very similar to my own. Two points of general concurrence, in particular, are worth noting. The first is that conventional academic wisdom agrees that terrorism is about generating a psychological impact over and above its physical effects, that the direct targets are not the intended recipients of the 'terrorist message' (one wonders, however, how many acts or threats of violence have been labelled terrorism when they do not satisfy this core criterion?). The second point is that most definitions of terrorism (perhaps surprisingly) do not explicitly include civilian or non-combatant targeting as indispensable to a definition—evident in Easson and Schmid's compilation of over 250 definitions[8] and Schmid and Jongman's sample in their study.[9] Notwithstanding those that see the targeting of civilians or non-combatants as indispensable to the concept the omission of these categories (as victims) from a definition, to reiterate, immediately renders the notion of terrorism as the peacetime equivalent of a war crime as inadequate.

Moreover, the view that anyone can be a victim of terrorism (including combatants of 'oppressive' regimes) brings into question zero-tolerance approaches to terrorism. Explicit condemnation of all terrorism and implicit sympathy for some is hardly a tenable stance. Would Washington and Westminster rush to condemn acts of terrorism carried out by the Free Syrian Army against those armed forces loyal to the Assad regime (including the notorious pro-state Shabiha militia), or indeed by the Kosovan Liberation Army against the military forces of Slobodan Milosevic? If one is to be dispassionate and impartial as to how one conceptualizes terrorism, then there may indeed be terrorisms that one sympathizes with—in particular those that refrain from targeting civilians or non-combatants and whose goal one might endorse. One could argue that these realities need to be honestly reflected in international approaches to the phenomenon.

A rarely acknowledged but formidable challenge arising from my (and many others') conceptualization of terrorism is that it is extremely difficult to *prove* what constitutes an act of terrorism because it is hard to know what the intent or purpose is behind the act of violence.[10] Roberta Senechal de la Roche argued that 'we evaluate a scientific definition solely by its usefulness in the ordering of facts.'[11] This clearly presents a problem—my definition, because it rests on intent, does not lend itself to the scrutiny of observable facts. Indeed, while there may be some cases where purported intent is expressed in relation to an act of political violence, this may not be the real intent and there are

---

[8] Appendix 2.1 in Schmid (ed.), *The Routledge Handbook of Terrorism Research*, pp. 99–157.

[9] Schmid and Jongman, *Political Terrorism*, pp. 34–7.

[10] This paragraph and the following three paragraphs have been reprinted with the permission of Taylor and Francis LLC, pp. 230–1 (see note 6).

[11] R. De la Roche, quoted in Schmid, 'The Definition of Terrorism', p. 90 (footnote 35).

many more examples where we do not even have purported intent. How do we know, for example, whether wider psychological impact is the intent more than the physical effects of an act of violence? Hence 'determining terrorist motives with any certainty remains difficult if not impossible, and subject to speculation at best.'[12]

Thus, there may have been many acts of violence that are labelled terrorism when, by my definition, there is little evidence that they are. This opens up a whole new subjective debate—*indeed, this is arguably where the real subjectivity problem lies within the definitional debate*. In the face of limited evidence, how do we know (and who decides) if an act of political violence is primarily designed to generate a wider psychological impact over its physical effect, and therefore whether it is an act of terrorism or another form of political violence? This is arguably the most fundamental problem with my conception of terrorism—and indeed, for some, it may justify the view that any serious endeavour to grapple with the definitional issue is indeed a waste of effort.

Perhaps we should simply define terrorism according to what is more readily observable in keeping with de la Roche's 'sole' function or purpose of a definition, and exclude the core element of intent altogether—possibly by focusing on tangibles such as incidents of the targeting of civilians (or non-combatants) in non-war environments (in keeping with international norms to do with the protection of civilians from any form of armed combat), and to gather data accordingly. But this would compromise what this author, and many others, believe an act of terrorism to be. If one is comfortable with one's conception of what terrorism is then the challenge is to empirically prove what acts constitute terrorism and which ones do not. As Shanahan has argued:

> Certainly, it cannot be required of a *definition* that it come packaged with specific empirical facts sufficient to establish that any given object, situation, or event is an instantiation. Definition and application are distinct. So, too, a definition of 'terrorism' should not be required to provide proof that a given attack was, in fact, an instance of terrorism. This is where ordinary methods of observation and interpretation are indispensable [original author's italics].[13]

There is unfortunately no simple answer to the problem of proving intent, to determine that the psychological dimension is the primary purpose behind an act of violence. Yet, there is also no escaping the fact that it is this psychological dimension, where the immediate victims are not the real target of the 'terrorist message', that conventional academic wisdom sees as the essence of

---

[12] Miller et al., 'The Complexity of Terrorism, Groups, Semiotics, and the Media', p. 58.
[13] Shanahan, 'Betraying a Certain Corruption of Mind: How (and How Not) to Define "Terrorism"'.

terrorism. Terrorism as a method is about intended psychological impact beyond the immediate target over and above anything else, and one should not alter its meaning simply to accommodate what might be more readily and conveniently observable, hence 'the onus is upon the social scientist to establish intent'.[14]

As I have suggested above, there may be many acts of political violence that have hitherto been presumed to be terrorism that may not be according to my conceptualization of terrorism. It is analytically dubious, for example, to simply label all acts of violence carried out by Al Qaeda or ISIS as acts of terrorism, by virtue of the fact that it is they who have carried them out. This does, of course, prompt the question as to what we call those acts of violence that are not intended to have psychological impact as their main purpose. It may be possible to classify much of this other violence as guerrilla warfare, or as more 'conventional' battles in the context of general insurgencies or civil wars where physical destruction or tangible territorial gain (or retention) may be the primary aim.

But what do we call those acts of violence in peacetime (that are not part of guerrilla, civil, or insurgency wars—in other words that have no hope of achieving 'parallel power'[15]) that also simply aim to cause physical destruction over and above any psychological impact? What if the motive is simply to 'hit back' and to inflict as much physical damage as possible, where any psychological impact is unintended or incidental? These cannot, by my own understanding of the phenomenon, be acts of terrorism. The notion that warfare has now become more intrastate rather than interstate[16] renders it more challenging to determine what is and what isn't terrorism within the spectrum of asymmetrical political violence. Yet, for the sake of analytical precision, it is an imperative task.

In order to further capture any distinctiveness about terrorism one thing seems to be essential—to understand it as a *method* independently from the cause. The ideology or cause may well be (and often is) important in providing the doctrinal parameters for the scale, lethality, and targeting of the violence and there are certainly what one might call terrorist ideologies where terrorism is, or becomes, embedded in the dogma itself. But, while terrorism may be intrinsic to some ideologies, these doctrines cannot claim ownership of the phenomenon—for it has been carried out in the name of many ideologies that are not themselves inherently violent, such as nationalism or single issue causes. Thus 'terrorism' cannot be confined to certain dogmas but should be

---

[14] Claridge, 'State Terrorism? Applying a Definitional Model', p. 51.

[15] Crelinsten, 'Analysing Terrorism and Counter-Terrorism: A Communication Model', p. 85.

[16] P. Champain, 'Tackling Violence: Are We Looking in the Right Place?', summary of seminar talk given at the University of East London, 12 December 2012.

viewed as a phenomenon that can, and has been, used as a method in pursuit of a plethora of different causes. As noted in the previous chapter, this helps us to steer clear of cause-based definitions that *confuse analysis of the activity* that one is trying to conceptualize.

My proposed general definition of terrorism above applies to all cases of terrorism. For many it may be excluding too much—that it is short of some key features of terrorism that are often included in the definitions of others. As I have argued above, it excludes features that may often or even usually apply. In order to capture these there may then be some merit in *describing* the phenomenon.[17] As Taylor has cautioned, '[w]e can try to draw together elements of a definition of terrorism, but inevitably what we will have is a list of attributes, rather than a water-tight definition...because not all of these attributes need necessarily always be present for us to view something as terrorism.'[18] Describing terrorism would allow us to draw attention to features of terrorism that 'often' or 'usually' apply but are not definitive of the concept. The Policy Working Group on the United Nations and Terrorism, for example, argued that: 'Without attempting a comprehensive definition of terrorism, it would be useful to delineate some broad characteristics of the phenomenon',[19] and in 2004 the UN ad hoc Committee on terrorism referred to a 'recommended "description"' of terrorism.[20] *Describing* terrorism, however, is not an *alternative* to defining or conceptualizing the phenomenon because it doesn't help us to classify what terrorism is or is not, or to determine what its parameters are—this needs a definition.[21]

There are doubtless more than a few assumptions and propositions in this work that many will find contentious. And there are dilemmas arising from some of the assumptions made that the author continues to grapple with that have not been adequately resolved here, and that perhaps require further thought. For example, where is the threshold that lies between those forms of state terror that intend to primarily generate a psychological impact beyond the immediate victims and terrorism? If one wants to ensure precision in our concepts then simply stating that such acts of state terror are of a wider scale is arguably vague enough to invite varying degrees of interpretation (even if

---

[17] See, for example, Jackson et al., *Terrorism, A Critical Introduction*, pp. 115–20.

[18] M. Taylor and E. Quayle, *Terrorist Lives* (London: Brassey's, 1994), p. 11.

[19] Policy Working Group on the United Nations and Terrorism, quoted in Schmid, 'The Definition of Terrorism', p. 56.

[20] Schmid, 'The Definition of Terrorism', p. 60. It has been argued that there is sometimes confusion between definition and description with Vladimir Lukov (commenting on Schmid's academic consensus definition) arguing that the 'definition is rather a description than a definition', although he believed that 'this "definition" is the most accurate description of the phenomenon in the literature' (V. Lukov, quoted in Schmid, 'The Definition of Terrorism', p. 61).

[21] The section beginning with 'would allow us to draw attention to features of terrorism...' to the end of the paragraph has been reprinted with the permission of Taylor and Francis LLC, p. 230 (see note 6).

I have suggested that some distinction needs to be made between the two). Also, to reiterate, how can one really prove the intent behind an act of violence? And where should one pitch the 'seriousness' threshold for an act of violence to be called terrorism?

There may be those who argue that this book does little more than illustrate that any such conceptual endeavour is indeed a waste of time, that any attempt to infuse some analytical quality into the concept is a forlorn task. Yet, I would also suggest, notwithstanding 'critical' perspectives that even question the use of the word 'terrorism' itself on the grounds that it has always been employed pejoratively,[22] that there are very few terrorism studies scholars who would argue that 'terrorism' is entirely devoid of analytical value, that there is something distinctive about our subject matter that we call 'terrorism' and that has spawned 'terrorism studies', and that it is a concept worth theorizing about.

A further challenge in conceptualizing terrorism is to ensure that ultimately the definition is resilient enough to warrant a sustainable 'shelf life'. Hence, rather than following the political exigencies of the day in moulding and remoulding what we mean by 'terrorism', and changing our meaning according to what the latest terrorist adversary is doing, we should hold true to what one believes is the core essence of terrorism, and if acts of violence do not satisfy the key criteria then they are not acts of terrorism. This is important for any meaningful, resilient, and sustainable theory building as to what terrorism is. There have also, as I have noted, been proclamations of the 'new terrorism' more than once in recent decades, including the contemporary 'new terrorism' of Al Qaeda and those inspired by it.[23] One should, however, draw a distinction between the *meaning* of terrorism and the evolving *physical manifestations* of terrorism. An important implication of one of my key assumptions in Chapter 5 (that there is no such thing as an act of violence that is in and of itself inherently terrorism—that the essence of terrorism therefore *lies in the intent behind the act*)—is that changes in the *physical acts* of terrorism should not alter the core essence and meaning of the concept.

One is often confronted with the perennial problem of the definition of terrorism at terrorism related conferences. In particular, students who are new to the field of terrorism studies pose the question of definition (paradoxically, 'what is terrorism' can be both an ignorant question from a complete newcomer to the subject or a sophisticated one posed by a seasoned scholar of terrorism studies). The silent pause that often follows reflects both the fact

---

[22] R. Jackson, 'Introduction: The Case for Critical Terrorism Studies', *European Political Science*, Vol. 6, No. 3, 2007, p. 247.

[23] For a discussion on this see Crenshaw, *Explaining Terrorism: Causes, Processes and Consequences*, Chapter 3.

that there is no short or simple answer, and also that there is an inescapable sense of unfulfilled obligation on the part of terrorism studies scholars. It may be that the task of proving intent behind acts of violence is too formidable a challenge—and that this problem alone would ultimately deem, for some, the conceptual endeavour a fruitless exercise. Yet, as Silke lamented, 'there can be few topics in the social sciences which cry out for better understanding.'[24] While aware of the many pitfalls and problems of defining terrorism, this discussion, in offering its own conceptualization of terrorism, does not attempt to 'speak truth' but does hope to reinvigorate the debate. The aim is to provoke discussion on how we conceive of, and understand, terrorism and how, in particular, we can infuse some sustainable analytical quality into the term in the hope that we may ultimately develop further the theoretical foundation as to what we mean by terrorism.

[24] A. Silke, 'An Introduction to Terrorism Research', in Silke (ed.), *Research on Terrorism: Trends, Achievements and Failures*, p. 2.

LIBRARY, UNIVERSITY O˜ CHESTER

Bibliography

Printed Sources

Acharya, U., 'War on Terror or Terror Wars: The Problem in Defining Terrorism', *Denver Journal of International Law and Policy*, Vol. 37, No. 4, 2008–2009.

Alexander, Y., Carlton, D., and Wilkinson, P. (eds.), *Terrorism: Theory and Practice* (Boulder, CO: Westview Press, 1979).

Alexander, Y. and Gleason, J. (eds.), *Behavioural and Quantitative Perspectives on Terrorism* (New York and Oxford: Pergamon Press, 1981).

Alexander, Y. and Pluchinsky, D., *Europe's Red Terrorists: The Fighting Communist Organizations* (London: Frank Cass, 1992).

Alleman, R., 'Definitional Aspects', *Studies in Conflict and Terrorism*, Vol. 3, Nos. 3–4, 1980.

Allen, R., 'Terrorism and Truth', *Alternative Law Journal*, No. 27, 2002.

Anderson, M., 'Georges Sorel: Reflections on Violence', *Terrorism and Political Violence*, Vol. 1, No. 1, 1989.

Arquilla, J. and Ronfeldt, D., 'Netwar Revisited: The Fight for the Future Continues', in R. Bunker (ed.), *Networks, Terrorism and Global Insurgency* (Abingdon: Routledge, 2005).

Badey, T., 'Defining International Terrorism: A Pragmatic Approach', *Terrorism and Political Violence*, Vol. 10, No. 1, 1998.

Bankoff, G., 'Regions of Risk: Western Discourses on Terrorism and the Significance of Islam', *Studies in Conflict & Terrorism*, Vol. 26, No. 6, 2003.

Bassiouni, M., *International Terrorism: Multilateral Conventions (1937–2001)* (New York: Transnational Publishers, 2001).

Baxter, R., 'A Skeptical Look at the Concept of Terrorism', *Akron Law Review*, Vol. 7, No. 3, 1973–74.

Begorre-Bret, C., 'The Definition of Terrorism and the Challenge of Relativism', *Cardozo Law Review*, Vol. 27, No. 5, 2005–2006.

Ben-Yehuda, N., 'Political Assassinations as Rhetorical Devices', *Terrorism and Political Violence*, Vol. 2, No. 3, 1990.

Beres, L. R., 'Meaning of Terrorism: Jurisprudential and Definitional Clarifications', *Vanderbilt Journal of Transnational Law*, Vol. 28, 1995.

Bessner, D. and Stauch, M., 'Karl Heinzen and the Intellectual Origins of Modern Terror', *Terrorism and Political Violence*, Vol. 22, No. 2, 2010.

Bishop, P. and Mallie, E., *The Provisional IRA* (London: Corgi, 1992).

Bjorgo, T. (ed.), *Root Causes of Terrorism* (Abingdon: Routledge, 2005).

Black, D., 'The Geometry of Terrorism', *Sociological Theory*, Vol. 22, No. 1, 2004.

Blackbourn, J., 'The Evolving Definition of Terrorism in UK Law', *Behavioral Sciences of Terrorism and Political Aggression*, Vol. 3, No. 2, 2011.

Blain, M., 'On the Genealogy of Terrorism', in D. Staines (ed.), *Interrogating the War on Terror: Interdisciplinary Perspectives* (Newcastle, UK: Cambridge Scholars Publishing, 2007).

Blakeley, R., 'Bringing the State Back into Terrorism Studies', *European Political Science*, Vol. 6, No. 3, 2007.

Blakeley, R., *State Terrorism and Neoliberalism* (Abingdon: Routledge, 2009).

Booth, K. (ed.), *Critical Security Studies and World Politics* (Boulder, CO: Lynne Rienner, 2005).

Brackett, D., *Holy Terror: Armageddon in Tokyo* (New York: Weatherhill, 1996).

Breen-Smyth, M., 'A Critical Research Agenda for the Study of Political Terror', *European Political Science*, Vol. 6, No. 3, 2007.

Broomhall, B., 'State Actors in an International Definition of Terrorism from a Human Rights Perspective', *Case Western Reserve Journal of International Law*, Vol. 36, Nos. 2 and 3, 2004.

Bryan, D., Kelly, L., and Templer, S., 'The Failed Paradigm of "Terrorism"', *Behavioral Sciences of Terrorism and Political Aggression*, Vol. 3, No. 2, 2011.

Burke, A., 'Metaterror', *International Relations*, Vol. 23, No. 1, 2009.

Bushnell, T., Shlapentokh, V., Vanderpool, C., and Sundram, J., 'State Organized Terror: Tragedy of the Modern State', in T. Bushnell, V. Shlapentokh, C. Vanderpool, and J. Sundram (eds.), *State Organized Terror* (Boulder, CO: Westview Press, 1991).

Caws, P., 'Terror: From the Armada to Al-Qaeda', in D. Staines (ed.), *Interrogating the War on Terror: Interdisciplinary Perspectives* (Newcastle, UK: Cambridge Scholars Publishing, 2007).

Chaliand, G. and Blin, A., *The History of Terrorism: From Antiquity to Al Qaeda* (Berkeley, Los Angeles, and London: University of California Press, 2007).

Chambers Giant Paperback Dictionary (Edinburgh: Chambers Harrap Publishers, 1997).

Claridge, D., 'State Terrorism? Applying a Definitional Model', *Terrorism and Political Violence*, Vol. 8, No. 3, 1996.

Coady, C., *Morality and Political Violence* (Cambridge: Cambridge University Press, 2008).

Coady, C., 'The Morality of Terrorism', in C. Gearty (ed.), *Terrorism* (Aldershot: Dartmouth Publishing, 1996).

Connolly, W., *The Terms of Political Discourse*, 2nd edn. (Oxford: Martin Robertson, 1983).

Coogan, T., *The IRA* (London: Fontana/HarperCollins, 1987).

Cooke, M., 'Academic Freedom: The "Danger" of Critical Thinking', *International Studies Perspectives*, Vol. 8, No. 4, 2007.

Cooper, H., 'Terrorism: The Problem of the Problem of Definition', *Chitty's Law Journal*, Vol. 26, No. 3, 1978.

Cox, R. and Sinclair, T., 'Social Forces, States, and World Orders', in *Approaches to World Order* (Cambridge: Cambridge University Press, 1996).

Crelinsten, R. D., 'Analysing Terrorism and Counter-Terrorism: A Communication Model', *Terrorism and Political Violence*, Vol. 14, No. 2, 2002.

Crelinsten, R. D. and Schmid, A., 'Western Responses to Terrorism: A Twenty-Five Year Balance Sheet', in A. Schmid and R. D. Crelinsten (eds.), *Western Responses to Terrorism* (Abingdon and New York: Frank Cass, 1993).

Crenshaw, M., 'The Concept of Revolutionary Terrorism', *The Journal of Conflict Resolution* (pre 1986), Vol. 16, No. 3, 1972.

Crenshaw, M., 'The Causes of Terrorism', *Comparative Politics*, Vol. 13, No. 4, 1981.

Crenshaw, M., 'Introduction: Reflections on the Effects of Terrorism', in *Terrorism, Legitimacy and Power: The Consequences of Political Violence* (Middletown, CT: Wesleyan University Press, 1983).

Crenshaw, M., 'The Logic of Terrorism: Terrorist Behaviour as a Product of Strategic Choice', in W. Reich (ed.), *Origins of Terrorism: Psychologies, Ideologies, Theologies, States of Mind* (Cambridge: Cambridge University Press, 1990).

Crenshaw, M., 'Current Research on Terrorism: The Academic Perspective', *Studies in Conflict and Terrorism*, Vol. 15, No. 1, 1992.

Crenshaw, M., *Explaining Terrorism: Causes, Processes and Consequences* (Abingdon: Routledge, 2011).

Dartnell, M., 'A Legal Inter-Network for Terrorism: Issues of Globalization, Fragmentation and Legitimacy', *Terrorism and Political Violence*, Vol. 4, No. 11, 1999.

De la Roche, R., 'Toward a Scientific Theory of Terrorism', *Sociological Theory*, Vol. 22, No. 1, 2004.

Der Derian, J., 'Imaging Terror: Logos, Pathos and Ethos', *Third World Quarterly*, Vol. 26, No. 1, 2005.

Drake, C., *Terrorists' Target Selection* (Basingstoke: Macmillan, 1998).

Dugard, J., 'International Terrorism: Problems of Definition', *International Affairs*, Vol. 50, No. 1, 1974.

Duvall, R. and Stohl, M., 'Governance by Terror', in M. Stohl (ed.), *The Politics of Terrorism* (New York: Marcel Dekker, 1988).

English, R., *Modern War: A Very Short Introduction* (Oxford: Oxford University Press, 2013).

English, R., *Terrorism: How to Respond* (Oxford: Oxford University Press, 2009).

Falk, R., 'Academic Freedom under Siege', *International Studies Perspectives*, Vol. 8, No. 4, 2007.

Fattah, E., 'Terrorist Activities and Terrorist Targets: A Tentative Typology', in Y. Alexander and J. Gleason (eds.), *Behavioural and Quantitative Perspectives on Terrorism* (New York and Oxford: Pergamon Press, 1981).

Faure, G. and Zartman, W. (eds.), *Negotiating with Terrorists: Strategy, Tactics, and Politics* (Abingdon: Routledge, 2010).

Fletcher, G.,'The Indefinable Concept of Terrorism', *Journal of International Criminal Justice*, Vol. 4, No. 5, 2006.

Freedman, D. and Thussu, D., 'Introduction: Dynamics of Media and Terrorism', in D. Freedman and D. Thussu (eds.), *Media and Terrorism: Global Perspectives* (London: Sage, 2012).

Fromkin, D., 'The Strategy of Terrorism', in C. Kegley (ed.), *International Terrorism: Characteristics, Causes, Controls* (New York: St Martin's Press, 1990).

Fussey, P. and Richards, A., 'Researching and Understanding Terrorism: A Role for Criminology?', *Criminal Justice Matters*, No. 73, 2008.

Gallie, W., 'Essentially Contested Concepts', *Proceedings of the Aristotelian Society for the Systematic Study of Philosophy* (London: Williams and Norgate, 1956).

Ganor, B., 'Defining Terrorism: Is One Man's Terrorist Another Man's Freedom Fighter?', *Police Practice and Research*, Vol. 3, No. 4, 2002, available at: <http://www. ict.org.il/Article/1123/Defining-Terrorism-Is-One-Mans-Terrorist-Another-Mans-Freedom-Fighter> (last accessed 27 November 2014).

Gearty, C., *Terror* (London: Faber and Faber, 1991).

Gearty, C. (ed.), *Terrorism* (Aldershot: Dartmouth Publishing, 1996).

Gearty, C., 'Terrorism and Morality', *European Human Rights Law Review*, No. 4, 2003.

George, D., 'Distinguishing Classical Tyrannicide from Modern Terrorism', *Review of Politics*, Vol. 50, 1988.

Githens-Mazer, J. and Lambert, R., 'Why Conventional Wisdom on Radicalization Fails', *International Affairs*, Vol. 86, No. 4, 2010.

Glover, J., 'State Terrorism', in *Violence, Terrorism and Justice* (Cambridge and New York: Cambridge University Press, 1991).

Golder, B. and Williams, G., 'What is Terrorism? Problems of Legal Definition', *University of New South Wales Law Journal*, Vol. 27, No. 2, 2004.

Goodin, R., *What's Wrong With Terrorism?* (Cambridge: Polity Press, 2006).

Goodwin, J., 'A Theory of Categorical Terrorism', *Social Forces*, Vol. 84, No. 4, 2006.

Gordon, A., 'Terrorism and the Scholarly Communication System', *Terrorism and Political Violence*, Vol. 13, No. 4, 2001.

Gressang IV, D., 'Audience and Message: Assessing Terrorist WMD Potential', *Terrorism and Political Violence*, Vol. 13, No. 3, 2001.

Gross, F., *Violence in Politics: Terror and Political Assassination in Eastern Europe and Russia* (The Hague: Mouton, 1972).

Gunning, J., 'Babies and Bathwaters: Reflecting on the Pitfalls of Critical Terrorism Studies', *European Political Science*, Vol. 6, No. 3, 2007.

Hauerwas, S. and Lentricchia, F. (eds.), *Dissent From the Homeland: Essays after September 11* (Durham, NC: Duke University Press, 2003).

Heath, R. and O'Hair, D., 'From the Eyes of the Beholder', in H. O'Hair, R. Heath, K. Ayotte, and G. Ledlow (eds.), *Terrorism, Communication and Rhetorical Perspectives* (Cresskill, NJ: Hampton Press, 2008).

Held, V., 'Terrorism and War', *The Journal of Ethics*, Vol. 8, 2004.

Herbst, P., *Talking Terrorism: A Dictionary of the Loaded Language of Political Violence* (Westport, CT: Greenwood Press, 2003).

Herman, E., *The Real Terror Network: Terrorism in Fact and Propaganda* (Boston, MA: South End Press, 1982).

Hewitt, C., 'Terrorism and Public Opinion', *Terrorism and Political Violence*, Vol. 2, No. 2, 1990.

Hoffman, B., 'Reply to Pluchinsky and Rapoport Comments', *Terrorism and Political Violence*, Vol. 9, No. 1, 1997.

Hoffman, B., 'Why Terrorists Don't Claim Credit', *Terrorism and Political Violence*, Vol. 9, No. 1, 1997.

Hoffman, B., *Inside Terrorism* (New York: Columbia University Press, 1998).

Hoffman, B., 'Defining Terrorism', in R. Howard and R. Sawyer (eds.), *Terrorism and Counterterrorism: Understanding the New Security Environment, Readings and Interpretations* (New York: McGraw-Hill, 2002).

Hoffman, B. and McCormick, G., 'Terrorism, Signaling, and Suicide Attack', *Studies in Conflict & Terrorism*, Vol. 27, No. 4, 2004.

Honderich, T., *After the Terror* (Edinburgh: Edinburgh University Press, 2002).

Horgan, J., *The Psychology of Terrorism* (Abingdon: Routledge, 2005).

Horgan, J., 'Individual Disengagement: A Psychological Analysis', in T. Bjorgo and J. Horgan (eds.), *Leaving Terrorism Behind* (Abingdon: Routledge, 2009).

Horgan, J. and Boyle, M., 'A Case against "Critical Terrorism Studies"', *Critical Studies on Terrorism*, Vol. 1, No. 1, 2008.

Howard, R. and Sawyer, R. (eds.), *Terrorism and Counterterrorism: Understanding the New Security Environment, Readings and Interpretations* (New York: McGraw-Hill, 2002).

Hughes, M., 'Terrorism and National Security', *Philosophy*, Vol. 57, 1982, reprinted in C. Gearty (ed.), *Terrorism* (Aldershot: Dartmouth Publishing, 1996).

Hurwood, B., *Society and the Assassin: A Background Book on Political Murder* (London: Macmillan, 1970).

Ilardi, J., 'Redefining the Issues: The Future of Terrorism Research and the Search for Empathy', in A. Silke (ed.), *Research on Terrorism: Trends, Achievements and Failures* (Abingdon and New York: Frank Cass, 2004).

Jackson, M., 'Terrorism, "Pure Justice" and Pure "Ethics"', *Terrorism and Political Violence*, Vol. 2, No. 3, 1990.

Jackson, R., 'Introduction: The Case for Critical Terrorism Studies', *European Political Science*, Vol. 6, No. 3, 2007.

Jackson, R., 'The Core Commitments of Critical Terrorism Studies', *European Political Science*, Vol. 6, No. 3, 2007.

Jackson, R., 'Knowledge, Power and Politics in the Study of Political Terrorism', in R. Jackson, M. Breen Smyth, and J. Gunning (eds.), *Critical Terrorism Studies: A New Research Agenda* (Abingdon: Routledge, 2009).

Jackson, R., 'In Defence of "Terrorism": Finding a Way through a Forest of Misconceptions', *Behavioral Sciences of Terrorism and Political Aggression*, Vol. 3, No. 2, 2011.

Jackson, R., Breen Smyth, M., and Gunning, J., 'Critical Terrorism Studies: Framing a New Research Agenda', in R. Jackson, M. Breen Smyth, and J. Gunning (eds.), *Critical Terrorism Studies: A New Research Agenda* (Abingdon: Routledge, 2009).

Jackson, R., Breen Smyth, M., and Gunning, J. (eds.), *Critical Terrorism Studies: A New Research Agenda* (Abingdon: Routledge, 2009).

Jackson, R., Jarvis, L., Gunning, J., and Breen Smyth, M., *Terrorism: A Critical Introduction* (Basingstoke: Palgrave Macmillan, 2011).

Jarvis, L., 'The Spaces and Faces of Critical Terrorism Studies', *Security Dialogue*, Vol. 40, No. 1, 2009.

Jenkins, B., 'The Study of Terrorism: Definitional Problems' in Y. Alexander and J. Gleason (eds.), *Behavioural and Quantitative Perspectives on Terrorism* (New York and Oxford: Pergamon Press, 1981).

Joseph, J., 'Critical of What? Terrorism and its Study', *International Relations*, Vol. 23, No. 1, 2009.

Kalyvas, S., 'The Paradox of Terrorism in Civil War', *The Journal of Ethics*, Vol. 8, No. 1, 2004.

Kassimeris, G. (ed.), *Playing Politics With Terrorism* (London: Hurst, 2007).

Kegley, C. (ed.), *International Terrorism: Characteristics, Causes, Controls* (New York: St Martin's Press, 1990).

Kennedy, R., 'Is One Person's Terrorist Another's Freedom Fighter? Western Approaches to "Just War" Compared', *Terrorism and Political Violence*, Vol. 11, No. 1, 1999.

Kepel, G. and Milelli, J.-P. (eds.), *Al Qaeda in its Own Words* (Cambridge, MA and London: Belknap Press of Harvard University Press, 2008).

Laqueur, W., *Terrorism* (London: Weidenfeld & Nicolson, 1977).

Laqueur, W., *A History of Terrorism* (New Brunswick, NJ: Transaction Publishers, 2001).

Laqueur, W., *No End to War: Terrorism in the Twenty-First Century* (New York: Continuum, 2004).

Leites, N., 'Understanding the Next Act', *Terrorism: An International Journal*, Vol. 3, 1979.

Levene, M. and Roberts, P. (eds.), *The Massacre in History* (New York and Oxford: Berghahn Books, 1999).

Levine, V., 'The Logomachy of Terrorism: On the Political Uses and Abuses of Definition', *Terrorism and Political Violence*, Vol. 7, No. 4, 1995.

Levitt, G., 'Is Terrorism Worth Defining?', *Ohio Northern University Law Review*, Vol. 13, No. 1, 1986.

McCauley, C., 'Terrorism, Research and Public Policy: An Overview', *Terrorism and Political Violence*, Vol. 3, No. 1, 1991.

McDonald, M., 'Emancipation and Critical Terrorism Studies', *European Political Science*, Vol. 6, No. 3, 2007.

Mayer, J.-F., 'Cults, Violence and Religious Terrorism: An International Perspective', *Studies in Conflict and Terrorism*, Vol. 25, No. 5, 2001.

Meisels, T., 'The Trouble with Terror: The Apologetics of Terrorism—a Refutation', *Terrorism and Political Violence*, Vol. 18, No. 3, 2006.

Merari, A., 'A Classification of Terrorist Groups', *Terrorism: An International Journal*, Vol. 1, Nos. 3 and 4, 1978.

Merari, A., 'Terrorism as a Strategy of Insurgency', *Terrorism and Political Violence*, Vol. 5, No. 4, 1993.

Michel, T. and Richards, A., 'False Dawns or New Horizons? Further Issues and Challenges for Critical Terrorism Studies', *Critical Studies on Terrorism*, Vol. 3, 2009.

Mickolus, E., 'International Terrorism', in M. Stohl (ed.), *The Politics of Terrorism* (New York: Marcel Dekker, 1988).

Miller, C., Matusitz, J., O'Hair, D., and Eckstein, J., 'The Complexity of Terrorism, Groups, Semiotics, and the Media', in H. O'Hair, R. Heath, K. Ayotte, and G. Ledlow (eds.), *Terrorism: Communication and Rhetorical Perspectives* (Cresskill, NJ: Hampton Press, 2008).

Monaghan, R., Antonius, D., and Justin Sinclair, S., 'Defining "Terrorism": Moving towards a More Integrated and Interdisciplinary Understanding of Political Violence', *Behavioral Sciences of Terrorism and Political Aggression*, Vol. 3, No. 2, 2011.

Mulaj, K., 'Resisting an Oppressive Regime: The Case of Kosovo Liberation Army', *Studies in Conflict & Terrorism*, Vol. 31, No. 12, 2008.

Myers, P. and Stohl, M., 'Terrorism, Identity and Group Boundaries', in H. Giles, S. Reid, and J. Harwood (eds.), *The Dynamics of Intergroup Communication* (New York: Peter Lang, 2010).

Nacos, B., 'The Terrorist Calculus behind 9-11: A Model for Future Terrorism?', *Studies in Conflict & Terrorism*, Vol. 26, No. 1, 2003.

Narveson, J., 'Terrorism and Morality', in R. Frey and C. Morris (eds.), *Violence, Terrorism and Justice* (Cambridge: Cambridge University Press, 1991).

Neilson, K., 'Commentary: On the Moral Justifiability of Terrorism (State and Other Wise)', *Osgoode Hall Law Journal*, Summer/Fall, 2003.

O'Hair, H., Heath, R., Ayotte, K., and Ledlow, G. (eds.), *Terrorism: Communication and Rhetorical Perspectives* (Cresskill, NJ: Hampton Press, 2008).

O'Hair, H., Heath, R., Ayotte, K., and Ledlow, G., 'The Communication and Rhetoric of Terrorism', in H. O'Hair, R. Heath, K. Ayotte, and G. Ledlow (eds.), *Terrorism: Communication and Rhetorical Perspectives* (Cresskill, NJ: Hampton Press, 2008).

O'Lear, S., 'Environmental Terrorism: A Critique', in S. Brunn (ed.), *11 September and its Aftermath* (London: Frank Cass, 2004).

Omand, D., *Securing the State* (London: Hurst, 2010).

Onuf, N., 'Making Terror/ism', *International Relations*, Vol. 23, No. 1, 2009.

Palmer Harik, J., *Hezbollah: The Changing Face of Terrorism* (London: I. B. Tauris, 2005).

Pearlstein, R. M., *Fatal Future? Transnational Terrorism and the New Global Disorder* (Austin, TX: University of Texas Press, 2004).

Pillar, P., 'The Dimensions of Terrorism and Counterterrorism', in R. Howard and R. Sawyer (eds.), *Terrorism and Counterterrorism: Understanding the New Security Environment, Readings and Interpretations* (New York: McGraw-Hill, 2002).

Primoratz, I., 'What is Terrorism?', *Journal of Applied Philosophy*, Vol. 7, No. 2, 1990, reprinted in C. Gearty (ed.), *Terrorism* (Aldershot: Dartmouth Publishing, 1996).

Ranstorp, M. (ed.), *Mapping Terrorism Research: State of the Art, Gaps and Future Direction* (Abingdon: Routledge, 2007).

Ranstorp, M., 'Mapping Terrorism Studies after 9/11', in R. Jackson, M. Breen Smyth, and J. Gunning (eds.), *Critical Terrorism Studies: A New Research Agenda* (Abingdon: Routledge, 2009).

Rapin, A.-J., 'What is Terrorism?', *Behavioral Sciences of Terrorism and Political Aggression*, Vol. 3, No. 3, 2011.

Rapoport, D., 'To Claim or Not to Claim; That is the Question—Always!', *Terrorism and Political Violence*, Vol. 9, No. 1, 1997.

Reich, W. (ed.), *Origins of Terrorism: Psychologies, Ideologies, Theologies, States of Mind* (Cambridge: Cambridge University Press, 1990).

Richards, A., 'Countering the Psychological Impact of Terrorism: Challenges for UK Homeland Security', in A. Silke (ed.), *The Psychology of Counter-Terrorism* (Abingdon: Routledge, 2011).

Richards, A., 'The Problem with "Radicalization": The Remit of "Prevent", and the Need to Refocus on *Terrorism* in the UK', *International Affairs*, Vol. 87, No. 1, 2011.

Richards, A., 'Conceptualizing Terrorism', *Studies in Conflict and Terrorism*, Vol. 37, No. 3, 2014.

Richards, A., Fussey, P., and Silke, A. (eds.), *Terrorism and the Olympics: Lessons for 2012 and beyond* (Abingdon: Routledge, 2011).

Richardson, L., 'Terrorists as Transnational Actors', in M. Taylor and J. Horgan (eds.), *The Future of Terrorism* (Abingdon: Routledge, 2000).

Richardson, L., *What Terrorists Want* (London: John Murray, 2006).

Roach, K., 'The Case for Defining Terrorism With Restraint and Without Reference to Political or Religious Motive', in A. Lynch, E. Macdonald, and G. Williams (eds.), *Law and Liberty in the War on Terror* (Sydney: The Federation Press, 2007).

Rodin, D., 'Terrorism without Intention', *Ethics*, Vol. 114, No. 4, 2004.

Romanov, V., 'The United Nations and the Problem of Combating International Terrorism', *Terrorism and Political Violence*, Vol. 2, No. 3, 1990.

Rostow, N., 'Before and After: The Changed UN Response to Terrorism since September 11th', *Cornell International Law Journal*, Vol. 35, No. 3, 2002.

Roth, 'The Law of War in the War on Terror', *Foreign Affairs*, Vol. 83, No. 1, 2004.

Sartori, G., 'Concept Misformation in Comparative Politics', *The American Political Science Review*, Vol. 64, No. 4, 1970.

Saul, B., 'Two Justifications for Terrorism: A Moral Legal Response', *Alternative Law Journal*, Vol. 30, No. 5, 2005.

Saul, B., *Defining Terrorism in International Law* (Oxford: Oxford University Press, 2006).

Saul, B., 'The Legal Response of the League of Nations to Terrorism', *Journal of International Criminal Justice*, Vol. 4, No. 1, 2006.

Saul, B., 'Defining Terrorism to Protect Human Rights', in D. Staines (ed.), *Interrogating the War on Terror: Interdisciplinary Perspectives* (Newcastle, UK: Cambridge Scholars Publishing, 2007).

Saul, B., 'The Curious Element of Motive in Definitions of Terrorism: Essential Ingredient or Criminalising Thought?' in A. Lynch, E. Macdonald, and G. Williams (eds.), *Law and Liberty in the War on Terror* (Sydney: The Federation Press, 2007).

Scharf, M. P., 'Defining Terrorism as the Peace Time Equivalent of War Crimes: A Case of Too Much Convergence Between International Humanitarian Law and International Criminal Law?', *ILSA Journal of International and Comparative Law*, Vol. 7, 2001.

Scharf, M. P., 'Defining Terrorism as the Peace Time Equivalent of War Crimes: Problems and Prospects', *Case Western Reserve Journal of International Law*, Vol. 36, Nos. 2–3, 2004.

Schmid, A., *Political Terrorism: A Research Guide to Concepts, Theories, Data Bases and Literature* (New Brunswick, NJ: Transaction Books, 1983).

Schmid, A., 'Terrorism and the Media: The Ethics of Publicity', *Terrorism and Political Violence*, Vol. 1, No. 4, 1989.

Schmid, A., 'Repression, State Terrorism, and Genocide: Conceptual Clarifications', in T. Bushnell, V. Shlapentokh, C. Vanderpool, and J. Sundram (eds.), *State Organized Terror* (Boulder, CO: Westview Press, 1991).

Schmid, A., 'The Response Problem as a Definition Problem', *Terrorism and Political Violence*, Vol. 4, No. 4, 1992.

Schmid, A., 'Frameworks for Conceptualising Terrorism', *Terrorism and Political Violence*, Vol. 17, No. 2, 2004.

Schmid, A., 'Terrorism: The Definitional Problem', *Case Western Reserve Journal of International Law*, Vol. 36, Nos. 2 and 3, 2004.

Schmid, A., 'The Definition of Terrorism', in A. Schmid (ed.), *The Routledge Handbook of Terrorism Research* (Abingdon: Routledge, 2011).

Schmid, A. (ed.), *The Routledge Handbook of Terrorism Research* (Abingdon: Routledge, 2011).

Schmid, A. and de Graaf, J., *Insurgent Terrorism and the Western News Media* (Leiden: Centrum Onderzock Meatschappelijke Tegenstelliugen, 1980).

Schmid, A. and Jongman, A., *Political Terrorism: A New Guide to Actors, Authors, Concepts, Databases, Theories and Literature*, 3rd edn. (New Brunswick, NJ: Transaction Books, 2008 [1988]).

Shanahan, T., *The Provisional Irish Republican Army and the Morality of Terrorism* (Edinburgh: Edinburgh University Press, 2009).

Shanahan, T., 'Betraying a Certain Corruption of Mind: How (and How Not) to Define "Terrorism"', *Critical Studies on Terrorism*, Vol. 3, No. 2, 2010.

Shultz, R., 'Conceptualizing Political Terrorism', in C. Kegley (ed.), *International Terrorism: Characteristics, Causes, Controls* (New York: St Martin's Press, 1990).

Silke, A., 'Terrorism and the Blind Men's Elephant', *Terrorism and Political Violence*, Vol. 8, No. 3, 1996.

Silke, A., 'Beating the Water: The Terrorist Search for Power, Control and Authority', *Terrorism and Political Violence*, Vol. 12, No. 2, 2000.

Silke, A., 'The Devil You Know: Continuing Problems with Research on Terrorism', *Terrorism and Political Violence*, Vol. 13, No. 4, 2001.

Silke, A. (ed.), *Terrorists, Victims and Society* (Chichester: John Wiley, 2003).

Silke, A., 'An Introduction to Terrorism Research', in A. Silke (ed.), *Research on Terrorism: Trends, Achievements and Failures* (London: Frank Cass, 2004).

Silke, A. (ed.), *Research on Terrorism: Trends, Achievements and Failures* (London: Frank Cass, 2004).

Silke, A., 'The Road Less Travelled: Recent Trends in Terrorism Research', in A. Silke (ed.), *Research on Terrorism: Trends, Achievements and Failures* (London: Frank Cass, 2004).

Silke, A., 'Contemporary Terrorism Studies: Issues in Research', in R. Jackson, M. Breen Smyth, and J. Gunning (eds.), *Critical Terrorism Studies: A New Research Agenda* (Abingdon: Routledge, 2009).

Silke, A., *Terrorism* (London: Hodder & Stoughton, 2014).

Simeonidou-Kastanidou, E., 'Defining Terrorism', *European Journal of Crime, Criminal Law and Criminal Justice*, Vol. 12, No. 1, 2004.

Singer, E., 'Terrorist Attacks on Nationals: The Lawful Use of Force Against Terrorist Bases on Foreign Soil', *Terrorism and Political Violence*, Vol. 1, No. 4, 1989.

Sloan, J., 'Political Terrorism in Latin America', in M. Stohl (ed.), *The Politics of Terrorism* (New York: Marcel Dekker, 1988).

Smith, M., *Fighting for Ireland: The Military Strategy of the Irish Republican Movement* (London and New York: Routledge, 1995).

Sorel, J.-M., 'Some Questions About the Definition of Terrorism and the Fight Against its Financing', *European Journal of International Law*, Vol. 14, 2003.

Spaaij, R., 'The Enigma of Lone Wolf Terrorism: An Assessment', *Studies in Conflict & Terrorism*, Vol. 33, No. 9, 2010.

Sproat, P., 'Can the State Commit Acts of Terrorism? An Opinion and Some Qualitative Replies to a Questionnaire', *Terrorism and Political Violence*, Vol. 9, No. 4, 1997.

Staines, D. (ed.), *Interrogating the War on Terror: Interdisciplinary Perspectives* (Newcastle, UK: Cambridge Scholars Publishing, 2007).

Stampnitsky, L., *Disciplining Terror* (Cambridge: Cambridge University Press, 2013).

Stephens, A. and Vaughan-Williams, N., 'Introduction: London, Time, Terror', in A. Stephens and N. Vaughan-Williams (eds.), *Terrorism and the Politics of Response* (Abingdon: Routledge, 2009).

Stohl, M., 'Demystifying Terrorism: The Myths and Realities of Contemporary Political Terrorism', in M. Stohl (ed.), *The Politics of Terrorism* (New York: Marcel Dekker, 1988).

Stohl, M., 'National Interests and State Terrorism in International Affairs', *Political Science*, Vol. 36, No. 1, 1984.

Stohl, M. (ed.), *The Politics of Terrorism* (New York: Marcel Dekker, 1988).

Stokes, D., 'Ideas and Avocados: Ontologising Critical Terrorism Studies', *International Relations*, Vol. 23, No. 1, 2009.

Taylor, M., *The Terrorist* (London: Brassey's, 1988).

Taylor, M. and Quayle, E., *Terrorist Lives* (London: Brassey's, 1994).

Taylor, P., *States of Terror* (London: BBC Books, 1993).

Teichman, J., 'How to Define Terrorism', *Philosophy*, Vol. 64, 1989, reprinted in C. Gearty (ed.), *Terrorism* (Aldershot: Dartmouth Publishing, 1996).

Thornton, T., 'Terror as a Weapon of Political Agitation', in H. Eckstein (ed.), *Internal War* (Toronto: Collier-Macmillan, 1964).

Tiefenbrun, S., 'A Semiotic Approach to a Legal Definition of Terrorism', *ILSA Journal of International and Comparative Law*, Vol. 9, No. 2, 2003.

Tilly, C., 'Terror, Terrorism, Terrorists', *Sociological Theory*, Vol. 22, No. 1, 2004.

Toros, H. and Gunning, J., 'Exploring a Critical Theory Approach to Terrorism Studies', in R. Jackson, M. Breen Smyth, and J. Gunning (eds.), *Critical Terrorism Studies: A New Research Agenda* (Abingdon: Routledge, 2009).

Townshend, C., *Terrorism: A Very Short Introduction* (Oxford: Oxford University Press, 2002).

Turk, A., 'Sociology of Terrorism', *Annual Review of Sociology*, Vol. 30, 2004.

Waldron, J., 'Terrorism and the Uses of Terror', *The Journal of Ethics*, Vol. 8, 2004.

Walker, C., 'Briefing on the Terrorism Act 2000', *Terrorism and Political Violence*, Vol. 12, No. 2, 2000.

Walker, C., *Blackstone's Guide to the Anti-Terrorism Legislation* (Oxford: Oxford University Press, 2002).

Walzer, M., *Just and Unjust Wars* (Harmondsworth: Penguin, 1977).

Wardlaw, G., *Political Terrorism* (Cambridge: Cambridge University Press, 1990).

Wardlaw, G., 'The Nature and Purpose of Terrorism', in A. Thompson (ed.), *Terrorism and the 2000 Olympics* (Canberra: Australian Defense Studies Centre, 1996).

Weinberg, L., *Global Terrorism: A Beginner's Guide* (London: Oneworld, 2005).

Weinberg, L. and Eubank, E., 'Everything that Descends Must Converge: Terrorism, Globalism and Democracy', in A. Silke (ed.), *Research on Terrorism: Trends, Achievements and Failures* (London: Frank Cass, 2004).

Weinberg, L. and Eubank, E., 'Problems with the Critical Studies Approach to the Study of Terrorism', *Critical Studies on Terrorism*, Vol. 1, No. 2, 2008.

Weinberg, L., Pedahzur, A., and Hirsch-Hoefler, S., 'The Challenges of Conceptualising Terrorism', *Terrorism and Political Violence*, Vol. 16, No. 4, 2004.

Wellman, C., 'On Terrorism Itself', *Journal of Value Enquiry*, Vol. 13, 1979.

Whittaker, D. (ed.), *The Terrorism Reader* (New York and London: Routledge, 2001).

Wilkinson, P., 'Can a State be "Terrorist"?', *International Affairs*, Vol. 57, No. 3, 1981.

Wilkinson, P., 'The Media and Terrorism: A Reassessment', *Terrorism and Political Violence*, Vol. 9, No. 2, 1997.

Wilkinson, P., *Terrorism versus Democracy: The Liberal State Response* (London: Frank Cass, 2002).

Williams, B., 'The CIA's Covert Predator Drone War in Pakistan, 2004–2010: The History of an Assassination Campaign', *Studies in Conflict & Terrorism*, Vol. 33, No. 10, 2010.

Zeidan, S., 'Desperately Seeking Definition: The International Community's Quest for Identifying the Specter of Terrorism', *Cornell International Law Journal*, Vol. 36, No. 3, 2003–2004.

Web and Other Sources

Ahmad, E., edited transcript of public talk, in E. Ahmad, *Terrorism, Theirs and Ours* (New York: Seven Stories Press, 2001), available at: <http://books.google.co.uk/books?hl= en&lr=&id=qcRX4prGAUAC&oi=fnd&pg=PA6&dq=The+Definition+of+Terrorism& ots=sqF2W3Ktk3&sig=_TxT2gSYS7uEH0RXNIjX7MtCeDY#v=onepage&q=The% 20Definition%20of%20Terrorism&f=false> (last accessed 27 November 2014).

Alexander, D. (Independent Reviewer of Terrorism Legislation), 'The Meaning of Terrorism', Clifford Chance University of Essex Lecture, 13 February 2013, available at: <https://terrorismlegislationreviewer.independent.gov.uk/wp-content/uploads/2013/ 04/clifford-chance-lecture.pdf> (last accessed 27 November 2014).

Arnold, J. et al., 'A Proposed Universal Medical and Public Health Definition of Terrorism', *Prehospital and Disaster Medicine*, Vol. 18, No. 2, available at: <http://journals. cambridge.org/action/displayAbstract?fromPage=online&aid=8227349> (last accessed 27 November 2014).

Arquilla, J. and Ronfeldt, D., *Networks and Netwars: The Future of Terror, Crime and Militancy* (Santa Monica, CA: RAND Corporation, 2001), available at: <http://www. rand.org/pubs/monograph_reports/MR1382/index.html> (last accessed 27 November 2014).

Associated Press, 'Taliban Bomber in Kabul Kills 17 at Supreme Court', 11 June 2013, available at: <http://bigstory.ap.org/article/kabul-police-large-explosion-hits-near-us-embassy> (last accessed 27 November 2014).

Bartlett, J., Birdwell, J., and King, M., *The Edge of Violence: A Radical Approach to Extremism* (London: Demos, 16 April 2010), available at: <http://www.demos.co.uk/files/Edge_of_Violence_-_web.pdf?1271346195> (last accessed 27 November 2014).

BBC News online, 'Activists cleared over Brighton weapons factory raid', 2 July 2010, available at: <http://www.bbc.co.uk/news/10489356> (last accessed 27 November 2014).

BBC News online, 'Afghan policeman kills three British soldiers', 2 July 2012, available at: <http://www.bbc.co.uk/news/uk-18670175> (last accessed 27 November 2014).

BBC News online, 'Afghanistan "rogue" attack: Four US soldiers killed', 16 September 2012, available at: <http://www.bbc.co.uk/news/world-asia-19614911> (last accessed 27 November 2014).

BBC News online, 'India "Maoist" train attack kills more than 100', 28 May 2010, available at: <http://www.bbc.co.uk/news/10178967> (last accessed 27 November 2014).

BBC News online, 'Islamic State crisis: US House approves Obama's Syria Plan', 18 September 2014, available at: <http://www.bbc.co.uk/news/world-us-canada-29248955> (last accessed 27 November 2014).

BBC News online, 'Libyan leader Muammar Gaddafi appears on state TV', 11 February 2011, available at <http://www.bbc.co.uk/news/world-africa-12533069> (last accessed 27 November 2014).

BBC News online, 'Pakistan bomber kills 17 in attack on police', 12 January 2011, available at: <http://www.bbc.co.uk/news/world-south-asia-12174011> (last accessed 27 November 2014).

BBC News online, 'Special Report: Hijack at Stansted', 14 February 2000, available at: <http://news.bbc.co.uk/1/hi/uk/636375.stm> (last accessed 27 November 2014).

Bouhana, N. and Wikstrom, P., 'Al-Qa'ida influenced radicalisation: A rapid evidence assessment guided by Situational Action Theory', Home Office, November 2011, available at: <http://www.homeoffice.gov.uk/publications/science-research-statistics/research-statistics/counter-terrorism-statistics/occ97> (last accessed 27 November 2014).

Brennan, J., Assistant to the president for homeland security and counterterrorism, Press Briefing by Press Secretary Jay Carney and Assistant to the President for Homeland Security and Counterterrorism John Brennan, 5 February 2011, available at: <http://www.whitehouse.gov/the-press-office/2011/05/02/press-briefing-press-secretary- jay-carney-and-assistant-president-homela> (last accessed 27 November 2014).

Carlile, A., 'The Definition of Terrorism', 15 March 2007, available at: <http://www.official-documents.gov.uk/document/cm70/7052/7052.pdf> (last accessed 27 November 2014).

Carney, J., Press Briefing by Press Secretary Jay Carney, 5 March 2011, available at: <http://www.whitehouse.gov/the-press-office/2011/05/03/press-briefing-press-secretary-jay-carney-532011> (last accessed 27 November 2014).

Champain, P., 'Tackling Violence: Are We Looking in the Right Place?', summary of seminar talk given at the University of East London, 12 December 2012.

Chapman, D., 'Defining Terrorism: A Thought Experiment', *State of Nature*, Spring 2009, available at: <http://www.stateofnature.org/definingTerrorism.html> (last accessed 27 November 2014).

Chittal, N., 'Sen. Mitch McConnell: Julian Assange is a "High Tech Terrorist"', Mediaite website, 5 December 2010, available at: <http://www.mediaite.com/tv/mitch-mcconnell-julian-assange-is-a-high-tech-terrorist/> (last accessed 27 November 2014).

CNN, transcript of George Bush State of the Union Address, 29 January 2003, available at: <http://edition.cnn.com/2003/ALLPOLITICS/01/28/sotu.transcript/> (last accessed 27 November 2014).

Columbia International Affairs online, 'Producing Jihad: The Al Qaeda Recruitment Tape', Reel 2, Excerpt 3, available at: <http://www.ciaonet.org/cbr/cbr00/video/excerpts/reel2.html?i"> (last accessed 27 November 2014).

Columbia International Affairs online, 'Producing Jihad: The Al Qaeda Recruitment Tape', Reel 3, excerpt 10, available at: <http://www.ciaonet.org/cbr/cbr00/video/excerpts/reel3.html?p> (last accessed 27 November 2014).

Communities and Local Government Committee, 'Preventing Violent Extremism', 30 March 2010, available at: <http://www.publications.parliament.uk/pa/cm200910/cmselect/cmcomloc/65/65.pdf> (last accessed 27 November 2014).

'Contest: The United Kingdom's Strategy for Countering Terrorism', July 2011, available at: <http://www.homeoffice.gov.uk/publications/counter-terrorism/counter-terrorism-strategy/strategy-contest?view=Binary> (last accessed 27 November 2014).

'Countering International Terrorism: The United Kingdom's Strategy', July 2006, available at: <http://tna.europarchive.org/20100419081706/http://security.homeoffice.gov.uk/news-publications/publication-search/contest/contest-strategy-2006?view=Binary> (last accessed 27 November 2014).

Daily Mail, 'Two British tourists escape with their lives after eight holidaymakers are killed in terrifying Manila bus siege', 24 August 2010, available at: <http://www.dailymail.co.uk/news/article-1305389/Manila-bus-siege-Hostage-taker-Rolando-Mendoza-shot-dead-7-tourists-killed.html> (last accessed 27 November 2014).

Daily Mail, G. Owen, 'David Miliband: there are circumstances in which terrorism can be justifiable', *Mailonline*, 16 August 2009, available at: <http://www.dailymail.co.uk/news/article-1206833/David-Miliband-There-circumstances-terrorism-justifiable.html> (last accessed 27 November 2014).

European Commission Sixth Framework Programme Project, 'Defining Terrorism' (WP3 Deliverable 4), 1 October 2008, available at: <http://www.transnationalterrorism.eu/tekst/publications/WP3%20Del%204.pdf> (last accessed 27 November 2014).

FBI Reports and Publications, *Terrorism 2002–2005*, available at: <http://www.fbi.gov/stats-services/publications/terrorism-2002-2005> (last accessed 27 November 2014).

Freedman, B., 'Officially Blacklisted Extremist/Terrorist (Support) Organizations: A Comparison of Lists from Six Countries and Two International Organizations', *Perspectives on Terrorism*, Vol. 4, No. 2, 2010, available at: <http://www.terrorismanalysts.com/pt/articles/issues/PTv4i2.pdf> (last accessed 27 November 2014).

Ganor, B., 'Defining Terrorism: Is One Man's Terrorist Another Man's Freedom Fighter?', International Institute for Counter-Terrorism, August 1998, available at: <http://www.ict.org.il/Article/1123/Defining-Terrorism-Is-One-Mans-Terrorist-Another-Mans-Freedom-Fighter> (last accessed 27 November 2014).

Ganor, B., 'Terrorism: No Prohibition Without Definition', 7 October 2001, available through Google search, no URL address/link on the actual document (last accessed 27 November 2014).

Gearty, C., 'Situating International Human Rights Law in an Age of Counter-Terrorism', April 2008, available at: <http://www.conorgearty.co.uk/pdfs/EU_UN_textFINAL.pdf> (last accessed 27 November 2014).

Geneva Conventions of 1949 and their Additional Protocols, available at International Committee of the Red Cross website: <http://www.icrc.org/eng/war-and-law/treaties-customary-law/geneva-conventions/index.jsp> (last accessed 27 November 2014).

Gordon, N., 'Defining Terrorism', *Palestine-Israel Journal*, Vol. 6, No. 1, 1999, available at: <http://www.israeloccupation.info/files/Defining%20Terrorism.pdf> (last accessed 27 November 2014).

Griset, P. and Mahan, S., *Terrorism in Perspective* (Thousand Oaks, CA and London: Sage, Thousand, 2003), available at: <http://books.google.co.uk/books?hl=en&lr=&id=YpmZ76zRW2oC&oi=fnd&pg=PR9&dq=defining+terrorism&ots=mN6SlK4htr&sig=YT9v2D6lMm8eKpHIcszBCfU9mUM#v=onepage&q=defining%20terrorism&f=false> (last accessed 27 November 2014).

Guardian, text of G. W. Bush speech, 20 September 2001, available at: <http://www.guardian.co.uk/world/2001/sep/21/september11.usa13> (last accessed 27 November 2014).

Harries, J., 'Labelling the Terrorist in Ancient Rome', Terrorism: Interdisciplinary Perspectives, CSTPV Seminar Series, University of St Andrews, 10 February 2010.

Horgan, J., 'Deradicalization or Disengagement?', *Perspectives on Terrorism*, Vol. 2, No. 4, 2008, available at: <http://www.terrorismanalysts.com/pt/articles/issues/PTv2i4.pdf> (accessed 27 November 2014).

Human Rights Watch, 'Military Assistance to the Afghan Opposition', 5 October 2001, available at: <http://www.hrw.org/legacy/backgrounder/asia/afghan-bck1005.pdf> (last accessed 27 November 2014).

Intelligence and Security Committee, Report into the London Terrorist Attacks on 7th July 2005, May 2006, available at: <https://www.gov.uk/government/uploads/system/uploads/attachment_data/file/224690/isc_terrorist_attacks_7july_report.pdf> (last accessed 27 November 2014).

International Summit on Democracy, Terrorism and Security, 'Addressing the Causes of Terrorism', Volume 1, 8–11 March 2005, The Club de Madrid Series on Democracy and Terrorism, available at: <http://www.clubmadrid.org/img/secciones/Club_de_Madrid_Volume_I_The_Causes_of_Terrorism.pdf > (last accessed 27 November 2014).

International Summit on Democracy, Terrorism and Security, The Causes of Terrorism, 8–11 March 2005, The Club de Madrid Series on Democracy and Terrorism, available at: <http://english.safe-democracy.org/causes/> (last accessed 16 July 2014).

International Terrorism, HC Deb, Vol. 372 cc689–810, 4 October 2001, available at: <http://hansard.millbanksystems.com/commons/2001/oct/04/international-terrorism> (last accessed 27 November 2014).

Jackson, R., 'An Argument for Terrorism', *Perspectives on Terrorism*, Vol. 2, No. 2, 2008, available at: <http://www.terrorismanalysts.com/pt/articles/issues/PTv2i2.pdf> (last accessed 27 November 2014).

Jackson, R., 'State Terror, Terrorism Research and Knowledge Politics', British International Studies Association paper 2008, available at: <http://cadair.aber.ac.uk/dspace/bitstream/handle/2160/1949/BISA-Paper-2008-Jackson-FINAL.pdf?sequence=1> (last accessed 27 November 2014).

Jenkins, B., 'Terrorism Works—Sometimes', RAND Corporation, April 1974, available at: <http://www.rand.org/content/dam/rand/pubs/papers/2006/P5217.pdf> (last accessed 27 November 2014).

Jenkins, B., 'The Study of Terrorism: Definitional Problems', RAND Corporation, December 1980, available at: <http://www.rand.org/content/dam/rand/pubs/papers/2006/P6563.pdf> (last accessed 27 November 2014).

Jongman, A., 'Internet Websites and Links for (Counter-)Terrorism Research', *Perspectives on Terrorism*, Vol. 5, No. 1, 2011, available at: <http://www.terrorismanalysts.com/pt/articles/issues/PTv5i1.pdf> (last accessed 27 November 2014).

Kelly, R., 'Is Terrorism Always Wrong?', *Perspectives on Terrorism*, Vol. 1, No. 1, 2007, available at: <http://www.terrorismanalysts.com/pt/articles/issues/PTv1i1.pdf> (last accessed 27 November 2014).

League of Arab States, Arab Convention on the Suppression of Terrorism (1998) (translated by the United Nation English translation service), available at Council on Foreign Relations website at: <http://www.cfr.org/terrorism-and-the-law/arab-convention-suppression-terrorism-cairo-declaration/p24799> (last accessed 27 November 2014).

Linton, M., Interview, 'The Terror in the French Revolution', available at: <http://www.port.ac.uk/special/france1815to2003/chapter1/interviews/filetodownload,20545,en.pdf> (last accessed 27 November 2014).

Lutz, J., 'A Critical View of Critical Terrorism Studies', *Perspectives on Terrorism*, Vol. 4, No. 6, 2010, available at: <http://www.terrorismanalysts.com/pt/index.php/pot/article/view/130> (last accessed 27 November 2014).

Maher, S. and Soliman, A., ICSR Insight: 'Al Qaeda confirms death of bin Laden', International Centre for the Study of Radicalisation and Political Violence, May 2011, available at: <http://icsr.info/2011/05/icsr-insight-al-qaeda-confirms-death-of-bin-laden/> (last accessed 27 November 2014).

National Counterterrorism Center (US), 'Annex of Statistical Information', US Department of State, available at: <http://www.state.gov/j/ct/rls/crt/2008/122452.htm> (last accessed 27 November 2014).

National Counterterrorism Center (US), *Country Reports on Terrorism 2005*, Statistical Annex, 7 April 2006, available at: <http://www.state.gov/documents/organization/65489.pdf> (last accessed 27 November 2014).

New York Times, Donald Rumsfeld quoted in 'A Nation Challenged: The Rebels; Bush Approves Covert Aid for Taliban Foes', 1 October 2001, available at: <http://www.nytimes.com/2001/10/01/world/a-nation-challenged-the-rebels-bush-approves-covert-aid-for-taliban-foes.html> (last accessed 27 November 2014).

Odom, W. (former head of the US National Security Agency), 'American Hegemony: How to Use It, How to Lose It', available at: <http://www.middlebury.edu/media/view/214721/original/OdomPaper.pdf> (last accessed 27 November 2014).

Organization of African Unity, Convention on the Prevention and Combating of Terrorism (1999), available at: <https://treaties.un.org/doc/db/Terrorism/OAU-english.pdf> (last accessed 27 November 2014).

Organization of African Unity, Protocol to the Convention on the Prevention and Combating of Terrorism (2004), available at: <http://www.au.int/en/sites/default/files/PROTOCOL_OAU_CONVENTION_ON_THE_PREVENTION_COMBATING_TERRORISM.pdf> (last accessed 27 November 2014).

Organization of Islamic Cooperation, Convention on Combating International Terrorism (1999), available at: <http://www.cfr.org/terrorism-and-the-law/convention-organization-islamic-conference-oic-combating-international-terrorism/p24781> (last accessed 27 November 2014).

'Prevent Strategy', June 2011, available at: <http://www.homeoffice.gov.uk/publications/counter-terrorism/prevent/prevent-strategy/prevent-strategy-review?view=Binary> (last accessed 27 November 2014).

'"Pursue, Prevent, Protect, Prepare": The United Kingdom's Strategy for Countering International Terrorism', March 2009, available at: <http://webarchive.nationalarchives.gov.uk/20100418065544/> <http://security.homeoffice.gov.uk/news-publications/publication-search/contest/contest-strategy/contest-strategy-2009?view=Binary> (last accessed 27 November 2014).

Quakers in Britain, 'Memorandum to Lord Carlile's independent review of the definition of terrorism in UK law', available at: <http://www.quaker.org.uk/definition-terrorism-uk-law> (last accessed 27 November 2014).

Ramsay, G., 'Targeting, Rhetoric, and the Failure of Grassroots Jihad', *Journal of Terrorism Research*, Vol. 3, No. 1, 2012, available at: <http://ojs.st-andrews.ac.uk/index.php/jtr/article/view/415/375> (last accessed 27 November 2014).

Richards, A., 'Characterising the UK Terrorist Threat: The Problem with Non-Violent Ideology as a Focus for Counter-Terrorism and Terrorism as the Product of "Vulnerability"', *Journal of Terrorism Research*, Vol. 3, No. 1, 2012, available at: <http://ojs.st-andrews.ac.uk/index.php/jtr/article/view/415/375> (last accessed 27 November 2014).

Santos, S., 'Terrorism: Toward a Legal Definition', *The Manila Times*, 5 October 2002, available at: <http://www.i-p-o.org/Manila-Times1.htm> (last accessed 1 December 2014).

Scheinin, M., United Nations Commission on Human Rights, Sixty-second session, Item 17, Promotion and Protection of Human Rights, Report of the Special Rapporteur on the promotion and protection of human rights and fundamental freedoms while countering terrorism, E/CN.4/2006/98, 28 December 2005, available at: <http://www2.ohchr.org/english/bodies/chr/docs/62chr/E.CN.4.2006.98.Add.1.pdf> (last accessed 27 November 2014).

Schmid, A., 'Terrorism as Psychological Warfare', *Democracy and Security*, No. 1, 2005, available at: <http://www.tandfonline.com/doi/pdf/10.1080/17419160500322467> (last accessed 27 November 2014).

Sinai, J., 'How to Define Terrorism', *Perspectives on Terrorism*, Vol. 2, No. 4, available at: <http://www.terrorismanalysts.com/pt/articles/issues/PTv2i4.pdf> (last accessed 27 November 2014).

South Asian Association for Regional Cooperation (SAARC), Regional Convention on the Suppression of Terrorism (1987) and its Additional Protocol (2004), available at: <http://www.saarc-sec.org/areaofcooperation/detail.php?activity_id=21> (last accessed 27 November 2014).

The Economist, 'Green-on-Blue blues', 1 September 2012, available at: <http://www.economist.com/node/21561943> (last accessed 27 November 2014).

Townsend, C., 'Terrorism: in search of the definite article', Open Democracy website, 3 July 2007, available at: <http://www.opendemocracy.net/conflicts/democracy_terror/what_is_terrorism> (last accessed 27 November 2014).

United Kingdom Terrorism Act 2000, available at: <http://www.legislation.gov.uk/ukpga/2000/11/section/1> (last accessed 27 November 2014).

United Nations, *In Larger Freedom: Towards Development, Security and Human Rights for All*, Chapter 3 ('Freedom from Fear'), available at: <http://www.unmillenniumproject.org/documents/Inlargerfreedom.pdf> (last accessed 27 November 2014).

United Nations, Press Release SG/SM/7977 GA9920, 'Secretary-General, Addressing Assembly on Terrorism, Calls for "Immediate, Far-Reaching Changes" in UN Response to Terror', 1 October 2001, available at: <http://www.un.org/en/terrorism/sg-statements.asp> (last accessed 27 November 2014).

United Nations, 'UN Action to Counter Terrorism', available at: <http://www.un.org/terrorism/> (last accessed 27 November 2014).

United Nations Conventions against terrorism, available at: <http://www.un.org/en/terrorism/instruments.shtml> (last accessed 27 November 2014).

United Nations High-Level Panel on Threats, Challenges and Change, Report: 'A More Secure World: Our Shared Responsibility', 2 December 2004, available at: <http://www.un.org/en/peacebuilding/pdf/historical/hlp_more_secure_world.pdf> (last accessed 27 November 2014).

US White House address after killing of bin Laden, transcript available at: <http://www.whitehouse.gov/blog/2011/05/02/osama-bin-laden-dead> (last accessed 27 November 2014).

Walter, C., 'Defining Terrorism in National and International Law', in *Terrorism as a Challenge for National and International Law: Security versus Liberty?* (Berlin: Springer-Verlag, 2004), conference paper version available at: <https://www.unodc.org/tldb/bibliography/Biblio_Int_humanitarian_law_Walter_2003.pdf> (last accessed 27 November 2014).

Washington Post, 'Text: Bin Laden Discusses Attacks on Tape', 13 December 2001, available at: <http://www.washingtonpost.com/wp-srv/nation/specials/attacked/transcripts/binladentext_121301.html> (last accessed 27 November 2014).

Whittaker, B., 'The Definition of Terrorism', *The Guardian*, 7 May 2001, available at: <http://www.guardian.co.uk/world/2001/may/07/terrorism> (last accessed 27 November 2014).

Wight, C., 'Theorising Terrorism: The State, Structure and History', *International Relations*, Vol. 23, No. 1, 2009, available at: <http://ire.sagepub.com/content/23/1/99.full.pdf> (last accessed 27 November 2014).

Wilkinson, B. and Barclay, J., 'The Language of Jihad, Narratives and Strategies of Al Qa'ida in the Arabian Peninsula and UK Responses', The Royal United Services Institute, Whitehall Report Series, December 2011, available at: <http://www.rusi.

org/downloads/assets/Language_of_Jihad_web.pdf> (last accessed 27 November 2014).

Young, R., 'Defining Terrorism: The Evolution of Terrorism as a Legal Concept in International Law and Its Influence on Definitions in Domestic Legislation', *Boston International and Comparative Law Review*, Vol. 29, No. 1, available at: <http://lawdigitalcommons.bc.edu/cgi/viewcontent.cgi?article=1054&context=iclr&sei-redir=1&referer=http%3A%2F%2Fwww.google.co.uk%2Furl%3Fsa%3Df%26rct%3Dj%26url%3Dhttp%3A%2F%2Flawdigitalcommons.bc.edu%2Fcgi%2Fviewcontent.cgi%253Farticle%253D1054%2526context%253Diclr%26q%3Dreuven%2Byoung%2Bdefining%2Bterrorism%26ei%3DMUuzUOjiKMbJ0QXyvICgDw%26usg%3DAFQjCNEcsH5VLKed6BQj4s7kolL8yIoOHA#search=%22reuven%20young%20defining%20terrorism%22> (last accessed 27 November 2014).

Index

Index

Index